心灵鸡汤

——致天下有情人

CHICKEN SOUP FOR THE COUPLE'S SOUL

Jack Canfield　Mark Victor Hansen
Barbara De Angelis, Ph.D.　Mark Donnelly
Chrissy Donnelly

Inspirational Stories About Love and Relationships

安徽科学技术出版社

Health Communications, Inc.

[皖]版贸登记号:1200055
图书在版编目(CIP)数据

心灵鸡汤.致天下有情人:英文/(美)坎费尔德,(美)汉森著.—合肥:安徽科学技术出版社,2000.10
ISBN 7-5337-2051-2

Ⅰ.心… Ⅱ.①坎… ②汉… Ⅲ.英语-语言读物,文学 Ⅳ.H319.4:Ⅰ

中国版本图书馆CIP数据核字(2000)第48665号

*

安徽科学技术出版社出版
(合肥市跃进路1号新闻出版大厦)
邮政编码:230063
电话号码:(0551)2833431
E-mail: yougoubu@sina.com
yougoubu@hotmail.com
网址: www.ahstp.com.cn
新华书店经销 合肥远东印刷厂印刷

*

开本:889×1194 1/32 印张:11.875 字数:292千
2004年9月第9次印刷
印数:5 000
ISBN 7-5337-2051-2/H·314 定价:19.00元

We are each of us angels with only one wing.
And we can fly only by embracing each other.

Luciano de Crescenzo

From our hearts to yours,
we dedicate this book to everyone
who has ever been in love, or
hopes to be in love again.

Contents

1. LOVE AND INTIMACY

2. FINDING TRUE LOVE

3. ON COMMITMENT

4. UNDERSTANDING EACH OTHER

5. OVERCOMING OBSTACLES

6. ON FAMILY

7. THE FLAME THAT STILL BURNS

8. ETERNAL LOVE

Acknowledgments

Chicken Soup for the Couple's Soul has taken more than three years to write, compile and edit. At times it has been a marathon, at times a sprint. At all times, it has been a work of love and joy. It has been a process of building strong relationships and benefiting unexpectedly from existing friendships. But most of all, it has been a project that we could not have completed without the loving assistance of many people. We would like to thank the following: Kim Kirberger, whose expert matchmaking skills helped bring this project through a pivotal phase. Kim, you have been our angel, and we are forever grateful for your friendship and love.

Patty Hansen, who helped bring us back to center and reminded us what *Chicken Soup* is about. Elisabeth and Melanie, thanks for your love and acceptance.

Georgia Noble, thanks for opening up your home and giving us such warm, loving support. Christopher Canfield, thanks for sharing your dad with us.

Bob Proctor, for providing the fertile creative environment that helped us refine the original idea. Without you, this would be a different story (literally)!

John Assaraf, for being the trunk of the success tree that led us to all of the other branches.

Phyllis and Don Garsham, thank you for always being a source of unconditional love, inspiration and unwavering support.

Bob and Jan Donnelly, for being there whenever we needed you, and for being great parents and good friends.

Jeanne Neale, for being a great mom and much needed sounding board. You're the best!

Hilda Markstaller, for being the fountain of wisdom that you are.

Mac Markstaller, for your tireless support in researching stories, your consistent optimism, and your ongoing belief that dreams can and do become reality.

Alison Betts, for being so resourceful and tireless in bringing the manuscript and permissions together, and for being our communications link throughout the project.

Patty Aubery, your support and your friendship have been a source of strength and inspiration for us in bringing this project home. You are the original multitasker, and the *Chicken Soup* recipe is awesome because you are, too! Jeff Aubery, J. T. and Chandler, thanks for your friendship and support!

Nancy Mitchell, thank you for your encouragement and direction from start to finish. Thanks also for leading us through the uncharted waters of the permission process.

Heather McNamara, for your expert assistance in guiding us from manuscript to finished book. Thanks for coming through for us, under incredible pressure—you're the best!

Leslie Forbes, for pitching in wherever we needed help, and for all of your hard work when permissions were due yesterday.

Veronica Romero, Teresa Esparza and Robin Yerian, for doing such a professional job of running Self-Esteem

Seminars.

Ro Miller, for being the ultimate team player. Which one of us is taking care of Chandler when Patty leaves the room?

Lisa Williams and Laurie Hartman at Mark Victor Hansen's office, for being so supportive of the project and guiding us through the maze.

Everyone at Health Communications, our publisher, for being so easy to work with and so enthusiastic about the project. Peter Vegso, Tom Sand and Terry Burke for putting together and leading such a wonderful team.

Christine Belleris, Matthew Diener, Lisa Drucker and Allison Janse for your expert work in editing the book. Larissa Hise, for your help with the creative and original cover design.

Diana Chapman, your tireless support and belief from day one have been invaluable. Your friendship and insights have kept us on track and sustained us through those inevitable lonely periods. Thank you.

Matt Eggers, Marty Rauch, Chris McDevitt, Amy and Neal Fanelli, James and Sherry Sandford, Lillian and Frank Kew, and DeJais Collel, who were true believers from the start. Your hearts are so big and so open to others that your good deeds will surely come back to you many times over.

Arielle Ford, for being such an avid supporter of this book. Thanks to you, too, Brian Hilliard!

Marci Shimoff and Jennifer Hawthorne, fellow coauthors extraordinaire, who provided key guidance and blessed us with your tremendous experience and good energy. We're glad to be on the same team.

Jann Mitchell, for getting the ball rolling with that article you wrote in *The Oregonian* three years ago.

We want to send a special thank-you to the many people

who took hours reading our top two hundred stories, providing grades and valuable feedback that helped us choose the final stories: Bonnie Block, Christine Clifford, Lisa Drucker, Beverly Kirkhart, Peggy Larson, Inga Mahoney, Lillian Wagner, Nancy Mitchell, Robbin O'Neill, Krista Buckner, Diana Chapman, Patrick Collins, Yvonne Fedderson, Dionne Fedderson, Tom Krause, Cristi Leahs, Heather McNamara, Jeanne Neale, Annie Slawik, Jilian West, Lynne Cain, Nance Dheifetz, Cindy Dadonna, Sherry Grimes, Tom Lagana, Laura Lagana, Barbara LoMonaco, Linda Mitchell, Ron Nielsen, Robin Stephens, Karen Lisko, Jean Soberick, Bud Grossmann, Rabbi Avi Magid, Robert Shapard, Ph. D., Dr. Ian MacMillan, Robert P. Barclay, Elizabeth Reveley, Connie Fueyo, Shore Slocum, Randy Heller, Lisa Molina, Barbara Rosenthal, Amy Rosenthal, Debbie Robins, Hubert La Bouillerie, Sharon Dupont and Jean Nero.

We also want to acknowledge the hundreds and hundreds of people who submitted stories, letters, poems and quotes for possible inclusion in *Chicken Soup for the Couple's Soul*. While it wasn't possible to use everything you sent in, we were all deeply moved by your sharing of such poignant and moving pieces. Your feelings and intentions about love and relationships were a constant source of inspiration for all of us. Thank you!

Because of the scope and duration of this project, we may have neglected to mention people who helped us along the way. If so, please accept our apologies, and know that you are appreciated.

We are deeply grateful for the many caring hands and heartfelt intentions that have touched this project. Without you it wouldn't have been possible. We love you all!

Introduction

Love is the most powerful, magical force in the universe, and there is nowhere it displays its beauty and wonder more than in the intimate relationship between two people. We wrote *Chicken Soup for the Couple's Soul* hoping to capture that mystery and wonder in words, words that will deeply touch and open your heart if you have ever been in love, or hope to be in love. This is a book for husbands and wives and lovers and anyone who dreams of finding their soul's true mate.

Some loves between two people endure a lifetime. Others are destined to only last for a while; then, the two lovers are separated, either by choice or by fate. But one thing is true: No matter what the outcome of a relationship, when love enters our lives, it never leaves without transforming us at the very depth of our being.

Each story in this book was written by someone who has been transformed by love. We were transformed when we read these stories, and our wish is that you will be, too. Perhaps some of the stories will help you renew the bond of trust and intimacy in your relationship, or better understand your partner; perhaps others will help you appreciate all of the ways love has enabled you to grow into a better human being; and still other stories will remind and reassure you that although love challenges and blesses each of us in unique ways, you are never alone in what you go through.

What defines our intimate relationships? What signs should we look for to discover how love is revealing itself? The stories you will read answer these questions with insight and eloquence: Sometimes love reveals itself in the unmatched level of understanding and friendship we share with our mate and no one else. Sometimes it is in what is said, and sometimes, what is not said but deeply felt. Sometimes it is in the obstacles we must face together. Sometimes it is in how the joy we feel with our partner spills over to our children and family members. And sometimes it is in where the relationship takes us inside ourselves—places we would never go willingly; but for love, we will do anything.

Intimate relationships are also powerful teachers, as these stories illustrate so beautifully. They teach us to be compassionate, caring and forgiving. They teach us when to hold on more tightly, and when to let go. They give us the opportunity to develop great virtues such as courage, patience, loyalty and trust. When we allow them to, our relationships will show us all the ways we need to grow as a person. In this way, love will never enter our lives without changing us for the better.

There are moments when love can be experienced as quite ordinary, expressed in a simple smile of acceptance from your beloved. And in other moments, love seems utterly sublime, inviting you into new worlds of passion and oneness you've never known before. Like love itself, the stories in this book reflect every season and mood, and every color of emotion: sweet beginnings; challenging and deepening intimacy; moments of grief when we are forced to say good-bye to our soul mate; moments of astonishment when we rediscover a love we thought we'd lost.

Some stories will make you laugh. Some will make you cry. But above all, the stories in *Chicken Soup for the Couple's Soul* pay tribute to love's ability to endure, beyond years, beyond difficulty, beyond distance, beyond even death.

There is no miracle greater than love. It is God's most precious gift to us. We offer this book as our gift to you. May it open your heart, uplift your mind, inspire your spirit, and be a sweet companion on your own heart's journey. And may your life always be blessed with love.

1

LOVE AND INTIMACY

Love is a force more formidable than any other.
It is invisible — it cannot be seen or measured — yet is powerful enough to transform you in a moment, and offer you more joy than any material possession ever could.

Barbara De Angelis, Ph. D.

Thinking of You

To live in hearts we leave behind is not to die.

Thomas Campbell

Sophie's face faded into the gray winter light of the sitting room. She dozed in the armchair that Joe had bought for her on their fortieth anniversary. The room was warm and quiet. Outside it was snowing lightly.

At a quarter past one the mailman turned the corner onto Allen Street. He was behind on his route, not because of the snow, but because it was Valentine's Day and there was more mail than usual. He passed Sophie's house without looking up. Twenty minutes later he climbed back into his truck and drove off.

Sophie stirred when she heard the mail truck pull away, then took off her glasses and wiped her mouth and eyes with the handkerchief she always carried in her sleeve. She pushed herself up using the arm of the chair for support, straightened slowly and smoothed the lap of her dark green housedress.

Her slippers made a soft, shuffling sound on the bare floor

as she walked to the kitchen. She stopped at the sink to wash the two dishes she had left on the counter after lunch. Then she filled a plastic cup halfway with water and took her pills. It was one forty-five.

There was a rocker in the sitting room by the front window. Sophie eased herself into it. In a half-hour the children would be passing by on their way home from school. Sophie waited, rocking and watching the snow.

The boys came first, as always, running and calling out things Sophie could not hear. Today they were making snowballs as they went, throwing them at one another. One snowball missed and smacked hard into Sophie's window. She jerked backward, and the rocker slipped off the edge of her oval rag rug.

The girls dilly-dallied after the boys, in twos and threes, cupping their mittened hands over their mouths and giggling. Sophie wondered if they were telling each other about the valentines they had received at school. One pretty girl with long brown hair stopped and pointed to the window where Sophie sat watching. Sophie slipped her face behind the drapes, suddenly self-conscious.

When she looked out again, the boys and girls were gone. It was cold by the window, but she stayed there watching the snow cover the children's footprints.

A florist's truck turned onto Allen Street. Sophie followed it with her eyes. It was moving slowly. Twice it stopped and started again. Then the driver pulled up in front of Mrs. Mason's house next door and parked.

Who would be sending Mrs. Mason flowers? Sophie wondered. *Her daughter in Wisconsin? Or her brother? No, her brother was very ill. It was probably her daughter. How nice of her.*

Flowers made Sophie think of Joe and, for a moment, she let the aching memory fill her. Tomorrow was the fifteenth. Eight months since his death.

The flower man was knocking at Mrs. Mason's front door. He carried a long white and green box and a clipboard. No one seemed to be answering. Of course! It was Friday—Mrs. Mason quilted at the church on Friday afternoons. The delivery man looked around, then started toward Sophie's house.

Sophie shoved herself out of the rocker and stood close to the drapes. The man knocked. Her hands trembled as she straightened her hair. She reached her front hall on his third knock.

"Yes?" she said, peering around a slightly opened door.

"Good afternoon, ma'am," the man said loudly. "Would you take a delivery for your neighbor?"

"Yes," Sophie answered, pulling the door wide open.

"Where would you like me to put them?" the man asked politely as he strode in.

"In the kitchen, please. On the table." The man looked big to Sophie. She could hardly see his face between his green cap and full beard. Sophie was glad he left quickly, and she locked the door after him.

The box was as long as the kitchen table. Sophie drew near to it and bent over to read the lettering: "NATALIE'S Flowers for Every Occasion." The rich smell of roses engulfed her. She closed her eyes and took slower breaths, imagining yellow roses. Joe had always chosen yellow. "To my sunshine," he would say, presenting the extravagant bouquet. He would laugh delightedly, kiss her on the forehead, then take her hands in his and sing to her "You Are My Sunshine."

It was five o'clock when Mrs. Mason knocked at Sophie's front door. Sophie was still at the kitchen table. The flower box was now open though, and she held the roses on her lap, swaying slightly and stroking the delicate yellow petals. Mrs. Mason knocked again, but Sophie did not hear her, and after several minutes the neighbor left.

Sophie rose a little while later, laying the flowers on the kitchen table. Her cheeks were flushed. She dragged a step-stool across the kitchen floor and lifted a white porcelain vase from the top corner cabinet. Using a drinking glass, she filled the vase with water, then tenderly arranged the roses and greens, and carried them into the sitting room.

She was smiling as she reached the middle of the room. She turned slightly and began to dip and twirl in small slow circles. She stepped lightly, gracefully, around the sitting room, into the kitchen, down the hall, back again. She danced till her knees grew weak, and then she dropped into the armchair and slept.

At a quarter past six, Sophie awoke with a start. Someone was knocking on the back door this time. It was Mrs. Mason.

"Hello, Sophie," Mrs. Mason said. "How are you? I knocked at five and was a little worried when you didn't come. Were you napping?" She chattered as she wiped her snowy boots on the welcome mat and stepped inside. "I just hate the snow, don't you? The radio says we might have six inches by midnight, but you can never trust them, you know. Do you remember last winter when they predicted four inches and we had twenty-one? Twenty-one! And they said we'd have a mild winter this year. Ha! I don't think it's been over zero in weeks. Do you know my oil bill was $263 last month? For my little house!"

Sophie was only half-listening. She had remembered the roses suddenly and was turning hot with shame. The empty flower box was behind her on the kitchen table. What would she say to Mrs. Mason?

"I don't know how much longer I can keep paying the bills. If only Alfred, God bless him, had been as careful with money as your Joseph. Joseph! Oh, good heavens! I almost forgot about the roses."

Sophie's cheeks burned. She began to stammer an apology, stepping aside to reveal the empty box.

"Oh, good," Mrs. Mason interrupted. "You put the roses in water. Then you saw the card. I hope it didn't startle you to see Joseph's handwriting. Joseph had asked me to bring you the roses the first year, so I could explain for him. He didn't want to alarm you. His 'Rose Trust,' I think he called it. He arranged it with the florist last April. Such a good man, your Joseph..."

But Sophie had stopped listening. Her heart was pounding as she picked up the small white envelope she had missed earlier. It had been lying beside the flower box all the time. With trembling hands, she removed the card.

"To my sunshine," it said. "I love you with all my heart. Try to be happy when you think of me. Love, Joe."

Alicia von Stamwitz

Someone to Watch Over Me

The passengers on the bus watched sympathetically as the attractive young woman with the white cane made her way carefully up the steps. She paid the driver and, using her hands to feel the location of the seats, walked down the aisle and found the seat he'd told her was empty. Then she settled in, placed her briefcase on her lap and rested her cane against her leg.

It had been a year since Susan, thirty-four, became blind. Due to a medical misdiagnosis she had been rendered sightless, and she was suddenly thrown into a world of darkness, anger, frustration and self-pity. Once a fiercely independent woman, Susan now felt condemned by this terrible twist of fate to become a powerless, helpless burden on everyone around her. "How could this have happened to me?" she would plead, her heart knotted with anger. But no matter how much she cried or ranted or prayed, she knew the painful truth—her sight was never going to return.

A cloud of depression hung over Susan's once optimistic spirit. Just getting through each day was an exercise in frustration and exhaustion. And all she had to cling to was her husband Mark.

Mark was an Air Force officer and he loved Susan with all of his heart. When she first lost her sight, he watched her sink into despair and was determined to help his wife gain the strength and confidence she needed to become independent again. Mark's military background had trained him well to deal with sensitive situations, and yet he knew this was the most difficult battle he would ever face.

Finally, Susan felt ready to return to her job, but how would she get there? She used to take the bus, but was now too frightened to get around the city by herself. Mark volunteered to drive her to work each day, even though they worked at opposite ends of the city. At first, this comforted Susan and fulfilled Mark's need to protect his sightless wife who was so insecure about performing the slightest task. Soon, however, Mark realized that this arrangement wasn't working—it was hectic, and costly. *Susan is going to have to start taking the bus again*, he admitted to himself. But just the thought of mentioning it to her made him cringe. She was still so fragile, so angry. How would she react?

Just as Mark predicted, Susan was horrified at the idea of taking the bus again. "I'm blind!" she responded bitterly. "How am I supposed to know where I'm going? I feel like you're abandoning me."

Mark's heart broke to hear these words, but he knew what had to be done. He promised Susan that each morning and evening he would ride the bus with her, for as long as it took, until she got the hang of it.

And that is exactly what happened. For two solid weeks, Mark, military uniform and all, accompanied Susan to and from work each day. He taught her how to rely on her other senses, specifically her hearing, to determine where she was and how to adapt to her new environment. He helped her befriend the bus drivers who could watch out for her, and save her a seat. He made her laugh, even on those not-so-good days when she would trip exiting the bus, or drop her briefcase full of papers on the aisle floor.

Each morning they made the journey together, and Mark would take a cab back to his office. Although this routine was even more costly and exhausting than the previous one, Mark knew it was only a matter of time before Susan would be able to ride the bus on her own. He believed in her, in the Susan he used to know before she'd lost her sight, who wasn't afraid of any challenge and who would never, ever quit.

Finally, Susan decided that she was ready to try the trip on her own. Monday morning arrived, and before she left, she threw her arms around Mark, her temporary bus riding companion, her husband, and her best friend. Her eyes filled with tears of gratitude for his loyalty, his patience, and his love. She said good-bye, and for the first time, they went their separate ways.

Monday, Tuesday, Wednesday, Thursday ... Each day on her own went perfectly, and Susan had never felt better. She was doing it! She was going to work all by herself.

On Friday morning, Susan took the bus to work as usual. As she was paying her fare to exit the bus, the driver said, "Boy, I sure envy you."

Susan wasn't sure if the driver was speaking to her or not. After all, who on earth would ever envy a blind woman who had struggled just to find the courage to live for the past year? Curious, she asked the driver, "Why do you say that you envy me?"

The driver responded, "It must feel so good to be taken care of and protected like you are."

Susan had no idea what the driver was talking about, and again asked, "What do you mean?"

The driver answered, "You know, every morning for the past week, a fine looking gentlemen in a military uniform has been standing across the corner watching you when you get off the bus. He makes sure you cross the street safely and he watches until you enter your office building. Then he blows you a kiss, gives you a little salute and walks away. You are one lucky lady."

Tears of happiness poured down Susan's cheeks. For although she couldn't physically see him, she had always felt Mark's presence. She was lucky, so lucky, for he had given her a gift more powerful than sight, a gift she didn't need to see to believe — the gift of love that can bring light where there had been darkness.

Sharon Wajda

Hungry for Your Love

It is cold, so bitter cold, on this dark, winter day in 1942. But it is no different from any other day in this Nazi concentration camp. I stand shivering in my thin rags, still in disbelief that this nightmare is happening. I am just a young boy. I should be playing with friends; I should be going to school; I should be looking forward to a future, to growing up and marrying, and having a family of my own. But those dreams are for the living, and I am no longer one of them. Instead, I am almost dead, surviving from day to day, from hour to hour, ever since I was taken from my home and brought here with tens of thousands of other Jews. *Will I still be alive tomorrow*? *Will I be taken to the gas chamber tonight*?

Back and forth I walk next to the barbed wire fence, trying to keep my emaciated body warm. I am hungry, but I have been hungry for longer than I want to remember. I am always hungry. Edible food seems like a dream. Each day, as more of us disappear, the happy past seems like a mere dream, and I sink deeper and deeper into despair.

Suddenly, I notice a young girl walking past on the other side of the barbed wire. She stops and looks at me with sad eyes, eyes that seem to say that she understands, that she, too, cannot fathom why I am here. I want to look away, oddly ashamed for this stranger to see me like this, but I cannot tear my eyes from hers.

Then she reaches into her pocket, and pulls out a red apple. A beautiful, shiny red apple. *Oh, how long has it been since I have seen one!* She looks cautiously to the left and to the right, and then with a smile of triumph, quickly throws the apple over the fence. I run to pick it up, holding it in my trembling, frozen fingers. In my world of death, this apple is an expression of life, of love. I glance up in time to see the girl disappearing into the distance.

The next day, I cannot help myself — I am drawn at the same time to that spot near the fence. *Am I crazy for hoping she will come again? Of course.* But in here, I cling to any tiny scrap of hope. She has given me hope and I must hold tightly to it.

And again, she comes. And again, she brings me an apple, flinging it over the fence with that same sweet smile.

This time I catch it, and hold it up for her to see. Her eyes twinkle. *Does she pity me?* Perhaps. I do not care, though. I am just so happy to gaze at her. And for the first time in so long, I feel my heart move with emotion.

For seven months, we meet like this. Sometimes we exchange a few words. Sometimes, just an apple. But she is feeding more than my belly, this angel from heaven. She is feeding my soul. And somehow, I know I am feeding hers as well.

One day, I hear frightening news: we are being shipped to another camp. This could mean the end for me. And it definitely means the end for me and my friend.

The next day when I greet her, my heart is breaking, and I can barely speak as I say what must be said: "Do not bring me an apple tomorrow," I tell her. "I am being sent to another camp. We will never see each other again." Turning before

I lose all control, I run away from the fence. I cannot bear to look back. If I did, I know she would see me standing there, with tears streaming down my face.

Months pass and the nightmare continues. But the memory of this girl sustains me through the terror, the pain, the hopelessness. Over and over in my mind, I see her face, her kind eyes, I hear her gentle words, I taste those apples.

And then one day, just like that, the nightmare is over. The war has ended. Those of us who are still alive are freed. I have lost everything that was precious to me, including my family. But I still have the memory of this girl, a memory I carry in my heart and gives me the will to go on as I move to America to start a new life.

Years pass. It is 1957. I am living in New York City. A friend convinces me to go on a blind date with a lady friend of his. Reluctantly, I agree. But she is nice, this woman named Roma. And like me, she is an immigrant, so we have at least that in common.

"Where were you during the war?" Roma asks me gently, in that delicate way immigrants ask one another questions about those years.

"I was in a concentration camp in Germany," I reply.

Roma gets a far away look in her eyes, as if she is remembering something painful yet sweet.

"What is it?" I ask.

"I am just thinking about something from my past, Herman," Roma explains in a voice suddenly very soft. "You see, when I was a young girl, I lived near a concentration camp. There was a boy there, a prisoner, and for a long while, I used to visit him every day. I remember I used to bring him apples. I would throw the apple over the fence, and he would be so happy."

Roma sighs heavily and continues. "It is hard to describe how we felt about each other—after all, we were young, and we only exchanged a few words when we could—but I can tell you, there was much love there. I assume he was killed like so many others. But I cannot bear to think that, and so I try to remember him as he was for those months we were given together."

With my heart pounding so loudly I think it will explode, I look directly at Roma and ask, "And did that boy say to you one day, 'Do not bring me an apple tomorrow. I am being sent to another camp'?"

"Why, yes," Roma responds, her voice trembling.

"But, Herman, how on earth could you possibly know that?"

I take her hands in mine and answer, "Because I was that young boy, Roma."

For many moments, there is only silence. We cannot take our eyes from each other, and as the veils of time lift, we recognize the soul behind the eyes, the dear friend we once loved so much, whom we have never stopped loving, whom we have never stopped remembering.

Finally, I speak: "Look, Roma, I was separated from you once, and I don't ever want to be separated from you again. Now, I am free, and I want to be together with you forever. Dear, will you marry me?"

I see that same twinkle in her eye that I used to see as Roma says, "Yes, I will marry you," and we embrace, the embrace we longed to share for so many months, but barbed wire came between us. Now, nothing ever will again.

Almost forty years have passed since that day when I found my Roma again. Destiny brought us together the first time during the war to show me a promise of hope, and now it had reunited us to fulfill that promise.

Valentine's Day, 1996. I bring Roma to the *Oprah Winfrey Show* to honor her on national television. I want to tell her in front of millions of people what I feel in my heart every day:

"Darling, you fed me in the concentration camp when I was hungry. And I am still hungry, for something I will never get enough of: *I am only hungry for your love.*"

Herman and Roma Rosenblat
As told to Barbara De Angelis, Ph. D.

Shmily

My grandparents were married for over half a century, and played their own special game from the time they had met each other. The goal of their game was to write the word "shmily" in a surprise place for the other to find. They took turns leaving "shmily" around the house, and as soon as one of them discovered it, it was their turn to hide it once more.

They dragged "shmily" with their fingers through the sugar and flour containers to await whoever was preparing the next meal. They smeared it in the dew on the windows overlooking the patio where my grandma always fed us warm, homemade pudding with blue food coloring. "Shmily" was written in the steam left on the mirror after a hot shower, where it would reappear bath after bath. At one point, my grandmother even unrolled an entire roll of toilet paper to leave shmily on the very last sheet.

There was no end to the places "shmily" would pop up. Little notes with "shmily" scribbled hurriedly were found on dashboards and car seats, or taped to steering wheels. The notes were stuffed inside shoes and left under pillows. "Shmily" was written in the dust upon the mantel and traced in the ashes of the fireplace. This mysterious word was as much a part of my grandparents' house as the furniture.

It took me a long time before I was able to fully appreciate my grandparents' game. Skepticism has kept me from believing in true love—one that is pure and enduring. However, I never doubted my grandparents' relationship. They had love down pat. It was more than their flirtatious little games; it was a way of life. Their relationship was based on a devotion and passionate affection which not everyone is lucky enough to experience.

Grandma and Grandpa held hands every chance they could. They stole kisses as they bumped into each other in their tiny kitchen. They finished each other's sentences and shared the daily crossword puzzle and word jumble. My grandma whispered to me about how cute my grandpa was, how handsome an old man he had grown to be. She claimed that she really knew "how to pick 'em." Before every meal they bowed heads and gave thanks, marveling at their blessings: a wonderful family, good fortune, and each other.

But there was a dark cloud in my grandparents' life: my grandmother had breast cancer. The disease had first appeared ten years earlier. As always, Grandpa was with her every step of the way. He comforted her in their yellow room, painted that color so she could always be surrounded by sunshine, even when she was too sick to go outside.

Now the cancer was once again attacking her body. With the help of a cane and my grandfather's steady hand, they still went to church every morning. But my grandmother grew steadily weaker until, finally, she could not leave the house anymore. For a while, Grandpa would go to church alone, praying to God to watch over his wife. Then one day, what we all dreaded finally happened. Grandma was gone.

"Shmily." It was scrawled in yellow on the pink ribbons of my grandmother's funeral bouquet. As the crowd thinned and the last mourners turned to leave, my aunts, uncles, cousins and other family members came forward and gathered around Grandma one last time. Grandpa stepped up to my grandmother's casket and, taking a shaky breath, he began to sing to her. Through his tears and grief, the song came, a deep and throaty lullaby.

Shaking with my own sorrow, I will never forget that moment. For I knew then that, although I couldn't begin to fathom the depth of their love, I had been privileged to witness its unmatched beauty.

S-h-m-i-l-y: See How Much I Love You.

Thank you, Grandma and Grandpa, for letting me see.

Laura Jeanne Allen

"Henry is so sweet.
He's drawn hearts on my antacid tablets."

Reprinted by permission of George B. Abbott.

An Irish Love Story

That which is loved is always beautiful.

Norwegian Proverb

Let's call him Ian. That's not his real name—but in Northern Ireland these days you have to be careful about revealing names. There have been more than twenty-four hundred sectarian murders since the recent flare-up of ancient troubles between Catholics and Protestants. So there's no sense taking risks.

And Ian has had misery enough for his twenty-four years of life.

He came from good Protestant stock, the sort that goes to church twice every Sunday as regular as clockwork. His father, a welder in the Belfast shipyards, steady as they come. Mother kept a clean and tidy house, baked the best bread in the neighborhood and ruled the family with the sharp edge of her tongue. Two elder brothers, both unemployed laborers.

Ian did well at school and was now earning good money as a craftsman in a production plant. Quiet, serious, fond of walking through the countryside during the green evenings and golden weekends of summer, he liked few things better than a book by the roaring fire during the long loneliness of winter. Never had much to do with girlfriends—though men tend to marry late in Ireland.

Two years ago, on his twenty-second birthday, he was walking home from work when a terrorist hurled a bomb from a speeding car...and left Ian babbling in the nightmare of sudden blindness.

He was rushed to a hospital, operated on immediately for internal injuries and broken bones. But both eyes were destroyed.

The other wounds healed in their own time, though their scars would disfigure his flesh the rest of his days. But the scars on his mind, though invisible, were even more obvious.

He hardly spoke a word, hardly ate or drank, hardly slept. He simply lay in bed, brooding and sightless. Nearly four months.

There was one nurse who seemed to be able to draw some small spark of human response from him. Let's call her Bridget — a fine Irish name. Good Catholic stock, the sort that goes to Mass first thing every Sunday morning.

Her father, a carpenter, mostly worked away from home over in England. A decent man — loved his family, spent weekends with them whenever he could afford the fare. And they loved him as only an absent father can be loved.

Mother kept a clean but untidy house, cooked the best stew in the neighborhood and ruled the family with a quick hand and a soft heart.

Six brothers, four sisters—with the youngest of them all, Mary, eleven, her father's darling.

Bridget did well at school, had trained as a nurse at a

famous London hospital, and now, at the age of twenty-one, was a staff nurse in Belfast's biggest hospital.

Lively, though fundamentally serious, a singer with a sweet and gentle voice and a way of her own with folk songs. Never had much to do with boyfriends — though it wasn't from any lack of young men who'd set their caps at her.

But now her heart was moved by Ian, for there was something of the little-boy-lost about him that brought tears to her eyes. True, he couldn't see the tears, yet she was afraid that her voice would betray her emotions.

In a way she was right about her voice, because it was the lilt and the laughter of it that dragged him back from the depths of depression and self-pity, the warmth and gentleness and strength of her words, the blessed assurance with which she spoke to him of the love of Jesus Christ.

And so, as the long dark of his days turned to weeks and months, he would listen for her footsteps and turn his sightless face toward her coming like a flower bending for the sun.

At the end of his four months in the hospital he was pronounced incurably blind, but what he now knew as their love gave him the courage to accept his affliction. Because, despite everything against them—religion, politics, the opposition of their families — they were in love and wandering in that young and singing landscape.

He was discharged and began the weary months of rehabilitation: how to wash and shave and dress without help, how to move around the house without cracking his shins on every chair, how to walk through the streets with a white stick, how to read Braille, how to survive the crushing pity he could sense in the very air he breathed. Their love gave him the hope to go on living and trying.

Not that they were able to spend much of their lives together: an occasional evening, perhaps an afternoon when her duties allowed. But they lived for those brief encounters and knew the beginnings of deep peace and joys.

Their families were appalled. Thinking of getting married? The very law of God forbade it, surely.

"What fellowship hath the children of light with the children of darkness?" thundered his father. "You'll not be marrying her whilst I'm drawing breath!"

"The Roman Catholic Church," stated her priest, "discourages mixed marriages, so you can be putting the idea from you!"

So, by all manner of pressures — constant arguments, threats, promises and even downright lies—they were driven apart. And, eventually, they quarreled, said hurtful things in their black misery, and one evening, with the rain drizzling and their hearts cold, she walked away from him on the weeping street.

He withdrew into his perpetual night. Days and weeks of bitterness. "You'll not be regretting it in the long run," he was told. "You'd have been inviting trouble by yoking with an unbeliever!"

She withdrew into her work, too sick at heart to remember. Weeks and months of numbed agony. "You'll live to praise the Almighty," she was told. "You'd have been asking for hell on earth marrying a Protestant!"

The months drained into a year. And the bombings continued, to the grief of Ireland.

Then one evening, as Ian sat alone in the house, there came a frantic hammering at the door. "Ian, come you quick!"

By the voice, hysterical, choked, with tears, he recognized young Mary, Bridget's sister. "A bombing! She's trapped and half-dead, so she is! Screaming after you. Come you, Ian! In the name of God, please come!"

Without even shutting the door behind him, he took her hand. And she led and stumbled and cried with him through the merciless streets.

The bomb had devastated a little restaurant where Bridget had been eating supper with three other nurses. The others had managed to scramble out from under the shifting rubble. But she was trapped by the legs. And the fire was spreading, licking towards her.

They could hear her screaming, but couldn't yet reach the pit where she lay. Firemen, soldiers, lights and special equipment were on the way.

Ian moved into the chaos. "You can't go in there!" shouted the official in charge.

"She's my girl," said Ian.

"Don't be a raving lunatic!" shouted the officer. "You'll not be seeing your hand in front of your face in the darkness!"

"What difference does darkness make to a blind man?" asked Ian.

And he turned toward the sound of her voice, and moved through that black inferno with all the skills and instincts of the blind, all the urgency of love. "I'm coming, Bridget! I'm coming!"

And he found her and cradled her head in his yearning arms, and kissed her.

"Ian," she whispered, "Ian ..." and lapsed into unconsciousness like a tired child.

And with her blood soaking into his clothes, the fire

reaching them, he held her until their rescuers chopped a way through. What he didn't see, being blind, was that the side of her lovely face had been seared by fire.

In time, a long time, she recovered. Despite cosmetic surgery, though, her face would always be scarred. "But," she said, "the only man I love will never have the seeing of it, so what difference does it make to me?" And they took up their love from where they had never really left it.

True, both families fought it every step of the way. One dramatic confrontation almost led to a fistfight: shouted abuse, insults, desperate threats. But, in the middle of it, Bridget took Ian's hand. And together they walked out of that place of hatred.

Yes, they would marry. All the conventional wisdom warns of failure. But do you know a more excellent way than love? And what other healing is there?

George Target

Berry Mauve or Muted Wine?

He found me weeping bitterly in the hospital room. "What's wrong?" Richard asked, knowing that we both had reason to cry. In the past forty-eight hours, I learned that I had a cancerous lump in my breast that had spread to my lymph nodes, and there was a possible spot on my brain. We were both thirty-two with three young children.

Richard pulled me tight and tried to comfort me. Our friends and family had been amazed at the peace that had overwhelmed us. Jesus was our Savior and comfort before I found out I had cancer, and he remained the same after my diagnosis. But it seemed to Richard that the terrifying reality of my situation had finally crashed in on me in the few moments he was out of the room.

As he held me tight, Richard tried to comfort me. "It's all been too much, hasn't it Suz?" he said.

"That's not it," I cried and held up the hand mirror I had just found in the drawer. Richard looked puzzled.

"I didn't know it would be like this," I cried, as I stared in shock at my reflection in the mirror. I didn't recognize myself. I was horribly swollen. After the surgery, I had groaned as I lay asleep and well-meaning friends had freely pushed the self-dispensing medication to ease what they thought was pain. Unfortunately I was allergic to morphine and had swelled like a sausage. Betadine from the surgery stained my neck, shoulder and chest and it was too soon for a bath. A tube hung out of my side draining the fluid from the surgical site. My left shoulder and chest were wrapped tightly in gauze where I had lost a portion of my breast. My long, curly hair was matted into one big wad. More than one hundred people had come to see me over the past forty-eight hours, and they had all seen this brown-and-white, swollen, makeup-less, matted-haired, gray-gowned woman who used to be me. Where had I gone?

Richard laid me back on the pillow and left the room. Within moments he came back, his arms laden with small bottles of shampoo and conditioner that he confiscated from the cart in the hall. He pulled pillows out of the closet and dragged a chair over to the sink. Unraveling my IV, he tucked the long tube from my side in his shirt pocket. Then he reached down, picked me up and carried me—IV stand and all—over to the chair. He sat me down gently on his lap, cradled my head in his arms over the sink and began to run warm water through my hair. He poured the bottles over my hair, washing and conditioning my long curls. He wrapped my hair in a towel and carried me, the tube, and the IV stand back over to the bed. He did this so gently that not one stitch was disturbed.

My husband, who had never blow-dried his hair in his life, took out a blow-dryer and dried my hair, the whole while entertaining me as he pretended to give beauty tips. He then proceeded, based on the experience of watching me for the past twelve years, to fix my hair. I laughed as he bit his lip, more serious than any beauty-school student. He bathed my shoulder and neck with a warm washcloth, careful to not disturb the area around the surgery, and rubbed lotion into my skin. Then he opened my makeup bag and began to apply makeup. I will never forget our laughter as he tried to apply my mascara and blush. I opened my eyes wide and held my breath as he brushed the mascara on my lashes with shaking hands. He rubbed my cheeks with tissue to blend in the blush. With the last touch, he held up two lipsticks. "Which one? Berry mauve or muted wine?" he asked. He applied the lipstick like an artist painting on a canvas and then held the little mirror in front of me.

I was human again. A little swollen, but I smelled clean, my hair hung softly over my shoulders and I recognized myself.

"What do you think?" he asked. I began to cry again, this time because I was grateful. "No, baby. You'll mess up my makeup job," he said and I burst into laughter.

During that difficult time in our lives, I was given only a 40 percent chance of survival over five years. That was seven years ago. I made it through those years with laughter, God's comfort and the help of my wonderful husband. We will celebrate our nineteenth anniversary this year, and our children are now in their teens. Richard understood what must have seemed like vanity and silliness in the midst of tragedy. Everything I had ever taken for granted had been shaken in those hours—the fact that I would watch my children grow, my health, my future. With one small act of kindness, Richard gave me normalcy. I will always see that moment as one of the most loving gestures of our marriage.

T. Suzanne Eller

A Gentle Caress

What comes from the heart, touches the heart.

Don Sibet

Michael and I hardly noticed when the waitress came and placed the plates on our table. We were seated in a small deli tucked away from the bustle of Third Street, in New York City. Even the smell of our recently arrived blintzes was no challenge to our excited chatter. In fact, the blintzes remained slumped in their sour cream for quite some time. We were enjoying ourselves too much to eat.

Our exchange was lively, if not profound. We laughed about the movie that we had seen the night before and disagreed about the meaning behind the text we had just finished for our literature seminar. He told me about the moment when he had taken the drastic step into maturity by becoming Michael and refusing to respond to "Mikey." Had he been twelve or fourteen? He couldn't remember, but he did recall that his mother had cried and said he was growing up too quickly. As we bit into our blueberry blintzes, I told him about the blueberries that my sister and I used to pick when we went to visit our cousins in the country. I recalled that I always finished mine before we got back to the house, and my aunt would warn me that I was going to get a very bad stomachache. Of course, I never did.

As our sweet conversation continued, my eyes glanced across the restaurant, stopping at the small corner booth where an elderly couple sat. Her floral-print dress seemed as faded as the cushion on which she had rested her worn handbag. The top of his head was as shiny as the soft-boiled egg on which he very slowly nibbled. She also ate her oatmeal at a slow, almost tedious pace.

But what drew my thoughts to them was their undisturbed silence. It seemed to me that a melancholy emptiness permeated their little corner. As the exchange between Michael and me fluctuated from laughs to whispers, confessions to assessments, this couple's poignant stillness called to me. *How sad*, I thought, *not to have anything left to say. Wasn't there any page that they hadn't yet turned in each other's stories? What if that happened to us?*

Michael and I paid our small tab and got up to leave the restaurant. As we walked by the corner where the old couple sat, I accidentally dropped my wallet. Bending over to pick it up, I noticed that under the table, each of their free hands was gently cradled in the other's. They had been holding hands all this time!

I stood up and felt humbled by the simple yet profound act of connection I had just been privileged to witness. This man's gentle caress of his wife's tired fingers filled not only what I had previously perceived as an emotionally empty corner, but also my heart. Theirs was not the uncomfortable silence whose threat one always feels just behind the punch line or at the end of an anecdote on a first date. No, theirs was a comfortable, relaxed ease, a gentle love that knew it did not always need words to express itself. They had probably shared this hour of the morning with each other for a long time, and maybe today wasn't that different from yesterday, but they were at peace with that, and with each other.

Maybe, I thought as Michael and I walked out, it wouldn't be so bad if someday that was us. Maybe, it would be kind of nice.

Daphna Renan

The Metal Box

Last weekend, we celebrated my parents' fiftieth wedding anniversary. This morning, they left on a long-awaited trip to Hawaii. They were as excited as if it were their honeymoon.

When my parents married, they had only enough money for a three-day trip fifty miles from home. They made a pact that each time they made love, they would put a dollar in a special metal box and save it for a honeymoon in Hawaii for their fiftieth anniversary.

Dad was a policeman, and Mom was a schoolteacher. They lived in a modest house and did all their own repairs. Raising five children was a challenge, and sometimes money was short, but no matter what emergency came up, Dad would not let Mom take any money out of the "Hawaii account." As the account grew, they put it in a savings account and then bought CDs.

My parents were always very much in love. I can remember Dad coming home and telling Mom, "I have a dollar in my pocket," and she would smile at him and reply, "I know how to spend it."

When each of us children married, Mom and Dad gave us a small metal box and told us their secret, which we found enchanting. All five of us are now saving for our dream honeymoons. Mom and Dad never told us how much money they had managed to save, but it must have been considerable because when they cashed in those CDs they had enough for airfare to Hawaii plus hotel accommodations for ten days and plenty of spending money.

As they told us goodbye before leaving, Dad winked and said, "Tonight, we are starting an account for Cancun. That should only take twenty-five years."

Ann Landers

Tell Her That You Love Her

What love we've given, we'll have forever. What love we fail to give, will be lost for all eternity.

Leo Buscaglia

I shall call him Dr. Case. He was an old-school country doctor, and a close friend of mine twenty years ago. In the years that followed, I often stopped in his little Colorado town to see him when I went west, and sometimes he would tell me stories about people we both had known. He told me about John and Louise.

John was a ranchman, big, quiet, unlettered and strong as a horse. He had begun with fifty head of sheep. Ambitious and frugal, in ten years he owned two thousand ewes and ample pasture for them. Next, he bought an alfalfa farm at the edge of town and fattened his lambs. By the time he was forty-five he was a prosperous man.

Then he married. Louise was a local girl who had finished high school and gone to work as a waitress in the restaurant in town. John met her there the summer she was twenty. Soon he began driving in from his alfalfa farm every day for a ten o'clock cup of coffee. You could set your watch by the time he drove up and parked in front of the restaurant. John was methodical as a windmill, dependable as the seasons.

Louise chattered to him about the weather, the crops and harmless local gossip. John merely watched her and smiled and nodded his head; finally he would say, "Got to get to work. So long."

This went on for three months. Then one morning—Doc Case had stopped in for coffee after a call and heard it—John said, "Louise, I want you to marry me." Louise caught her breath and almost spilled the coffee. Doc said it was as though the two of them, John and Louise, were all alone. Louise said, "John, maybe I will. But I want a day or two to think about it." John nodded and drank his coffee and said, "Got to get to work. So long."

They were married two weeks later. After a honeymoon in Colorado Springs they settled down on the alfalfa farm, and Louise had the house painted and papered and refurnished with things from Denver. All that first year John had workmen out there, putting in a new kitchen, building a screened porch.

But Doc Case knew things weren't going right. Twice John called him out to see Louise, and he discovered that Louise wasn't happy. She wasn't well, either; she said she had frightful headaches, but there was nothing that Doc could put his finger on. The second time he went out to see her he asked her if John was treating her right. Louise answered that John was the best husband any woman could ask for, only—well, he didn't say much, and a woman wants to be talked to. After that things seemed to straighten out. When Doc saw her in town a few weeks later, Louise said, "I guess I was just imagining a lot of aches and pains. I've decided to be big and strong, like John!"

It was not until eighteen months later that Doc heard from them again. At 3:30 one morning, a banging on his door wakened him. John was there, his car out front with the motor running. "Doc," he said, "Louise is awful sick. You got to do something quick!" Louise was in the car, almost fainting with pain. They had been out at John's sheep ranch for a few days and the pain had struck her late that evening. She tried to shrug it off, but it got so bad she couldn't stand it. She fainted on the thirty-mile drive to town.

The doctor took her over to his four-bed hospital and operated. Her appendix had burst, but she rallied by dawn and Doc Case thought he had won. He told John they wouldn't know for twenty-four hours, but it looked as if the worst was over. John cried like a baby. "She's got to get well, Doc," he said. "She's got to!"

By evening her condition was worse. Doc gave her two plasma transfusions during the night, yet she weakened steadily. "I'm just not strong enough," she whispered to the doctor.

"What do you mean?" Doc demanded. "I thought you were going to be big and strong like John."

Louise smiled wanly. "John is so strong he doesn't need me. If he did he'd say so, wouldn't he?"

"Louise," Doc told her, "John does need you, whether he says so or not."

She shook her head and closed her eyes.

In the office, Doc said to John, "She doesn't *want* to get well."

"She's *got* to get well!" John exclaimed. "Look, Doc, how about a transfusion?"

The doctor explained that he had given her plasma.

"I mean *my* blood, Doc. I'm strong enough for both of us!"

The doctor led him down the hall. "Do you love that girl, John?" he asked.

"Wouldn't have married her if I didn't," John said.

"Have you ever told her so?"

John's eyes were baffled. "Haven't I given her everything I could? What more can a man do?"

"Talk to her," Doc said.

"I'm not a talking man, Doc. Hell, she knows that!" He gripped Doc's shoulders. "Give her some of my blood!"

The doctor thought a moment. Then he led John to the little laboratory, took a blood sample and typed it. At last he said, "All right, John. In ten minutes."

The doctor went to Louise's room and told her that John wanted to give her a transfusion, and there was a flicker of interest. He took her pulse. It was weak and fluttering slightly. He knew there was only a slim chance. Calling the nurse into the hall, he told her what he was going to do.

In a few moments he led John into Louise's room. The operating table had been placed beside her bed, and a curtain rigged up between bed and table. The nurse held the curtain aside as John lay down on the table. He put out a big, awkward hand and took Louise's hand and said, "Now *I'm* going to make you well, Louise."

Without looking at him, she whispered, "Why?"

"Why do you suppose?" John exclaimed.

"I don't know," she said.

"You're my wife, ain't you?"

There was no answer. The nurse lowered the curtain, swabbed John's arm and inserted a needle. John flexed the muscle proudly. "Here it comes," he said to Louise. A moment later he asked, "How's she taking it, Doc?"

Beyond the curtain, Doc Case had inserted a needle in Louise's wrist and relaxed the clamp on the tube. His fingers were on the pulse in her other wrist.

"Okay, John," he said.

"How does it feel, Louise?" John asked.

"All right," she whispered.

"Get a gallon of this blood in you," John said, "and you'll talk as loud as I do."

Her pulse seemed to strengthen slightly.

"John," she whispered.

"Yes?"

"I love you, John."

There was a moment of silence. Then John said, "Louise! You got to get well!"

"Why?" she whispered.

"You've got to do it for me. I need you." John hesitated, and his voice choked. "I love you."

Her pulse almost surged.

"You never told me," she said.

He said, "I never thought I had to." The pulse was steady now.

"John," she said, "tell me again."

He hesitated, then repeated the words: "I love you, Louise. More than anything in the world. I love you and I need you, and by God, I'm going to make you well!"

The doctor removed the needle from her wrist and took the plasma bottle from the rack beneath the towel and set them aside. He checked her pulse again. It was impossible, but there it was —steady and strong.

"How you doing over there?" John asked, his voice under control again. But Louise couldn't answer. She was weeping.

"She's coming along fine," Doc Case said. "You've done it,

John!"He signaled to the nurse, who pulled the needle from John's arm, removed the jar from beside the operating table and drew the curtain aside. Then she and the doctor went out into the hall.

When the doctor returned several minutes later, John was sitting with both of Louise's hands in his, talking to her.

"She was still a mighty sick girl," Doc said when he told me the story, "but I knew she was going to get well. And she did."

Doc shook his head. "It was enough that the miracle happened. John's blood was the wrong type for her, probably would have killed her. What did it matter if she got another pint of plasma while his blood went into a glass jar? What that girl needed was John. And she got him."

Hal Borland

The Greatest Gift of All

It took me a long time to understand the difference between a present and a gift. For years, I thought of the two as the same thing.

I grew up in a household where presents marked special occasions. There was always a beribboned box for each of us under the tree at Christmas or at our place at the table on our birthdays.

Additionally, Dad always gave Mom something each Valentine's Day and anniversary—cards, a box of chocolates, some token, eagerly offered. He loved to shop and would carefully plan his excursions to find just the right thing—a sweater in "her color", a velvet skirt for Christmas, some flattering expansion of her wardrobe.

I often accompanied him on these shopping expeditions. His joy in the hunt was infectious, proof of the pleasure of giving and of his love for her. I came to see these presents as the desirable norm, the tangible expression of a husband's devotion, their absence a visible lack.

So when I married a man who did not give presents on a regular basis, it was an adjustment. I wrestled with my ingrained expectations. Gary did not wholly eschew gift-giving. Sometimes he would return from sea armed with a brown paper bag inside of which was something he had found that reminded him of me—a meat cleaver on our first Christmas, a paring knife on our fifth.

Once, in acknowledgment of how many hours I spend on the telephone — for both work and pleasure — he brought home a shoulder pad for the telephone receiver. But mostly, he ignored holidays, refusing to shop for a thing to present to me as a sign of his affection.

I could not reconcile this present-less marriage with the one I had grown up observing. I tried to change him by example. I knitted him sweaters, socks, hats and gloves for Christmas; made him shirts; and bought books for his birthdays. He appreciated the caring these gifts represented, but refused to reciprocate in kind.

I dropped hints, they fell on deaf ears. I pouted, complained, explained and ranted. Nothing changed.

I began to tell him what I wanted, giving specific instructions. When Gary left for the local auction one Saturday (my birthday, as it happened), I asked him to find me a piece of jewelry, a bracelet or diamond earrings, as a birthday gift. He came home with a road scraper. I was stunned that he had missed the mark by so much. He attached the rusted blade to the back of the ancient tractor, then enthusiastically showed me how to use it, oblivious to the fact that I was not grateful.

But when the blizzard hit later that year and he was at sea, I used the road scraper to plow out both our drive and our neighbor's, thinking, as I rumbled along, how useless earrings would have been. Gary had wisely chosen not the thing that I wanted, but the thing that he knew I would need.

It was then that I finally realized that he had been giving me gifts all along. He would not be cajoled or coerced into handing over a scheduled token, an arbitrary tax on his affections. But the gestures, large and small, born of his caring and concern for me, for our children and for our lives together were the gifts that he gave daily.

His teaching me to manage my own earnings was a means of ensuring my capability and independence, a gift that bore other fruit when I used it to help my father sort out his tangled affairs.

Gary encourages my work, makes obvious his pleasure in our time together, willingly cooks, runs errands, does laundry, vacuums and chauffeurs the children—gifts to the whole family and an expression of our partnership.

The day before he leaves for sea, he stacks a month's worth of firewood against the chimney outside my office, and a week's worth inside, a labor of time and effort that frees me of a disliked, time-consuming, but absolutely necessary chore.

We struggle to teach others how to love us. In that struggle, we often forget how to appreciate the love they already give us as only they can give it. There are two parts to a gift—the giving and the accepting. Neither can be dictated.

I finally began to understand the difference between a present and a gift. A present is a thing. But a gift is broader and often intangible. It is a small act of kindness, the willingness to bend to another's needs, the sacrifice of time and effort. Love is a gift. Any expression of it, freely given, is an offering from the heart that is immeasurably better than a present.

My insistence on presents must have seemed to Gary a lack of appreciation for the gifts he had been giving all along, but he never stopped giving them.

Gary will be home this Christmas, but I don't expect a present. I already have the greatest gift.

Nancy Taylor Robson

What Does It Mean to Be a Lover?

Presence is more than just being there.

Malcolm Forbes

What does it mean to be a lover? It is more than just being married to or making love to someone. Millions of people are married, millions of people have sex — but few are real lovers. To be a real lover, you must commit to and participate in a perpetual dance of intimacy with your partner.

You are a lover when you appreciate the gift that your partner is, and celebrate that gift every day.

You are a lover when you remember that your partner does not belong to you — he or she is on loan from the universe.

You are a lover when you realize that nothing that happens between you will be insignificant, that everything you say in the relationship has the potential to cause your beloved joy or sorrow, and everything you do will either strengthen your connection or weaken it.

You are a lover when you understand all this, and thus wake up each morning filled with gratitude that you have another day in which to love and enjoy your partner.

When you have a lover in your life, you are richly blessed. You have been given the gift of another person who has chosen to walk beside you. He or she will share your days and your nights, your bed and your burdens. Your lover will see secret parts of you that no one else sees. He or she will touch places on your body that no one else touches. Your lover will seek you out where you have been hiding, and create a haven for you within safe, loving arms.

Your lover offers you an abundance of miracles every day. He has the power to delight you with his smile, his voice, the scent of his neck, the way he moves. She has the power to banish your loneliness. He has the power to turn the ordinary into the sublime. She is your doorway to heaven here on earth.

Barbara De Angelis, Ph. D.

My Sergei

Not long ago I heard someone ask a friend, "If you had to live your life over again, what would you do differently?" I've thought about this, and for me, I'd like to live my life over again backward. I'd like to live in a world where tomorrow would be yesterday, the day after tomorrow two days ago, and so on. Any day I'm living now, I would exchange for any day in the past because I know that for me to find the kind of happiness I had with Sergei isn't possible. It's like trying to find the comet that was in the night sky last spring, which passes Earth once in seventeen thousand years. No matter what lies ahead, the best years of my life will have been with my Seriozha, and those years are now laid to rest.

With Sergei and me, everything was natural, almost inevitable. First we were skating partners. Then we were friends. Then we were close friends. Then we were lovers. Then husband and wife. Then parents. I lived in a world in which I always had my favorite thing to do, which was skate. Then, God took Sergei away from me at the age of twenty-eight. Sergei died without warning of a heart attack on November 20, 1995, during a routine training session in Lake Placid, New York. I lost my husband and best friend, the father of my daughter. I lost my favorite thing to do, because now I had no skating partner. It's like I was living in a fairy tale before,and now I've been abandoned in a wild forest.

That is what life with Sergei was like,a fairy tale. It began the year I turned eleven. The pairs coach at the Central Red Army Club in Moscow,where I had skated since I was four, told me to come early to practice one day. He had chosen a skating partner for me. I was very excited because I knew it was going to be Sergei.

I had never spoken to him. I remembered seeing him on the ice with the older boys,and he was slender and narrow and handsome. But sergei was so much older than me—four years,which at that age seems like a lifetime—that I'd never thought it possible that we'd someday be paired together.

As a pairs skater,you have to learn everything you learned as a singles skater over again because you have to align your body with your partner's. Sergei and I practiced the jumps endlessly. I was never scared of the lifts because I always felt very safe in Sergei's arms. I'm not sure why, but once we were paired,I always believed Sergei was the only one who could skate with me.

Several years passed,we both grew up some more,and we began preparing for the 1988 Olympics. As the games approached,everything became a little more stressful,a little more intense. In mid-November,during practice for an exhibition,Sergei caught his blade in a soft rut in the ice while holding me aloft and dropped me. The first part of my body to hit the ice was my forehead.

I didn't feel any pain at first,then my entire head felt like it was splitting apart. I blacked out and was driven to the hospital. I ended up staying for six days. I'd suffered quite a serious concussion. I lay there worrying about missing practice and the Olympics, and I was mad at Sergei because I thought this fall was his mistake. Then, there was a knock on the door, and it was Sergei.

He was carrying a dozen roses, and he was very, very upset. It was the first time he'd given me flowers. I was surprised, even happy to see how distressed he was. It was another week before I was allowed on the ice, and Sergei continued to visit me at home every day. When at last I could skate again, I immediately noticed a change in the way he was holding me. Something had happened in those two weeks, and I realized that his thoughts for me had changed. Before we had been like two skaters. After that, we were a pair.

On December 31, we were spending New Years with my family. Sergei and I sat at a table and talked. He said, "I want to tell you something." But whatever it was, he was having trouble saying it. Then, he said, "Why don't we kiss?" Something like that. It wasn't really a question. He could probably see I wanted it, too. He gave me a gentle kiss on the mouth, and when he saw that I liked it, he gave me one that was longer.

I remember walking afterward and listening to the cold crunching of the snow beneath our footsteps. The fields were all blanketed in white, and the moon gave us shadows. It was so beautiful, and I was so happy. I wondered, why me? Why am I so lucky? I was so young and small and shy, and Sergei could have had any nice long-legged girl. Why should he choose me? I believed he would love me just for a little while, and then it would be over.

We went on to win the gold medal at the 1988 Olympics in Calgary, Canada. And the following year Sergei and I were married, and our daughter, Daria, was born a year and a half later. Then in 1994 we won our second Olympic gold medal in Lillehammer, Norway. The first gold medal we had won for the Soviet Union. This one we won for each other.

In 1995, we were training in Lake Placid for a fifty-five-city tour with the Stars on Ice. Our choreographer, Marina Zueva, was coming to help us work out the finishing touches on the program. We went over to the rink at about ten o'clock. We were both very happy with the changes she'd made in the program and decided we should skate through the whole number. At the beginning, I'm on one knee, and Sergei is on one knee, and we are face-to-face. I put my head on his shoulder, and I remember that his T-shirt smelled very clean. So I said, "Hmm, smells good."

And he said. "Yes, it's clean." Just that. They were to be his last words.

Then we started to skate. We did the early movements — the camel spin into a lift. Then we were supposed to do two crossovers before another lift. The full orchestra was just coming in, one of those high waves of music Marina liked so much. Sergei was gliding on the ice, but he didn't do the crossovers. His hands didn't go around my waist for the lift. I thought it was his back, which had been bothering him for some time. He was bent over slightly, and I asked him, "Is it your back?" He shook his head a little. He couldn't control himself. He tried to stop, but he kept gliding into the boards. He tried to hold on to the boards. He was dizzy, but he didn't tell me what was happening. Then he bent his knees and lay down on the ice very carefully.

I kept asking what was happening. "What's wrong, Seriozha? What's the matter?" But he didn't tell me. He didn't speak at all.

Marina stopped the music. When she came over to him, she knew right away it was something with his heart. It looked like he couldn't breathe anymore. She told me to call 911, and she started doing CPR on him. I was so scared. I was screaming. I don't know what. I forgot all the words in English. I couldn't remember the word for *help*. I ran, crying, to get someone to call 911 for me.

By the time I got back, everyone was around Sergei, and the medical people were working on him, trying to get his heart going. They wouldn't let me get close to him. The other skaters were holding me. They didn't want to let me watch what was happening. Then the medical people were taking him in the ambulance, and I only had time to get my skates off and pick up Sergei's bag. I sat in the front because they didn't want me to see as they worked on him in the back. I looked at the clock when we got to the hospital, and it was 11:35 A.M.

Then a doctor came out to talk to us. Her face was very serious. She said they had given him electric shocks. She said they had given him a shot of Adrenalin in the heart. But they had lost Sergei. At the age of twenty-eight he had died of a heart attack, the result of undiagnosed heart disease.

I can't describe the feelings that went through me when I walked into the room where Sergei was lying, still with his skates on. It looked like he was just sleeping. I talked to him, all the time thinking: *He will never stand up. He will never take me in his arms again, never hug me again, never hold my hand again.*

Then I started to take off his skates, and his feet were very cold. I tried to warm them up by rubbing them. I rubbed them and rubbed them. I tried to warm his hands, too. I loved his hands very much. I loved the way they were so big and soft. But I couldn't make them warm.

There was no question where the burial would be. Sergei

had a Russian soul. He was only comfortable there. Daria, of course, would come, too, and there was the question of what to say to her.

The next morning I sat Daria down and we talked. It was very, very difficult to start, difficult even for me to say these words: "Your father is dead; he's not coming back." Daria didn't cry or get upset. But she asked: "How can we see him?" So I told her that her father would come and see her whenever he wants and that sometimes she'd see him in her dreams. That he was like a little angel now. But that he'd never come back to her as we knew him and that it was very sad, and sometimes I would be crying, and that would be the reason.

I looked carefully into her eyes as I spoke these words, so she'd understand. And I think she did understand, at least as far as was possible. Because when we were back in Moscow, Daria wore a cross on a chain around her neck. And a few times she held this cross up to people and said, her face very said, "You know, God took my father."

I stayed in Moscow, living with my parents and taking one day at a time. I felt I was slowly losing myself. I had no purpose in my life, nothing to strive for. When I opened my eyes in the morning, I'd lie in bed wondering, *Why do I awaken? What do I have to get out of bed for?* I had no pressing responsibilities. Nothing to train for. No future I cared to think about. No Sergei. Always the thoughts ended there. No Sergei to lead me out of the unending darkness.

I began to realize that work was what could help me heal. I still had skating. I was always a skater first, and to lose both Sergei and skating was more than I could handle. A tribute to Sergei's memory had been arranged, a skating exhibition by all of our dear friends. It was to be held in the

Hartford Civic Center in Connecticut on February 27. It was difficult for me to imagine myself skating in front of people without holding Sergei's hand, without looking into Sergei's eyes, looking only at the audience, trying to fill that huge ice surface all by myself. But if I was to skate in the exhibition, that was how it would have to be. I wasn't going to skate with another partner. It was inconceivable to think of someone else's arms around me on the ice, touching me. Sergei's was the only hand I had held on the ice since I was eleven years old.

The tribute night arrived. I was waiting behind the curtain, not watching, for fear that I would cry and lose my composure. When I heard the music of Moonlight Sonata, so many memories came back. I found myself going through my movements for our free program from the 1994 Olympics in Lillehammer. Here Sergei throws me. Here we spin. Here we cross over...I couldn't stop myself. I didn't want to stop myself. I felt Sergei's spirit was beside me right then.

As the time neared for my solo number, a prayerful tribute to my union with Sergei, I thought about the words he used to say to me when we were getting ready to skate. We always kissed each other before we skated, we always hugged and touched each other. In the tunnel, waiting to go on the ice, I didn't have anyone to touch or kiss. It was a terrible feeling to be standing there by myself. Then I thought of what Marina had told me during my last practice: "Just trust Sergei. He will help you."

The lights rose, the people started to applaud and I had a feeling I'd never experienced before. I'd been worried that I'd be lost out there by myself, that I'd be so small no one would see me. But I felt so much bigger than I am. I felt huge, suddenly, like I filled the entire arena.

I thought, *I can't stop or I'll lose all this magic and power.* I just listened to my legs. And I listened to Sergei. It was like I had double power. I never felt so much power in myself, so much energy. I'd start a movement, and someone would finish it for me. I didn't have a thing in my head. It was all in my heart, all in my soul.

I'll never be able to skate this number as well again. I don't want to skate it again. It was such a special thing, and I don't know if Sergei would help me a second time.

Afterward I was supposed to say something, but as soon as I was handed the microphone, I couldn't think of any words. I thanked all the skaters, introduced Sergei's mother to the audience, thanked my own parents and then I remembered what I wanted to say: "I don't have enough words, but I want to wish to all of you: Try to find happiness in every day. At least once, smile to each other every day. And say just one extra time that you love the person who lives with you. Just say, 'I love you.'"

That is what Sergei taught me.

Ekaterina Gordeeva and E. M. Swift

2

FINDING TRUE LOVE

From every human being there rises a light that reaches straight to heaven, and when two souls that are destined to be together find each other, the streams of light flow together and a single brighter light goes forth from that united being.

Ba'al Shem Tov

Unforgettable Gracie

Our relationship was simple: I fed her straight lines and she fed me. Gracie Allen was my partner in our act, my best friend, my wife and lover, and the mother of our two children. We were a team, both on and off the stage.

When I met Gracie in 1923, she was a young woman living in New York City without a job. She had just quit a vaudeville act in New Jersey and heard I needed a partner. So she caught my act in Union City.

After the last show her roommate brought Gracie backstage to meet me. She was just a tiny thing, barely five feet tall and hardly more than 100 pounds. She had long hair, with curls that spun down over her shoulders. Her skin was that Irish peach-bloom, and she was wearing just a touch of makeup.

"Nattie," her roommate said (offstage everybody called me Nat or Nattie, since my real name was Nathan Birnbaum), "this is Grace Allen."

I remember looking down at her and thinking, *What a pretty little girl she is. I hope she'll work with me.* The next day her roommate told me Gracie was interested in joining up with me.

We billed ourselves "Burns and Allen" because it was my act, and I was going to be the comedian. We were booked into a theater in Newark, New Jersey.

There were maybe fifteen people in the audience when Grace Allen and I walked onstage together for the first time. I was nervous. She was cute, but who knew how she was going to do onstage?

The act did not go the way it was supposed to. Gracie fed me a straight line, and the audience chuckled. I answered with my topper; nothing. She gave me another line. This time people really laughed. I answered; again, nothing. By the time we finished our first show, Gracie was getting good laughs with lines like, "Oh, how stingy is her father?"

I didn't have to be a genius to understand that there was something wrong with a comedy act when the straight lines got more laughs than the punch lines. So I decided to give Gracie a few of my toppers, to see how the audience, reacted. They roared.

By the time we finished three days in Newark, Gracie had three-quarters of the punch lines. By month's end, Gracie was the whole act. My part had been reduced to little more than walking onstage with her and asking, "So, how's your brother?"

The audience created Gracie's character. I listened to the jokes they laughed at and gave Gracie more like that. The character was simply a dizzy dame, but what made her different was that Gracie played her as if her answers actually made sense. We called it illogical logic. For example, she would ask me, "Where do you keep your money?"

"In a bank," I'd respond.

"What interest do you get?"

"Four percent."

"Ha! I get eight."

"You get eight?"

"Yep. I keep it in two banks."

Like Gracie herself, her birdlike voice was unforgettable, and she was the most natural performer I've ever seen. She never tried to act, which was probably why she could make an audience believe that she really believed she could save electricity by shortening the vacuumcleaner cord.

In addition to our becoming successful, something else was happening. I was falling in love with Gracie.

It took me almost a year to tell her how I felt. I knew she was planning to marry Benny Ryan, a successful vaudevillian. I was afraid if I told her I loved her, she'd get upset and quit the act. So I kept my mouth shut.

I always kissed Gracie as part of the act, but I don't remember the first time I kissed her for real. It happened gradually. Instead of kissing her on the cheek, I kissed her lightly on the lips. The next time I pressed harder, and maybe the time after that I put my arms around her. Finally, it was for real. Only once, I remember, did she pull away. "It's not right, Nat," she told me. "What about Benny?"

"I'll kiss him later," I said. We eventually got married, of course, and years later Gracie and I remembered our wedding on radio. At the end of the show Gracie said, "I just want everyone to know one thing," she said. "I'm a very lucky woman. I was courted by the youngest, handsomest, most charming, most sought-after star in show business..."

"Thank you very much," I said. "...but I married George because I loved him."

I called her Googie. It started when she woke me up one night and asked me to make her laugh. So I looked at her and said, in baby talk, "Googie, googie, googie." (Look, when I was wide awake my material wasn't that great, so how much better could it have been in the middle of the night?) Gracie laughed, and from then on she was Googie to me.

Just as Gracie and I were becoming stars, vaudeville was dying. Fortunately, we had the perfect act for radio. Gracie's illogical logic clicked immediately. Women understood her. Men thought they were married to her. And everybody knew someone just like her.

After a few years on the air, our show, now named "The Adventures of Gracie" and later changed to "The George Burns and Gracie Allen Show," began attracting the biggest names in show business.

Gracie was on a first-name basis with America. Lovable, confusing Gracie, who claimed to have grown grapefruits so big it took only eight to make a dozen, who confessed to cheating on her driver's test by copying from the car in front of her and whose Uncle Barnham Allen had the water drained from his swimming pool before diving in because he knew how to dive but didn't know how to swim.

When I think of Gracie, I remember a little girl with more energy than anyone else around her; a strong, vibrant, sometimes tough woman. When I think of someone with a bad heart, that wasn't Gracie at all.

But she had suffered her first heart attack in the early '50s, and over the next several years she had other minor ones. Today they call her condition angina. Each time she had an episode, I'd hold her tightly in my arms and talk to her until the pain subsided.

Gracie kept working, but she talked about retiring. I didn't pay any attention. I thought she wanted to quit show business the way Jack Benny was stingy—it was just part of the act.

But during our last season I noticed little things. How she had an extra problem with a line, how she took a slightly longer break between takes.

One Sunday night as we were in our den watching television I asked her, "Do you really want to stop?"

"I really do," she said.

We filmed our final show on June 4, 1958. It was the last time we ever worked together. When Gracie finished, the crew gave her a standing ovation. Someone opened a bottle of champagne. Gracie took one sip, just to be polite, and said, "Okay, that's it." Then she paused, for just a second, took a long look around the set, added, "Thank you very much, everyone," and walked away. She never looked back.

For the first few years of her retirement, Gracie was very happy. She was well enough to go shopping and visit with friends and play cards and spend time reading and redecorating the house. But after a heart attack in 1961, she couldn't go out at night as much. She just didn't have the energy.

One night in August, we were home alone, watching the Democratic convention on TV. They were showing a tribute to President Kennedy, and Gracie was crying. When the convention went off the air, I went downstairs to work on a script. A little later, I heard Gracie calling for me. She was having trouble breathing. I phoned the doctor. As soon as he arrived, he listened to her heart. He turned to me. "I think we should call an ambulance, George."

When we got to the hospital, they rushed her upstairs. Not much later, the doctor came and told me, "I'm sorry, George. Gracie's gone."

He asked me if I wanted to see her. Of course I did. I wanted to talk to her for a few more minutes. I wanted to stand next to her onstage and hear the laughter of the audience. I wanted her to look up at me with her trusting eyes. I wanted to ask her just once more, "Gracie, how's your brother?"

So I went into the room. She was lying there, and she looked so peaceful. I didn't know what to do. So I did the only thing there was to do. I leaned over, and I kissed her and whispered, "I love you, Googie."

For the first time in forty years I was alone. I don't know of many couples who spent as much time together as we did. We'd get up together, go to the theater or studio together, come home together at night. We loved each other, we liked each other, and we respected each other.

People often ask me how to make a marriage work. I know all about the importance of respect and trust and honesty and generosity. But for me the answer still comes back to one thing: marry Gracie.

George Burns

A Test of Faith

Love cures people, both the ones who give it, and the ones who receive it.

Karl Menninger

A slight chill bit the night air as Wes Anderson climbed into his silver sedan. It was 8:30 on March 7, 1994, and the burly thirty-four-year-old minister of Carmichael Christian Church in Sacramento, California, had just finished a meeting with several church members.

"Have a good evening, Pastor," a member of his congregation called out.

"I will," Wes answered. Then chiding gently in his Tennessee twang, he added, "Hope to see y'all Sunday."

Wes had been studying criminal justice in college when he felt a call to the church. He came to Carmichael in 1992, and the 110-member congregation responded warmly to the easygoing man with the broad smile.

Driving home, Wes saw one of his congregants, seventy-eight-year-old Dorothy Hearst, locked in a three-car fender bender. Wes stopped to help, and he was relieved that she was only slightly shaken. Suddenly, fast-approaching headlights flashed toward them. "Dorothy!" Wes shouted. "He's going to hit us!" Wes shoved her out of the way just as a station wagon slammed into his right side, crushing him against Dorothy's car. His right leg exploded in pain. Then he lay writhing on the asphalt, his right leg nearly severed.

As the ambulance arrived at the University of California, Davis, Medical Center, a doctor thrust a surgical consent form into the pastor's hand. "There is no other way to say this," he said. "Your right leg may have to be amputated."

Shortly after surgery, Wes felt an agonizing cramp gnarled in his right calf. He reached down to rub the area, but recoiled. There was nothing there.

Phantom pain — physical sensation experienced by amputees when the brain signals that the limb is still there — would come and go like torturing ghosts. Each time, he winced from the sharp, shooting pangs in the leg that was no longer there. All of this because of James Allen Napier — a drunken driver who would spend only eight months in jail.

As the days wore on, Wes fell into depression. Surgeries left his remaining leg raked with scars. Red welts crisscrossed his stomach, a road map where tissue for skin grafts had been taken.

"It isn't fair," he complained to Mike Cook, his friend and the pastor of Carmichael Christian's sister church, Sylvan Oaks. "I wanted to have a wife and children someday. What woman could love me with all these injuries and scars?"

"Life isn't fair," Mike replied. "But is it supposed to be? You've seen terrible things happen to good people. Remember, Wes, you saved a life. I know it's hard to believe, but God has his reasons."

Wes looked away. He, too, counseled his flock to keep the

faith in times of trouble. "God always has a plan," he often told them. "Trust his will." But the words he once thought were so powerful suddenly seemed insignificant.

A reporter from the *Sacramento Bee* called, wanting to tell Wes's story. Wes's instinct was to say no; he didn't want to be portrayed as a hero. The reporter promised to simply recount what happened, and Wes finally gave in. *Who knows*, he thought. *Maybe it could do someone some good*.

Virginia Bruegger dropped the March 16, 1994, *Sacramento Bee* on a pile by her bed. As usual, making it through the day had been a scramble. First her car wouldn't start; then she missed the bus. For the past year and a half, the thirty-eight-year-old divorced mother had adopted a relentless schedule of classes, study and internships to earn a bachelor's degree in behavioral science at the University of California, Davis. Now, as midterms loomed in her last year, her shoestring budget was stretched to the limit.

Just as she settled in at her kitchen table that night to study, her sixteen-year-old son, Steven, became sick from food poisoning. At three o'clock in the morning, Virginia trudged to her room, exhausted. Suddenly the pressure felt crushing. *Am I doing the right thing*? She wondered. *Will I be able to find a job after graduation*?

A newspaper headline jumped out at her: "Pastor Loses Leg Saving Woman from Car Crash." She lifted the section and began reading.

My God, she thought, *what this man went through*. Virginia stopped at the quote the pastor gave as his reason for telling his story — that it might help get "people's lives spiritually on track."

It's as if he's speaking directly to me, she thought. As a girl, Virginia had a religious upbringing in the small town of

Bushton, Kansas. But since her divorce, she'd drifted away from her faith; until now, she could barely recollect a prayer.

As the morning sunlight arrived, classes loomed just hours away. *Not today*, Virginia thought. Something told her she had to meet this man.

Awakening from his seventh surgery in ten days, Wes didn't know what to make of the woman at his door with a potted ivy plant in her hand. Her sparkling brown eyes registered a shy look until she smiled — then her whole face brightened.

"I just wanted to thank you," Virginia began, groping for words. *What do I say to him*? She wondered. Dozens of cards crowded a bedside stand and clung to a wall next to the bed. Flowers sent by friends, family and Wes's congregation bloomed in every corner. His story had obviously touched many people, not just her.

"I read the article in the paper, and I had to let you know what your story did for me," Virginia said. "It changed my perspective on what I've been going through. I've been having kind of a tough time."

Do I sound whiny? She wondered. *This man, after all, has gone through a real trial — not just a few worries over bills and school*. Wes's expression reassured her. "Your story helped me realize that I needed to get my relationship back on track with the Lord."

Wes studied the stranger. Since he'd been in the hospital, Wes had barely had a moment free of pain. Now his mind was less on himself and more on how he could help. "Do you have a church?" he asked.

Virginia shook her head. Such a simple thing. *He got right to the problem*, she thought, and reached out to shake his hand. Wes took it, but he pulled away a little quickly. *I hope*

I haven't been too forward, she thought.

Wes hadn't meant to draw back. It was instinct; he still felt wounded, and he was exhausted. Funny, though, her thanking him. For some reason, it was he who felt better.

Within a week of meeting Wes, Virginia found a church near her home and sent Wes a note. She then visited him a second time two weeks later; they compared notes about their lives. They discussed her classes and job prospects, and talked about how his physical therapy was coming along.

He's so easy to talk to, Virginia mused on her way home. Every few days, she'd send him a note or drop by.

About two months after the accident, Virginia phoned Wes. "I'm being discharged today!" he said, his voice barely able to contain his excitement.

After they hung up, Virginia was struck by an inexplicable feeling. She hopped in her car and sped to the medical center.

"What are you doing here?" Wes asked, revealing his surprise.

"I'm not sure," Virginia replied, a bit shakily. "I just felt like I was supposed to be here."

"Well, I'm glad you are," he said, smiling.

As they approached his small A-frame church, Wes's eyes began to fill. On a black wrought-iron fence, dozens of yellow ribbons blossomed like bright flowers. Children from the church's elementary school jumped up and down, waving at his car. Banners proclaimed: "We love you! Welcome home, Mr. Anderson!"

Virginia felt tears, too.

In June, wearing a cap and gown, Virginia strode proudly down an auditorium aisle and accepted her degree. Unable to attend because of church obligations, Wes had sent congratulatory flowers. A few nights later, the two friends and their parents met for dinner. They had much in common. Both of their parents had been married for more than forty years; they were both raised in the Methodist Church.

"You even talk like me!" Wes chided.

"I may have a drawl," Virginia kidded back, "but I'm not that bad."

At home, Wes finished buttoning his shirt as he was getting ready to go to church. Suddenly he felt himself falling backward toward the floor. He landed directly on his stump and screamed in agony. Wes spent the next nine days in bed. He'd always prided himself on being independent, strong. Now, doubt and depression crashed over him.

He even began to question his relationship with Virginia. "I really like her," Wes told Mike. "I'm just worried that this might be some sympathy thing. I mean, I was never a Hollywood star, but look at me now."

"Wes, you're not any less of a person than you were before the accident," Mike said. "What's important is what's on the inside."

It had been several days since Virginia had heard from Wes. She thought about their last meeting, a visit to Muir Woods National Monument. *Did I do something wrong*? Virginia wondered. They had talked openly about her divorce eight years ago and her struggle to make a better life for herself and Steven. When she'd been out with other men, she'd worried where things were leading. With Wes, such things never crossed her mind. *He's different from any man I've ever known*, Virginia thought.

When Wes finally called, he asked Virginia to the state fair and surprised her by picking her up in his car, newly adapted for the loss of his leg. Under a star-filled sky they sat and watched the fireworks display. "I was starting to wonder when I'd see you again," Virginia said.

"I'm sorry," Wes replied. "It's just that I don't do a lot of dating. If I go out with someone, I look on it as something serious. I treasure our friendship, and I'd never want to jeopardize it. I just..."

Virginia interrupted. "Wes, before you go any further ..."

Wes looked down. *This is the part where she'll say let's just be friends.*

"You need to know I care about you as an individual," Virginia continued, "and not whether you have one leg or two. To me, you are a whole man, a complete person."

Wes listened stunned. "I love you," he said, his voice thick with emotion.

"I love you, too," Virginia replied. For the first time, they kissed.

That Easter, Wes and Virginia helped set up a sunrise service outdoors. Wes struggled through wet grass with his artificial leg and lost his balance. He slammed to the ground, feeling the old flames of anger, frustration and doubt.

Virginia rushed to his side, but Wes didn't look up, afraid of what he might see. *Fear*? *Pity*? He'd never doubted her, but he felt so vulnerable. A grown man, helpless.

At that moment the truth dawned on him. *I've focused on the outside, when it was my inside that really needed to heal.*

Virginia and a friend helped Wes up. He was shaken and embarrassed. But at last he wasn't afraid. *This is who I am*, he realized. *A man who will fall occasionally, but who will rise, each time stronger*.

On May 27, 1995, Wes came in through a side door to the altar of the Carmichael Christian Church, dressed in a white tuxedo and gripping a black cane. He looked to the entrance as Virginia, in a beaded white gown, came toward him, escorted by her parents.

The church was full as Mike Cook performed the wedding ceremony. "Two are better than one," Mike said, reading from Ecclesiastes. "If one falls down, his friend can help him up. But pity the man who falls and has no one to help him up."

As the service ended, Wes stood before a flight of stairs leading to the congregation. Holding hands with Virginia, he walked down, step by step, until they reached the bottom.

A little more than a year before, Wes had wondered about God's plan.

Now he knew.

Bryan Smith

Damaged Goods

The dust mites danced in the ray of sunshine that provided the only light in the rabbi's office. He rocked back in his office chair and sighed as he stroked his beard. Then he took his wire-rimmed glasses and polished them absent-mindedly on his flannel shirt.

"So," he said, "you were divorced. Now you want to marry this good Jewish boy. What's the problem?"

He nestled his grizzled chin in his hand and smiled softly at me.

I wanted to shriek. What's the problem? First of all, I'm Christian. Second, I'm older than he is. Third—and not least, by any means—I'm divorced! Instead, I looked back into his soft brown eyes and tried to form the words.

"Don't you think," I stuttered, "that being divorced is like being used? Like being damaged goods?"

He settled back in the office chair and stretched so that he was looking at the ceiling. He stroked the scraggly beard that covered his chin and his neck. Then, he returned to his spot behind the desk and leaned toward me.

"Say you have to have surgery. Say you have a choice between two doctors. Who are you going to choose? The one right out of medical school or the one with experience?"

"The one with experience," I said.

His face crinkled into a grin. "I would, too," he locked his eyes with mine. "So in this marriage, you will be the one with experience. That's not such a bad thing, you know.

"Often, marriages tend to drift. They get caught in dangerous currents. They get off course and head toward hidden sandbars. No one notices until it is too late. On your face, I see the pain of a marriage gone bad. You will notice the drift in this marriage. You'll call out when you see the rocks. You'll yell to watch out and pay attention. You'll be the person with experience," he sighed. "And believe me, that's not such a bad thing. Not bad at all."

He walked to the window and peeked between the slats of the blinds. "You see, no one here knows about my first wife. I don't hide it, but I don't make a big deal about it. She died early in our marriage before I moved here. Now, late at night I think of all the words I never said. I think of all the chances I let pass by in that first marriage, and I believe I'm a better husband to my wife today because of the woman I lost."

For the first time, the sadness in his eyes had meaning. Now I understood why I chose to come talk to this man about marriage instead of taking an easier route and getting married outside both our religions. The word "rabbi" means teacher. Somehow I sensed he could teach me, or even lend me, the courage I needed in order to try again, to marry again and to love again.

"I will marry you and your David," said the rabbi. "If you promise me that you will be the person who yells out when you see the marriage is in danger."

I promised him I would, and I rose to leave.

"By the way," he called to me as I hesitated in his doorway, "did anyone ever tell you that Joanna is a good Hebrew name?"

Sixteen years have passed since the rabbi married David and me on a rainy October morning. And, yes, I have called out several times when I sensed we were in danger. I would tell the rabbi how well his analogy has served me, but I cannot. He died two years after our wedding. But I will always be grateful for the priceless gift he gave me: the wisdom to know that *all* of our experiences in life make us not less valuable, but more valuable, not less able to love, but more able to love.

Joanna Slan

The Fortune Cookie Prophecy

There is no surprise more magical than the surprise of being loved; it is God's finger on man's shoulder.

Charles Morgan

I was married three times before I was seven years old.

My older brother Gary performed the ceremonies in our basement. Gary was good at entertaining the family and neighborhood kids with his creative ideas. Since I was the youngest boy in our group, I was often on the receiving end of his creativity.

What I remember most about those weddings is that all the girls were at least five years older than I was, and they all had beautiful eyes that sparkled when they laughed. Those weddings taught me to imagine what it would be like to find my soul mate one day and to be sure that I would know her by her beautiful eyes.

Puberty hit me late. I was still afraid of the opposite sex when I was fifteen, and yet I prayed every night for the girl I would marry. I asked God to help her do well in school and to be happy and full of energy—wherever and whoever she was.

I first kissed a girl when I was twenty-one. From that time forward, I dated many beautiful and talented young ladies, searching for the girl I had prayed for in my youth and still certain that I would know her by her eyes.

One day, my phone rang. "Don," it was my mother. "You know I told you about the Addisons, who moved in next door to us. Well, Clara Addison keeps asking me to invite you over for cards some night."

"Sorry, Mom, I've got a date that night."

"How could you? I haven't even told you what night it is?" my mother responded with exasperation.

"It doesn't matter when. I'm sure the Addisons are nice people, but I'm not going to waste an evening socializing with people who don't have any eligible daughters."

That's how stubborn I was—I was positive that there was no reason for me to go to visit the Addisons.

Years passed. I was twenty-six, and my friends were getting nervous about my prospects. They kept lining up blind dates for me. Many of these dates were fiascoes, and they were interfering with my social life. So I made up a few rules about blind dates:

1. No dates recommended by my mother (moms don't understand the sex-appeal factor).
2. No dates recommended by a female (they're too easy on each other).
3. No dates recommended by a single guy friend (if she's so awesome, how come he hasn't asked her out?).

In three simple steps, I eliminated 90 percent of all my blind dates, including one recommended by my old friend Karen. She called one evening to tell me that she had become good friends with a beautiful girl who reminded her of me.

She said she knew we would hit it off.

"Sorry," I said, "you're ruled out by rule number two."

"Don," she said, "you're crazy, and your silly rules are eliminating the girl you've been waiting for. But have it your way. Just take her name and phone number, and when you change your mind, call her."

To get Karen to stop bothering me about it, I said I would. The girl's name was Susan Maready. I never called her.

Just a couple of weeks later, I ran into my old buddy Ted in the university cafeteria. "Ted," I said. "You look like you're walking on air."

"Can you see stars under my feet?" he said, laughing. "The fact is, I just got engaged last night."

"Hey, congratulations!"

"Yeah," he said, "at thirty-two, I was beginning to wonder if any woman was going to have me." He pulled his wallet out of his pocket. "Here," he said, suddenly serious, "look at this."

It was a thin strip of paper from a fortune cookie. "You will be married within a year," it said.

"That's wild," I said. "They usually say something that would fit anyone, like 'You have a magnetic personality.' They were really taking a chance with that one."

"No kidding," he said. "And look at me now."

A few weeks later, my roommate Charlie and I were eating dinner at a Chinese restaurant. I shared this story about Ted's fortune cookie prediction, and his subsequent engagement. Just then, the waiter brought over our post-meal fortune cookies. Charlie laughed at the coincidence as we opened our cookies. Mine said, "You have a magnetic personality." His said, "You or a close friend will be married within a year." A chill ran up my spine. This was really strange. Something told me to ask Charlie if I could keep his fortune, and he handed it to me with a smile.

Not long afterward, my classmate Brian said he wanted to introduce me to a young woman named Susan Maready. I was sure I'd heard that name before, but couldn't remember how or where. Since Brian was married, and therefore I wouldn't be breaking my "rules" about being fixed up by single guys, I accepted his offer to meet Susan.

Susan and I spoke on the phone, and planned a bike ride and a cookout. Then, the meeting—and as soon as I saw her, my heart started beating hard and wouldn't stop. Her large green eyes did something to me I couldn't explain. But somewhere in me, I knew that it was love at first sight.

After that wonderful evening, I remembered that this hadn't been the first time someone tried to fix me up with Susan. It all came back to me. Her name had been popping up all over the place for a long time. So the next time I had a chance to talk to Brian alone, I asked him about it.

He squirmed and tried to change the subject.

"What is it, Brian?" I asked.

"You'll have to ask Susan," was all he'd say.

So I did.

"I was going to tell you," she said. "I was going to tell you."

"Come on, Susan," I said. "Tell me what? I can't stand the suspense."

"I've been in love with you for years," she said, "since the first time I saw you from the Addisons' living room window. Yes—it was me they wanted you to meet. But you wouldn't let anyone introduce us. You wouldn't let the Addisons set us up; you wouldn't take Karen's word for it that we would like each other. I thought I was never going to meet you."

My heart swelled with love, and I laughed at myself. "Karen was right," I said. "My rules were crazy."

"You're not mad?" she asked.

"Are you kidding?" I said. "I'm impressed. I've got only one rule for blind dating now."

She gave me a strange look. "What's that?"

"Never again," I said and kissed her.

We were married seven months later.

Susan and I are convinced that we are true soul mates. When I was fifteen and praying for my future wife, she was fourteen and praying for her future husband.

After we had been married a couple of months, Susan said to me, "Do you want to hear something really strange?"

"Sure," I said. "I love to hear strange things."

"Well, about ten months ago, before I'd met you, my friends and I were at this Chinese restaurant, and ..." She pulled a slip of paper from a fortune cookie out of her wallet:

"You will be married within a year..."

Don Buehner

Reprinted by permission of Benita Epstein.

Will Power

A minister had just finished giving a lecture on marriage at the local community center when he was approached by three couples. Impressed by his presentation, the couples asked if they could join his church.

"Are you married?" the minister inquired of them. Each couple assured him that they were, and again, asked if they could becomes members of his congregation. "Well, I am impressed by your sincerity," the minister responded. "But I need to know that you are serious about your commitment to spiritual discipline. So to prove this, you must pass a test."

"We'll do anything," all three couples insisted.

"All right," he explained "then here is your test: you must practice total abstinence from marital intimacy for three weeks." The couples agreed, and left, promising to return at the end of that time.

Three weeks later, the three couples met the minister in his study at the church. "I'm glad to see you again," the minister began. Turning to the first couple, he asked, "Well, how did you two do?"

"We've been married for almost thirty years," the husband answered. "So it was no problem."

"Splendid!" exclaimed the minister. "Welcome to my church."

Then he looked towards the second couple, and asked them how they had done with the test.

"Well I must admit, it wasn't easy," explained the wife. "You see, we've only been married for five years, so we were tempted, but we didn't give in, and I'm happy to say we lasted the whole three weeks."

"Good for you!" the minister responded with a smile. "Welcome to my church." The minister then turned to the third couple, who were newlyweds. "And you?" he asked gently. "How did you do with the test?"

"Well pastor, I can't lie to you," the husband began. "We were both doing okay until this morning right after breakfast when my wife bent over to pick up a box of cereal she'd dropped on the floor. We both reached down to pick it up at the same time, and our hands touched. Suddenly, we were so overcome with passion that we gave in to our desires right then and there!"

"I appreciate your honesty," the minister said to the couple. "But you did fail the test, and I'm afraid I just can't let you come to my church."

"That's okay, pastor," the man answered. "We aren't allowed back in that supermarket anymore either."

Barbara De Angelis, Ph. D.

Streaking for Love

On a warm spring night in April on Iraklion Air Station in Crete, I left my dorm with a girlfriend, and decided to check out a party that was happening on the base. Boyfriend-less at the time, my eyes automatically swept the crowd in search of "potential"—and stopped on Frank.

I'd seen him around the base before, and I'd always thought he was cute: Tall and thin. Curly black hair. Mustache. Kind of Jim Croce-looking. I parked myself next to him and engaged him in conversation.

As we spoke I found he had a sweet smile and a sexy New York accent. (Terribly exotic for a girl who'd grown up in the cornfields of Indiana.) But it wasn't just his good looks and accent that charmed me. He was a genuinely nice guy—easy to talk to, and best of all, he made me laugh.

I was so engrossed in Frank and his lively conversation that at first, I didn't notice the commotion around us. Too late, I looked up just in time to see a flash of bare skin disappear around the corner of the building. Everyone around us laughed hysterically and pointed in that direction. Suddenly, I realized what I'd missed.

"My first streakers!" I gasped. Then I turned to Frank accusingly. "And I missed them because of you!"

Frank looked properly contrite. "I'm sorry. But for you, I'll get them to do it again."

I didn't think Frank was serious, but before I could say a word, he scrambled up from the ground where we were sitting, and disappeared around the corner of the dorm.

A few minutes later, I heard a peal of shrill laughter from the crowd. I whipped my head around, and there they were—the two streakers, as naked as babes, running once again like mad demons down the span of lawn between the two dorms. Suddenly my eyes widened. A third streaker had joined the other two. He was tall and thin, with curly black hair and a mustache. Kind of Jim Croce-looking.

Oddly enough, Frank missed the whole thing, or so he said. He reappeared at my side a few minutes later slightly out of breath, acting as if nothing had happened.

"Thanks," I said dryly. "You didn't have to go to so much trouble to impress me."

He shrugged with a sly smile. "Well, I couldn't let you miss your first streakers."

What could I say? He'd done it for me.

That was the beginning of our relationship. It's been twenty-three years now, and we have two wonderful grown children. Frank doesn't streak anymore. He feels it no longer fits into his lifestyle—being a respected computer programmer and all.

Oh, he still gets naked—just not for the general public.

Everyone who knows the story of our first meeting thinks I saw something I liked that night when Frank streaked past me in the buff. I did ...

His personality.

Carole Bellacera

Lemonade and a Love Story

Love is the way I walk in gratitude.

A Course in Miracles

Driving down a deserted Indiana road, I saw a "fresh lemonade" sign and pulled over. I had expected a filling station or small store, but to my surprise, it was a house. An old man sat on the porch. I got out of my car; nobody else was around. He poured me some lemonade and offered me a seat. It was so peaceful; nothing but cornfields, sky and sun in view.

We talked about the weather and my trip. He asked if I had family. I explained that I had just gotten married and hoped to have children someday. He seemed pleased that family still mattered to some folks. Then he told me his story. I share it because it is one I cannot forget.

"There's something special about families. A wife, children, a home of your own. The peace of mind that comes with doing the right thing. I remember being your age," he said.

"I didn't think I'd have a chance at marriage. I didn't have the greatest family. But I persevered. Both parents loved me tremendously, and now I realize their intentions for me were good. But it was tough. Many nights I remember lying in bed, thinking, *I'm not going to risk having divorce happen to me. A wife? A family? Why?* I was convinced I would never risk exposing my kids to divorce.

"As a teenager, I experienced new emotions. I didn't believe in love, though. I thought it was only infatuation. I had this friend. In eighth grade she had a crush on me. We were afraid to let each other know how we felt, so we just talked. She became my best friend. All through high school we were like peas and carrots," he grinned.

"She had problems in her family, too. I tried to help her out. I did my best to take care of her. She was smart, and beautiful, too. Other young fellas wanted her to be theirs. And since this is between you and me," he winked, "I'll tell you—I wanted her to be mine, too."

"We tried going out once, but things blew up and we didn't talk for nine months. Then one day in class I got up the nerve to write her a note. She wrote back, and things slowly picked up again. Then she went to college."

The old man poured us more lemonade.

"She went to school in Minnesota, where her father lived," he reminisced. "I wanted to play baseball. I got turned down from school after school, and finally was accepted by a small school, also in Minnesota! It was so ironic. When I told her, she cried.

"We began dating. I remember kissing her for the first time in my room. My heart beat so fast, I was afraid of rejection. But our relationship grew. After college, I did get to play baseball. Then, I married that sweet girl of mine. I never would have believed I'd be walking down the aisle."

"Did you have children?" I asked.

"Four of 'em!" he smiled. "Put them through school, taught them the best way to live as far as we could tell. Now they're all grown with kids of their own. It made me proud to see them holding their babies. I knew then that life was worthwhile.

"When the kids left the house, my wife and I would go on trips together, holding hands like we were young again. That's the beauty of it, you see. As the years rolled on, my love for her continued to grow. Sure we fought, but love prevailed.

"I don't know how to explain the love I felt towards my wife," he said, shaking his head. "It never quit on us. It never died. It just got stronger. There've been lots of mistakes in my life, but I never regretted marrying her.

"Lord knows how tough life can be," he said, looking into my eyes. "I may be too old to understand how today's world works, but when I look back, I'm certain of this: nothing in this world is more powerful than love. Not money, greed, hate or passion. Words cannot describe it. Poets and writers try. They can't, because it is different for each of us. I love my wife so much, you see. I'll be long gone in the grave with her by my side, and that love will still be burning bright."

He looked at my empty glass. "I've kept you much longer than you had probably liked," he apologized. "I hope you enjoyed your lemonade. As you go, remember: love your wife and kids with everything you've got, every day of your life. 'Cause you never know when it may end."

Walking to my car, I felt the power of his words. It struck me that this man, who I assumed must have lost his wife years ago, still loved her with a passion. I was filled with sadness as I thought about how lonely he must be, with only his lemonade and an occasional guest.

As I set out on the road again, I couldn't get the man out of my mind. Suddenly, I realized I hadn't paid him for the lemonade, and so I turned the car around and drove back. As I approached the house, I saw a car in the driveway. I was surprised; someone else had stopped by.

I walked over to the porch. The man was nowhere to be found. I bent to put the money on his chair and happened to glance in the window. And there was the old man, in the middle of the living room, slow dancing with his wife!

I shook my head as I finally understood. He hadn't lost her after all. She had only been gone for the afternoon.

It's been years since that incident, yet I still think of that man and his wife. I hope to live the kind of life they lived and to pass our love on to my kids and grandchildren as they did. And, I hope to be a grandfather who can slow dance with his wife, knowing that indeed, there is no greater blessing than love.

Justin R. Haskin

"I have a great personality,
but I'm saving it for the woman I marry."

Reprinted by permission of Randy Glasbergen.

A Second Chance

The course of true love never did run smooth.

A Midsummer Night's Dream

Time leapt by. Year by year. First, a few years. Then a dozen years. Then two dozen. Marriages had come between them. Children came. Their lives had taken two courses, and yet they were so parallel. In honor of their love, Ingrid Kremeyer would descend the stairs to the basement and pull out an old box that sat between the jars of jam and apple crates.

There sat proof of their love, tucked away for so long in this box, told and retold in dozens of letters that had been written over a period of three years post-World War Ⅱ. The box moved from Germany to the United States and went with Ingrid everywhere she went for more than a half-century. The written words attested to a love so strong and so deep that time could not conquer it.

Even though the American soldier had sent her a "Dear Jane letter," she never doubted for an instant that he loved her — even forty-seven years later. She knew then and she knew now that they had been intended for one another, even if it meant only in their hearts and shadowed memories.

They had met during the Berlin airlift in 1949 where Ingrid worked with more than a dozen American soldiers at an Air Force base office in northern Germany. Because she spoke English, her clerical talents were needed, and she had no problem understanding the soldiers who constantly asked her on dates.

Most of the soldiers were only nineteen; her age. Not old enough as far as she was concerned to be taken seriously. But one American soldier with a charming Southern drawl intrigued her. Lee Dickerson was twenty-six, lean and attractive. She waited. But for months, he didn't ask her out. She tried not to be too hopeful. Perhaps he had a girlfriend.

When an American-style July 4 celebration was planned, Ingrid was spinning from the numerous requests she had for dates. At least seven soldiers had asked her to go. At least seven soldiers were rejected. She had hoped Lee would ask her, but she hadn't seen him all day.

He showed up just a few minutes before they were off work. Ingrid's heart thumped rapidly. Maybe this was it. He invited her. She would love to go, she explained, but she just couldn't face the other soldiers she had turned away.

"I'll fix that," Lee said as he opened the door and asked the others: "How about taking Ingrid to the celebration tonight?" And that's how Ingrid went, holding Lee's hand and escorted by a small brigade. The night was heaven. There were fireworks, and fireworks lit up in Ingrid's eyes. Lee had them, too. When he took her home, he kissed her good night. "That's when I knew, this is the guy for me," Ingrid said. "Right from the start. I knew what he was going to say before he'd even say it."

From that night on, the two were inseparable. But they

only had four months before Lee would be shipped back to the States.

Every free moment they spent together, strolling through parks or the woods, visiting the Air Force club or taking her parents out to dinner. There wasn't much to do in Celle at the time, so they found themselves sitting in small snack shops talking and talking.

The talk grew more serious. Lee wanted to marry. He wanted her to move to the United States. Ingrid was delighted, and so were her parents. The couple didn't foresee the future. The day Lee left to return to Hamilton Air Force Base north of San Francisco, they were both numb with loneliness, but content in the knowledge that as soon as Lee could arrange it, he would bring his future bride home.

What the pilot didn't know when he left Germany was that military personnel were not allowed to sponsor immigrants into the States. Lee was exasperated. He decided to return to Germany to see Ingrid and put in for reassignment. He was passed up several times. Finally, he was going to have the chance to return and he thought he had it made.

Instead, he had a severe attack of appendicitis and was hospitalized for several days. His units left without him. And then his new assignment came. He was going to be transferred to Asia for the next three years—perhaps to serve in the Korean War.

Making the hardest decision which felt "like cutting off my hand," Lee wrote to his love: "It just wasn't meant to be. I wish you a happy life."

And then they lost touch.

Years later, Ingrid moved to New York to live with an aunt who tried quickly to marry her off to an aging, wealthy man. When Ingrid refused his proposal, her aunt was so angry that Ingrid found herself on a plane headed to Chicago to meet the only other person she knew how to find in America. He was a former college classmate. They were close friends, and even though he always knew that she carried a torch for another man, he married her.

Ted and Ingrid had two sons, Karl and Kevin. Their marriage was good, but Ingrid still found herself descending the stairs to read Lee's letters. She cried a lot wondering what might have been. She cried harder when Ted, at the age of forty-one, died suddenly on Christmas Eve. He had been a good man and a good husband who understood her love for Lee. She decided then she wouldn't even think about another serious relationship and committed herself to her top priority, raising her two sons.

Love slipped by Ingrid for another two decades. She had plenty of time to think about it.

Lee had retired from his job as an aircraft contract manager at Hughes, had married twice and had two children. He had spent the last several years in total misery watching his second wife die slowly from pancreatic cancer. He didn't feel he had much to live for. He just carried on in isolation, feeling like he was walking through water, until the letter arrived.

He tore open the letter. It was from Ingrid. "You could have knocked me over with a feather. After all this time, she's in the United States. Here's my future, right here."

He sat down and wrote a response and mailed it that day.

Maybe there would be a chance for him to fall in love again. He had never forgotten Ingrid.

The last time Ingrid had pulled out the box and cried for an hour, she was retired and only working part-time teaching German at college. This time, she froze. Why shouldn't she find him? Her sons were grown and gone. Who knew what had happened in his life? For the next week, she was obsessed with tracking Lee down. Then she remembered that one of her students was a retired naval officer. She asked him and he provided her with a phone number for The Naval Retirement Center.

She sat on the phone breathlessly, waiting, her heart pounding for some thirty minutes. Yes, there were three Lee Dickersons that had retired, one from each branch in the military. It was obvious he was the one who'd served in the Air Force. The center would forward a letter. The fee was $3.50. In the letter, Ingrid wrote Lee that she had "a compelling desire" to find him and ended it with: "I hope I am not making a fool of myself by giving in to this urge."

When the letter arrived in her box, Ingrid knew immediately it was from Lee. Forty-seven years later, she could still recognize his handwriting in a second. She tore it open and could barely read it in her excitement. He told her he was retired, widowed and thrilled that she had found him. He had not forgotten her, but thought he should write rather than call to "rekindle an old flame."

Writing be hanged is the way Ingrid felt. She was still that peppy nineteen-year-old he'd met in Germany so many years ago. She'd never lost that. She dashed to the phone and called Lee, disappointed when a voice recorder picked up. That night, he called her back and the two talked for hours. They decided to meet in Tucson, because Ingrid was headed there to see her son and Lee's son lived in Arizona too.

On the plane ride, Ingrid began to panic. What had she done? Was she crazy? She should just forget this right now. If only she could figure out some way to get off the plane. But the emotions settled right after she disembarked.

She took one look at Lee, still tall and almost as slender he was at twenty-six. They melted into each other's arms and spent a week together trying to catch up. "It was as though forty-seven years had vanished," Ingrid said. "We hugged and kissed, and just held each other."

When they both returned home, they agreed to meet in a few months, but Ingrid couldn't stand the separation again. "It was so hard to part," she fumed. "It was just horrible."

Lee flew to Chicago to visit, but worried what her neighbors would think.

Ingrid responded, "Who cares about the neighbors? Hang the neighbors."

This time, Ingrid and Lee knew they would marry. There was nothing stopping them.

They married January 2, 1997, aboard the aging ocean-liner, the *Queen Mary*, in Long Beach. She wore a knee-length white dress. He wore his U. S. Air Force uniform with a major's oak leaf insignias. She was now sixty-seven. He was seventy-four. Their wedding was attended by some seventy relatives and international media keenly interested in the second-chance love affair.

And after all the buzzing news cameras and family went home, Lee and Ingrid settled into a quiet life that they had tried to start when they were so young.

The final chapter now ending so sweetly, Ingrid wrote:

"My heart is filled to overflowing with happiness in the knowledge that my first love will also be my last."

Diana Chapman

Against All Odds

They first laid eyes on one another in the spring of 1986, when they were both admitted to the cystic fibrosis wing of Dallas' Presbyterian Hospital.

Kimberley Marshall was then sixteen, thin, winter-pale and beautiful, her red hair falling down the back of her pink nightgown. David Crenshaw was eighteen, and wore his usual T-shirt and faded gray pajama pants. David would stand at one end of the hospital hallway, hoping Kim would come out of her room at the other end.

"No way," the wing's respiratory therapist would say. "No way she's going to look twice at you."

On the cystic wing of Presbyterian's third floor, about a dozen teenagers and young adults inhabit private rooms. Throughout the day, they receive vast amounts of antibiotics through intravenous injections. Some have thin oxygen tubes running into their noses; others use more-elaborate machines to open their bronchial passages. Respiratory therapists pound lightly on their chests and backs, hoping to dislodge the mucus in their lungs. And always there is the sound of coughing — dry, flinty coughing, spasms of coughing, the sound echoing up and down the corridor like a cold car engine trying to start.

Like a brilliant serial killer, CF is unstoppable: Although

an array of pulmonary treatments and medicines allows patients to live more productive, pain-free lives, few survive into their thirties.

It was hard enough to imagine a love affair developing between two cystic fibrosis patients, let alone one between Kim and David. But that is what is so magical about their story.

When Kim Marshall came to Presbyterian in the mid-1980s, she knew she was fortunate just to be alive. The doctors had been expecting her to die since the day she was born, July 10, 1969, when she took her first breath and immediately began to throw up a black-green mucus. Kim was wheeled into the operating room, where surgeons saved her by removing four feet of her intestine. But Dr. Kramer, who was then a young pediatrician, informed Kim's mother, Dawn, that it was only a temporary reprieve. At that time, before the advent of more-advanced treatments, 50 percent of kids born with CF were dead by the first grade; 80 percent were dead by their teens.

"This isn't supposed to happen to us," Dawn told Dr. Kramer. Dawn, a beautiful young housewife, and her husband, budding aeronautical engineer Bill Marshall, were a popular couple who attended Dallas debutante parties and saw their pictures printed on the society pages of the *Dallas Morning News*. "All of a sudden," she recalls, "it was like our lives stopped and we couldn't start again."

Desperate to keep Kim alive, Dawn carried her on a pillow and put her to bed in a mist tent. For a total of three hours a day, she gently thumped on her chest and back. Kim's skin was as white as a dove, and her bones stuck out so sharply in her arms that it seemed as if they would puncture her skin. To the astonishment of her doctors, however, she eventually became strong enough to go to elementary school. She even took ballet classes and joined a girl's soccer team.

But then came the days when Kim's body seemed to deflate, just like a rubber toy with a hole in it, and Dawn would return her to the hospital, wondering if this time she would be too sick to recover. The routine became all too familiar: a few months of remission followed by a trip to the CF wing. Kim always brought along her stuffed animals, her favorite pink blanket and her diary. As the children in the rooms around her would die, one by one, Kim would write down her impressions ("Wendy Winkles died at 8:10 this morning! She suffered all night. It's better this way. Poor little thing"). "Kim was always so optimistic, so willing to smile," Dawn says. "I think the diary was her way of preparing herself for what she knew would someday happen to her."

For a while, Kim did what she could to be like the "normals" (her nickname for kids without CF). In high school, she made A's and B's and always dressed superbly, wearing tea-length dresses to hide her spindly legs. If classmates asked why she had coughing spells, she would say she was suffering from asthma. Still, she could not ignore the reality of her life. Finally, during her senior year, she grew so weak that she had to stop attending classes and finish her course work at home. Just as her mother feared, she never got to go to a high school dance.

Kim became despondent. Over and over, she watched a videotape of *The Blue Lagoon*, the story of an adolescent boy and girl who are stranded on an island and fall in love. She went through a rebellious streak, smoking cigarettes, two packs of Marlboros a night, even though she knew the smoke would harm her already weak lungs. She would sneak her mother's car out at night, racing it up and down Forest Lane or the Dallas North Tollway.

One night, at the end of her rope, Dawn finally screamed, "What is the matter with you? Why are you trying to destroy yourself?" Kim buried her face in her hands and began to sob. "You know what's the matter," she said. "I have no life. You know I'll never have a life."

Dawn, who always tried to have a soothing answer for her daughter, for once couldn't think of anything to say.

David Crenshaw was something of a legend at Presbyterian. Loud and robust, he was famous for trying to impress girls with crude jokes. No one had ever heard of a CF patient doing the things David did. For instance, when he wasn't in the hospital, he raced midget cars at a local dirt track. "Our goal was to raise him as if he weren't sick," says David's father. "Maybe I thought if he stayed tough enough, he could beat it."

In truth, David never did act particularly sick. A prankster, he conducted wheelchair races and tomato-throwing competitions in the hospital's third-floor hallway. One night he took some CF patients to a go-cart track in 32-degree weather. "He had this sense of immortality about him," Dr. Kramer remembers.

For two years David stared at Kim. He would walk past her door, working up the courage to pop in and say hello. Kim would look at him in his tennis shoes, blue jeans, and white T-shirt, his eyeglasses held together by a piece of tape, and with a brief smile she would go back to reading her book.

David was undaunted. "When she was in the hospital and he was home," a respiratory therapist says, "he'd call me to find out how she was — even though she wouldn't give him the time of day."

For months and months, David waited patiently as Kim

was courted by other third-floor boys: blond-haired boys, sophisticated boys, richer boys.

Then, early in the fall of 1989, when he and Kim were out of the hospital, David made his move: He called her at home and asked her to dinner. Although she said no, David declared, "I'll be there at eight P.M., no buts about it," and then hung up. Horrified, Kim brought along a friend, whom she made sit with David in the front seat of his car; she sat in the back refusing to speak. She also remained silent throughout dinner and gave David a tortured look when he suggested they go dancing at a nightclub. When he took her home, Kim leapt out of the car, ran to her room, and shut the door.

But David kept showing up at Kim's house. He took her to Sound Warehouse to buy tapes. He took her bowling. He took her to watch him race. While she sat nervously on the metal bleachers at DFW Speedway—"Oh, God," she said to those around her, "he's going to die!"—David would speed around the track; then, after the race, he would blow her a kiss.

Despite seemingly impossible circumstances, love bloomed. On November 17, 1989, after her usual diary entries about her friends' deaths, Kim wrote:

"Tonight, David and I went out to the picnic tables in back of the hospital and kissed for the first time ...I have so many deep feelings for him because he is also my buddy, best friend, supporter, and he loves me as much as I him. God, please let this relationship work out."

To the shock of their families, friends, and doctors, Kim and David announced their engagement. "Both of you are sick," David's father told him, pleading with his son to reconsider. "You're sick! You two can't possibly take care of yourselves."

"Do you realize what will happen?" Kim's mother asked her tearfully, "Do you realize that one of you is going to die in the other's arms?"

"I think Kim realized this was going to be the last chance she had to experience love," Dawn says. "I still thought it was a little crazy. I had all those motherly questions about how they could handle their finances and insurance if they got married and who would take care of them if they both got too sick to get out of bed. But one day the chaplain at Presbyterian told me, 'Dawn, we don't know how long they have on this earth. At least let them have it together.' And I said, 'You're right.'"

On Kim and David's wedding day, the church was filled with the sound of coughing, as Dallas' CF community came out to see them vow to stay with each other in sickness and in health. Ushers had two stools ready for Kim and David in case they needed to sit down. But as everyone later said, Kim had never looked healthier or more beautiful. The shoulder pads in her wedding dress gave her body a fuller look. Her complexion was even a little pink.

After checking into the local hotel where they spent their wedding night, David asked the bellman to carry their oxygen bottles up to their room. "We might need them," he said with a confident grin, "in case we get too excited."

They lived on their meager monthly disability checks. Their one-bedroom apartment resembled a hospital room: It was crammed with oxygen tanks and boxes of syringes and medicines, and the refrigerator was stocked with IV bottles. Domestic tasks were made difficult by their inability to get around like normals. They needed a day to clean the apartment and do the laundry. Kim was too weak to lift the mattress and change the sheets. At the grocery store, she shuffled slowly down the aisles, carrying her portable oxygen bottle with the tubes stuck up her nostrils. By nighttime, they were exhausted. Kim would lie on the couch, while David would recline beside her in his easy chair.

Yet they kept insisting that they were happier than they ever could have imagined. He was constantly buying her huge four-color Hallmark cards, the mushier the better. She, in turn, would write him long love letters. "We are going to conquer the unconquerable."

By 1992, however, Kim was taking a turn for the worse. She had been stuck with IV needles so many hundreds of times that her veins had collapsed. Her clogged digestive system was causing constant diarrhea. She was losing feeling in her fingers and toes and had begun to walk with even more of a staggering gait.

Because her body was unable to absorb food, she was rapidly losing weight. She became ashamed to show herself in public. David wrote her a letter which said "I love your body just the way it is. Your perfect body puts mine to shame! You are the most beautiful woman I know inside and out. I love you with all my heart and soul! Please believe me!"

David never left Kim's side during her frequent trips to the hospital. At night, he slept on a cot in her room. Because she was so weak, he held the blow dryer to dry her hair. To entertain her, he wheeled her over to the hospital's maternity ward so she could look at the newborn babies. If she wanted butterscotch candy in the middle of the night, he drove to a store and bought her some.

But in early 1993, something changed: David's cough was growing louder and deeper. His face would turn purple; the veins in his neck would protrude. One afternoon, a nurse named Dana Thompson dropped by to see them. Kim was watching a soap opera while David sat quietly in his chair. Dana noticed that David didn't tease her the way he usually did. He just kept staring at one of the actors on TV. Finally he blurted out, "I wish I was that handsome."

"I said, 'David, you *are* handsome,'" Dana remembers. "But I looked at him and I realized he was changing. His face was getting puffy from fluid retention. He used to lift weights, and now all the muscles in his arms were gone. Kim just gave me this sad look and I thought to myself, 'My God, my God, it's David who's going to die first.'"

David tried to assure Kim that there was nothing to worry about; but he didn't tell her what the doctor had said after a recent checkup: The disease, which had been mostly dormant, had unexpectedly ambushed him. His lungs were becoming stiff with scar tissue. His bronchial tubes were closing up. His heart was not pumping enough oxygenated blood. If the assault continued, David would lose more and more oxygen and slowly start choking to death.

It was a race against time. David said he would not waste a single moment: In July, to celebrate their birthdays—David's twenty-sixth, Kim's twenty-fourth — he insisted that they take the week-long Florida vacation that they had always talked about. "Only once did they feel good enough to leave the condo and go to the beach," says Kim's sister, Mandy, who traveled with them. "They both carried their portable oxygen tanks. Kim couldn't get too deep into the water because of her balance problems, and David couldn't get in because of his lack of strength. They finally just sat on the beach and let the waves roll up to their feet. They knew it would be the last time they didn't have a care in the world. People would walk by and stare, but Kim and David just looked at one another, holding hands."

Three months later, David and Kim went to see Dr. Kramer for a checkup. While Kim waited in another room, Dr. Kramer studied David's oxygen levels. David couldn't say more than two or three words without needing to take a breath. "You've got to go into the hospital," Dr. Kramer said. "And this time, I don't think you'll be coming out." David managed only one response: "Make sure Kim is okay."

Dr. Kramer walked across the hall to tell her. After a long silence, she asked if David could go home for one more night, back to their little one-bedroom apartment, where she could cook him a meal. When Dr. Kramer softly said no, Kim dropped her head and tried not to cry. "Don't let him suffer," she said. During thirty years as a specialist in CF, Dr. Kramer had watched more than four hundred of his young patients die. For his own sanity, he distanced himself emotionally from cases like David's. But at that moment, he gathered Kim in his arms and wept.

David was admitted to the hospital on the afternoon of Wednesday, October 21. Throughout the ordeal, Kim sat by David's side. By Monday, David's lips and fingernails were turning blue, and nurses had put an oxygen mask over his face. When they brought in a morphine machine to relieve some of the pain, Kim knew it was over.

"David, not yet," she said, but he was unable to speak. All he could do was mouth "I love you" to his young wife and blow her a kiss. Just outside the door was the usual noise of the hospital: carts rolling by, people moving with quickened footsteps, doctors speaking in half-finished sentences. But at the bed, Kim and David stared at each other in silence, exchanging one long look of grief and love.

He died at 5:50 A.M. on October 26. Kim was the only one in the room. She wiped off his face with a tissue and then called for the nurse.

She had told everyone—her mother, the doctors, and everyone at the hospital—that she wanted to live. She said that she knew David would not want her to give up. But within twenty-four hours of David's funeral, Kim collapsed while taking a shower. She got up, walked to the kitchen, and fell again. Dawn managed to put Kim into bed, where she lay in semi-darkness, staring at a photograph on her nightstand of David with his arms around her.

It was all happening so quickly, a panicked Dawn thought. It was too cruel.

Kim was just beginning to mourn her husband's death; now she had to deal with her own death. Dawn put her daughter in the car and took her back to the third floor of Presbyterian. Kim, in her favorite pink nightgown with white hearts, clutched her pink blanket.

Those who knew Kim well said there was something mysterious and haunting about her final days. After Dr. Kramer stopped by to see Kim for the last time, he led Dawn and Kim's father, Bill, out to the hallway and offered a decidedly non-medical diagnosis. "Her body is giving up," he told them. "It's like she's dying of a broken heart."

When friends and relatives came to say good-bye, Kim whispered that she felt like she was getting better. In fact, her eyes were the color of ash, and her weight was down to sixty pounds. "Mom," she told Dawn. "I'm sorry I'm taking so long this time." Dawn walked to a corner of the room, not wanting her daughter to see her cry.

Kim was semi-comatose for the last two days of her life. The only sound in her room was the hiss of the oxygen machine. It will never be known for sure why one of her good friends, lying in a room down the hall, suddenly awoke at three in the morning on November 11 and called for a nurse. "I feel like something's happening," the friend said, scared. A couple of minutes later, Kim regained consciousness, opened her eyes, and began speaking in a kind of mumble—a peaceful, cooing kind of sound that no one could fully understand. A nurse in the room said it sounded as if Kim was talking to David. "Kim, what is it?" said Dawn, who was resting on a cot at the foot of the bed. But Kim had shut her eyes and died, still clutching her pink blanket.

She was buried in her white wedding dress. On her wrist was a watch that David had given her for Christmas; she wore ruby earrings, also a gift from David. She was placed beside her husband in a new section of Restland Cemetery.

Despite his limited income, David had been paying $47 a month for that plot ever since he and Kim were married. He had said it was important for him to know that they had a final resting place together. Their tombstone read:

"David S. (Bear) Crenshaw and Kimberley (Tigger) Crenshaw ... Together forever. Married three years."

For weeks afterward, Dawn halfheartedly sorted through their possessions, trying to decide what to keep and what to give away. Perhaps she found some solace one afternoon while going through some of Kim's papers. She came across the last card David sent Kim before he died:

"We are close even when we are apart," the front of the card read. "Just look up. We are both under the same starry sky."

Skip Hollandsworth

3

ON COMMITMENT

Now join your bands, and with your hands
your hearts.

William Shakespeare

You're Still You

The only genuine love worthy of a name is unconditional.

John Powell

Five days after the accident on Memorial Day weekend 1995, I became fully conscious and able to make sense. Dr. Scott Henson and Dr. John Jane, chief of neurosurgery at University of Virginia Hospital, explained my situation. They told me in detail about the extent of my injury and said that after the pneumonia cleared from my lungs they would operate to reconnect my skull to the top of my spine. They didn't know if the operation would be successful, or even if I could survive it. They had a plan, but it was extremely risky and they needed my consent. Dana had insisted (over the objections of some of the family) that the doctors discuss everything with me and that nothing be done without my permission.

I answered somewhat vaguely, "Okay, whatever you have to do." Ever since childhood I'd been used to solving my problems. Whatever scrape I would get myself into, I was always sure of a way out. So at first I thought this was just another temporary problem. I needed surgery, but I'd be up and around before long. It was only after the doctors left that I began to absorb what they had told me: This is a paralyzing injury.

Dana came into the room. We made eye contact. I mouthed my first lucid words to her: "Maybe we should let me go." She said, "I am only going to say this once: I will support whatever you want to do, because this is your life and your decision. But I want you to know that I'll be with you for the long haul, no matter what." Then she added the words that saved my life: "You're still you. And I love you."

If she had looked away or paused or hesitated even slightly, or if I had felt there was a sense of her being *noble*, or fulfilling some obligation to me, I don't know if I could have pulled through. Because it had dawned on me that I had ruined my life and everybody else's. But what Dana said made living seem possible, because I felt the depth of her love and commitment. I was even able to make a little joke. I mouthed, "This is way beyond the marriage vows — in sickness and in health." And she said, "I know." I knew then that she was going to be with me forever.

Christopher Reeve

Room at the Table

My wife, Marie, and I recently celebrated our fortieth wedding anniversary. We raised three children all of whom have been real joys in our lives. They've gone on to have families of their own, so we now have six grandchildren here on earth, and one already waiting for us in heaven. And I don't think any of the blessings I have known would have happened if my guardian angel hadn't saved my marriage one strange and awful night.

I grew up in the Midwest in an intensely Catholic family, one of six children. In our house we believed in angels; I mean, we really *believed*. In school the nuns taught us about them. At Mass, we let our guardian angel into the pew first. One of the first prayers I ever learned to say, after the Our Father, was "Angel of God, my guardian dear, to whom God's love entrusts me here, ever this day be at my side, to lead and guard, to light and guide, Amen."

Otherwise, my childhood was ordinary until I was fourteen. That year, my favorite brother, Frank, who was eight, became ill. I didn't know it at the time, but Frank had leukemia, an acute type that often strikes children. To cheer him up, I taught him how to ride my bike, but before long he couldn't even push the pedals.

One day my parents came home from the hospital crying.

The priest from our parish was with them. We all gathered together with much solemnity while the pastor told us that Frank's angel had taken him to heaven to be with Jesus. I was so sick at heart I just cried.

As soon as I had dried my tears for the moment, a slow and seething kind of anger began to grow in me, like a piece of metal turning gradually red, orange, yellow, and finally white hot. I felt as if I would explode. *Why didn't my parents tell me Frank was going to die. I never got a chance to say good-bye to him*? I screamed silently. *How could the God I believed in have allowed it*? *Where was his angel*? I hated Frank's angel. What a stupid thing to believe in.

My anger didn't go away. My father got me a punching bag, which I demolished in a week. I lashed out at everyone and even lost my best friend after beating him up.

When my grandmother tried to tell me about angels, I turned away. When my birthday came later that fall, and I was supposed to set the table for my guardian angel, I threw the plate at the kitchen window, breaking both with a loud crash.

Frank's death triggered an uncontrollable rage in me against anything that failed to reach perfection. I became obsessed with achieving all that I could as fast as possible. I went out for football and wrestling, and I blew off so much aggression in both sports that I became the best athlete on both teams out of sheer energy.

I had always been a good student, with something like a photographic memory and an especially keen ear for languages. I read as compulsively as I practiced wrestling falls, and when I finally graduated from high school, I was third in a class of nearly five hundred. I had twelve letters in sports and the school award for excellence in Latin and German. I also had a scholarship to the state university.

I got a summer sales job and worked seven days a week from morning to night. I still had my anger, although I was no longer throwing dishes through the windows. It was toward the end of that summer I met Marie. She came to the door to hear my passionate spiel about the tools and gadgets I was selling, and as soon as I looked up into her pretty round face with her big brown eyes and freckles, I was in love. I never did anything in a half-way fashion. I proposed to her on the spot. Marie laughed, but I knew she wasn't laughing at me, just at the situation. We were married two years later.

With my marriage and the distractions of school and a job, my pent-up energy found a positive outlet. After college my anger continued to burn. I worked for a import-export business and literally lived in my office for days on end. When I was at home, I was too tired to notice either my children or my wife. I had no friends, no social life, no outside interests. I lived and breathed the office, and at the time I truly believed I loved it. All that mattered to me were my own ambitions. I never even noticed that Marie and I were being forced apart by my obsession over work.

Over the Easter weekend in 1969, Marie came into the den, where I was working on some totally forgettable proposal, and said, without preamble, "Jack, I'm leaving you. I think I want a divorce."

She explained that our marriage was a disaster, with a husband who shut her out of his life entirely. "I've already taken the kids to Mother's, and I'm leaving to join them. It's up to you whether we come back." And she left, just like that.

I was so shocked I couldn't speak. It was like my brother

dying all over again, and once again I had no warning. I went to the kitchen and began smashing everything in sight. Glasses, plates and utensils all went flying, while I raged. *How dare she leave me. How could she do this to me*? I thought as I looked for more things to break.

I reached the last cabinet in the kitchen. It held some old dishes my mother had given us years before. They were the ones we had used when I was a child, and they brought back memories of my brother that made me want to cry. I brought out the stack of plates, set them on the kitchen table, and threw them forcefully at the sink. But when I came to the last dish, I couldn't pick it up. I tried with both hands to pry it up but I couldn't.

And then, while I stood there like a buffalo at bay, panting, sweating, my hands and face cut from flying glass and crockery, I heard a voice, a kind and compassionate voice that echoed all around me. It said, "Jack, make room for me at the table. Jack, make room for me at the table." It was the most beautiful voice, like an operatic soprano singing softly.

"Who are you?" I gasped.

"You know me, Jack, make room for me at your table." And the voice faded.

Numb as I was, I knew the voice. Without even thinking, I got up and brushed off the table. This time I picked up the plate without any problem, and set it at the end, where I usually sat. I retrieved a knife, fork, and spoon, and placed them around the plate, adding a napkin and an aluminum drinking glass that had survived my anger. Then I brushed off a chair and set it in place. I think I was saying, "Angel, please sit down; here, I'm making room for you."

As I sat back looking at the place setting, I felt the most incredible peace I had ever known. Then I bowed my head and prayed the prayer I had learned as a child: "Angel of God, my guardian dear ..."

When I had finished, I just started talking aloud to my angel about all the things that had been going on in my life, and most of all about Marie's leaving and taking the kids with her. I talked for a good hour without stopping. And I had the most extraordinary feeling that my guardian angel was right there, sitting across the table from me, even though I couldn't see her. And I felt that she was telling me, not just that I needed to change—I knew that—but that I could change, that the anger was gone that had skewed so much of my life.

The sky was just beginning to turn gray when I heard the sound of a key in the lock. It was my Marie. She pushed the door open, and as it opened, the sound of broken glass grated across the kitchen floor. She looked at me and at the kitchen, horrified; then she came across the room and threw her arms around me, and we both cried. "I couldn't sleep," she said. "Finally, it was like I heard a voice saying, 'Jack needs you, Marie.' It just kept repeating softly, over and over again. So I came."

I was so drained I felt like a little child again, needing to be led rather than to lead. Marie took me out of the kitchen and into the bathroom, where she washed my hands and bandaged the one that was badly cut. She put me to bed without saying another word, and I slept like a baby until nearly noon.

After I woke, I felt disoriented, as though I had had the worst nightmare of my life. Then I saw my hands, all cut up, and everything that had happened came back in a rush. I jumped up and went to look at the war zone that had been my kitchen. It was as neat as a pin, except for all the scratches and dents and broken windows. Marie, looking tired but at peace, smiled. "I would never have believed this mess if I hadn't seen it with my own eyes. It took me hours to clean it up. It filled bags and bags of trash."

I started to apologize, but she shook her head. "We'll talk later, Jack. Just tell me one thing—why did you break up everything in the kitchen and then go to the trouble of setting the table?"

She pointed, and I saw that the old plate and the aluminum glass were still where I had left them after my guardian angel had asked me to let her into my life again.

"Marie, I have to tell you what happened," I said.

When I had finished telling her, she looked thoughtful. "You do seem different somehow, Jack. The tension is gone; you seem relaxed in a way I've never seen."

"Marie, I hope this doesn't seem silly, but I want to keep that place setting on the table forever. I don't ever want to take it off. If my angel hadn't come to me last night, I don't know what I would have done. I want to thank her and keep reminding myself of something I knew when I was a kid and then forgot."

"I think we can arrange that," she smiled.

That strange night was more than twenty years ago, but its effects have stayed with me ever since. Marie and I took the first vacation we had had together since our honeymoon and began to rebuild our marriage. We talked and talked, and I found all my old priorities changing for the better. I left my job to start my own business and found pleasure, instead of compulsion, in work again.

And each night, I still set out the old plate and dented aluminum cup, the silverware and the napkin. They're my pledge to my guardian angel, and to God who sent her, that I will always welcome them at my table.

James DiBello

"Sure we're allowed to date now—
the church has loosened up a lot of the old rules."

Reprinted by permission of Randy Glasbergen.

The Promise

My lifetime listens to yours.

Muriel Ruckeyser

One evening I found myself at a conference in Washington, D. C. And as fate would have it, Bucky Fuller happened to be making a presentation that evening at another conference in the very same hotel. I got to the ballroom in time to hear the end of Bucky's lecture. I was in awe of this little man in his eighties, with his clear mind, deep wisdom and boundless energy. At the end of the talk, we walked together through the underground parking lot to his airport limousine.

"I've got to go to New York City tonight for another presentation," he said, looking at me with an anxiousness that I had rarely seen in Bucky.

"You know, Annie's not doing well. I'm very concerned about her."

We hugged.

Bucky Fuller had once confided to me that he had promised his wife Annie to die before she did, so that he could be there to welcome her when it was her turn. I took the comment as a hope, not a commitment. Which shows how greatly I underestimated Buckminster Fuller.

Shortly after Bucky's presentation in New York, he learned that Annie had lapsed into a coma in a hospital in Los Angeles. Doctors felt that there was a good chance she would not regain consciousness. Bucky took the first flight he could get. Upon arriving in Los Angeles, he went immediately to Annie's bedside. Sitting beside her, he closed his eyes.

And quietly died.

The power to choose life fully was something that Bucky exemplified. So much so that he had the power to choose death when it was time, peacefully, with arms wide open to the universe that he served. It was simply another courageous step forward.

Hours later, Annie peacefully joined him in death. He had kept his promise. He was waiting for her.

Thomas F. Crum

Fifty Ways to Love Your Partner

1. Love yourself first.
2. Start each day with a hug.
3. Serve breakfast in bed.
4. Say"I love you"every time you part ways.
5. Compliment freely and often.
6. Appreciate—and celebrate—your differences.
7. Live each day as if it's your last.
8. Write unexpected love letters.
9. Plant a seed together and nurture it to maturity.
10. Go on a date once every week.
11. Send flowers for no reason.
12. Accept and love each others' family and friends.
13. Make little signs that say"I love you"and post them all over the house.
14. Stop and smell the roses.
15. Kiss unexpectedly.
16. Seek out beautiful sunsets together.
17. Apologize sincerely.
18. Be forgiving.
19. Remember the day you fell in love—and recreate it.
20. Hold hands.
21. Say"I love you"with your eyes.
22. Let her cry in your arms.

23. Tell him you understand.
24. Drink toasts of love and commitment.
25. Do something arousing.
26. Let her give you directions when you're lost.
27. Laugh at his jokes.
28. Appreciate her inner beauty.
29. Do the other person's chores for a day.
30. Encourage wonderful dreams.
31. Commit a public display of affection.
32. Give loving massages with no strings attached.
33. Start a love journal and record your special moments.
34. Calm each others' fears.
35. Walk barefoot on the beach together.
36. Ask her to marry you again.
37. Say yes.
38. Respect each other.
39. Be your partner's biggest fan.
40. Give the love your partner wants to receive.
41. Give the love you want to receive.
42. Show interest in the other's work.
43. Work on a project together.
44. Build a fort with blankets.
45. Swing as high as you can on a swingset by moonlight.
46. Have a picnic indoors on a rainy day.
47. Never go to bed mad.
48. Put your partner first in your prayers.
49. Kiss each other goodnight.
50. Sleep like spoons.

Mark and Chrissy Donnelly

Saving My Husband's Life

Where love reigns the impossible may be attained.

Indian Proverb

It was a clear Friday morning, August 30, 1991. My husband, Deane, and I were enjoying a long-planned camping vacation in Montana's scenic Glacier National Park, our first trip since his retirement earlier that year. The previous week, we'd driven from our home in Holland, Michigan, and had explored various areas of the park. Today, we were about to start our eighth hiking trip. "Do you have your camera?" I asked Deane as we stepped from our small pop-up camper. "And what about the crackers for lunch?"

Deane nodded, grinning. "Yes, dear," he said teasingly, patting his small backpack. "We're ready to go." We started off slowly, enjoying the crisp coolness of the air as we followed a narrow trail up the steep wooded slope. Occasionally we'd wave to other campers on the trail or study a distant mountaintop through my binoculars. By 12:30 P.M. we had covered almost three miles and decided to stop for lunch.

After sharing a simple meal of cheese and crackers, we

were about to start back down toward camp when another couple appeared from the trail above us.

"You shouldn't stop now," the woman called. "At least see Iceberg Lake — it's only another couple of miles up the trail." We decided to continue upward as she suggested.

It was almost 3 P. M. when we reached Iceberg Lake — placid, crystal-clear, surrounded by a dizzying array of brightly colored wildflowers. In keeping with its name, small icebergs floated on its calm surface.

"Oh, Deane, isn't this *beautiful*!" I exclaimed. We stood hand in hand, drinking in the peaceful scene.

After forty-three years of marriage Deane was my best friend as well as my husband. We'd both grown up in the same small South Dakota town. Deane was sixteen and I was just eight months younger when we met in Sunday school. We started dating and were married within three years.

Now, five kids and fifteen grandchildren later, we were looking forward to spending our "golden years" together while we were young enough to enjoy getting out and doing things. At age sixty-two, I felt hardly older than I had at thirty-five. Although we had some health problems — Deane was a borderline diabetic, and I was on daily heart medication — staying active had kept us both in good shape.

Leaving Iceberg Lake, Deane and I started retracing our steps back down the mountain. We'd walked several hundred feet when we came to a bend in the trail. As we rounded the corner, I heard Deane gasp and felt his warning squeeze on my arm. I immediately saw why: just ahead of us, a mother grizzly and her two half-grown cubs were whirling around, startled, to face us.

They were less than forty feet away. The mother bear's ears were pointed sharply forward, her eyes fastened on us.

Without moving, she emitted a gruff "Woof!" sending her cubs scampering.

"My God," whispered Deane. "Lorraine, I think we're in trouble."

Just two nights before, we had attended a park ranger's lecture about bears in the wild. "Let's get down in a fetal position like they told us," I breathed. "We're supposed to play dead." Lowering myself to my knees, I tucked my head down, clasping my hands behind my neck. Beside me, I felt Deane doing the same.

But it was too late. I peeked up past my elbows, to see the bear charge. She sprang forward with a low, rumbling growl, her fangs bared. Muscles rippling beneath her thick brown coat, she covered the distance between us in three powerful leaps, her jaws working in an angry chomping motion. Beside me, Deane drew a sharp breath; then, in horror, I heard his agonized scream. The grizzly had pounced on him, sinking her teeth into his back and stomach. Gripping him in her jaws, she shook him violently from side to side, then savagely tossed him in the air like a rag doll. He'd barely hit the ground before she was on him again, growling and biting. I could hear her teeth puncturing his skin, making small popping noises as he shrieked in pain.

Still huddled on my knees, I was unable to believe what was happening. From the corner of my eye, I saw the huge animal toss him again; then clamping down on his right hand, she began to drag him away into the brush.

"Oh, dear God, not like this!" he was sobbing. "Please, not like this!"

Somehow, his despairing plea mobilized me. With a silent prayer I stood up and reached toward him. I had nothing to fight with, not even a stick. But as I looked down at my heavy binoculars, I suddenly remembered advice my father had once given me years before when I'd worked on our farm, which was often plagued by wolves and coyotes. "If you're ever cornered by a wild animal," Daddy told me, "go for its nose, where it's the most sensitive." I determined to use the binoculars as a weapon and "go for it" now.

I wrapped the thick plastic strap firmly around my right hand. Then, swinging the binoculars high in the air, I charged at the bear. My first blow landed squarely on her broad black nose. As I felt the binoculars hit, I jerked them downward, deliberately scraping them along her snout. She flinched but didn't release Deane. *Lord help me*, I prayed, then raised the binoculars and swung again. Although I could hear my husband moaning at my feet, I didn't dare look down at him. I kept my attention on the bear's nose, using all my aiming skills from playing golf and horseshoes to make each blow count.

Finally, after the fourth blow, the bear dropped Deane's hand and rose, enraged, to her full seven-foot height. I faced the animal across my husband's bloody body, my eyes level with her chest. Her yellow-black claws, long and curved, were poised in the air just inches from my face. I resisted the impulse to make eye contact, thinking that would further enrage her. Taking a breath, I swung the binoculars again.

This time she seemed to see the blow coming. With another muffled "Woof!" she abruptly dropped to all fours and retreated into the brush. I hesitated for a moment, certain she'd return to attack me. But as she noisily crackled her way through the thick brush, I realized she was really gone.

I finally looked down at Deane. He was lying on his back, his face turned away from me, his right arm still extended above his head. He was moaning softly, his breath coming in ragged gasps. As I saw for the first time the full extent of his injuries,I went cold with fear.

His clothes were shredded,his chest torn open,the gaping wound revealing corded muscles and fatty tissues. His right shoulder, bitten almost completely away, was bleeding profusely; blood vessels and nerves dangled from his right wrist. His right leg, back and stomach were also badly gashed. I bent over him,trying to get his attention.

"Deane!"I said. "Deane,it's me!"He didn't respond until my third call, then he turned his head toward me. Eyes glazed with pain,he hardly seemed aware of who I was."It's okay now. The bear is gone,"I said.

He slowly focused on my face. "No,it's not,"he murmured. Tears streaming,I assured him it was true.

"I've got to stop your bleeding,"I told him. "Just lie still. You'll be okay."

Fortunately,I was familiar with basic first-aid techniques; Deane had been a part-time volunteer fireman for more than twenty-eight years,and we had often studied his rescue manuals together. Now I tried to fight off panic and make myself think clearly. His right shoulder and wrist were both spurting blood,which might mean an artery had been cut. I needed to apply some kind of tourniquet.

My bra! I thought. Without hesitation I peeled off my top and unhooked my bra,then pulled the stretchy elastic around his upper arm,making sure it was snug. If the blood didn't start to clot within a few minutes,I'd use a stick to wind it even tighter. *Better for him to lose an arm than to bleed to death*,I thought desperately.

Then I turned my attention to his chest. I had some tissues in my waist-purse,and I quickly dropped them into the gaping wound. But it wasn't enough to stop the bleeding; I needed more bandages. I was reaching for my discarded top when Deane said weakly, "Use my shirt. Just help me get it off."

I eased him up, pulling his shirt off over his head, then ripped the fabric into four-inch strips. After binding up his chest and leg, I checked his right arm again. The blood was starting to clot.

Thank God, I thought, easing the tourniquet a bit. I finally took time to pull my top back on.

Now that the immediate danger had passed, I felt my determined calm starting to crack. What if the bear decided to return after all? Deane couldn't walk, and we were over four miles from our campsite. I decided my best bet was to start shouting; eventually, other hikers would surely hear me. "Help!" I shouted repeatedly. "Somebody help us!"

It seemed like an eternity when finally two young men appeared from around the bend. They immediately ran over.

"My husband's been attacked by a bear," I told them. "Can you run for help?"

"I can do it," one of the men said.

Deane spoke briefly, "Tell the rangers to send a helicopter." The young man nodded, then headed off down the trail at a fast trot.

It was only after he left that I remembered more advice from the park ranger about traveling in bear country. "Don't ever run. It's an open invitation to attack." Worriedly, I bit my lip. *Oh Lord*, I prayed, *please keep him safe.*

Over the next hour, eleven more people came down the trail; they included three nurses, a doctor and a ski patrol paramedic. One nurse gave Deane some pills for pain while the others dressed his wounds with clean bandages. It seemed an amazing coincidence to have that many medical professionals show up on this remote mountainside.

Deane was taken to the hospital in an air ambulance, and since there was not enough room for me and the medics, I followed in a smaller helicopter.

By the time I got to the hospital, Deane was already in surgery. It was almost 3 A. M. when his surgeon wearily emerged from the operating room and pulled me aside.

"Your husband is one lucky man," he said, shaking his head. "That bear just missed several major arteries and nerves. He had a very close call." He also told me Deane's deep wounds would require over two hundred stitches.

Nine days later, Deane was discharged from the hospital, and we returned home.

Now, back in Michigan, I'm sometimes still astonished about what happened to us. When I think about how close I came to losing Deane, tears spring to my eyes. But thanks to the mercy of God—and a sturdy pair of binoculars—my husband is still alive today.

Lorraine Lengkeek
As told to Deborah Morris

Just Dial 911

Marie and Michael had been dating for some time, and felt fortunate that even though they had different jobs, they were able to talk with each other through their work almost every day — Michael is a police officer, and Marie is a "911" dispatcher, both working for the same police department.

One day, Marie received a call from Michael who said he was out on the road in his patrol car.

"Marie, would you do me a favor?"

"Sure," Marie answered, happy to have an excuse to talk to him.

"Could you check a license plate for me? I need to see if this guy has any outstanding warrants," Michael explained.

"Okay, spell it for me."

Michael phonetically spelled out the license plate, using code names, as all police officers do, so Marie would be sure to get the right letter:

William
Ida
Lincoln
Lincoln
Young
Ocean
Union

Mary
Adam
Robert
Robert
Young

Mary
Edward

As she did hundreds of times a day, Marie wrote down the letters on a piece of paper, typed them into her computer, and started to run the license check. At first, she was puzzled—this license plate number was too long, even for a personalized plate. Her coworkers, who were in on Michael's "plan", finally had to say, "Marie, what do those letters spell?"

This time, Marie read just the first letters of each word out loud: W-I-L-L Y-O-U M-A-R-R-Y M-E?

With a cry of joy, Marie was all smiles as she got back on the phone to Michael, who was obviously not following any fictitious "driver" with the fictitious plates, but was anxiously waiting in his patrol car for her response.

"Michael, are you there?" Marie began. "Yes, Marie?" he responded, his voice cracking a bit with nervousness.

"My answer is: Affirmative!"

There was no "copping out" on this proposal!

Cynthia C. Muchnick
101 Ways to Pop the Question

A Prayer for Couples

Dear God,
Please make of our relationship a great and holy adventure.
May our joining be a sacred space.
May the two of us find rest here,
a haven for our souls.

Remove from us any temptation to judge one another
or to direct one another.
We surrender to You our conflicts and our burdens.
We know You are our Answer and our rock.
Help us to not forget.

Bring us together in heart and mind as well as body.
Remove from us the temptation to criticize or be cruel.
May we not be tempted by fantasies and projections,
but guide us in the ways of holiness.
Save us from darkness.

May this relationship be a burst of light.
May it be a fount of love and wisdom for us,
for our family, for our community, for our world.
May this bond be a channel for Your love and healing,

a vehicle of Your grace and power.
As lessons come and challenges grow,
let us not be tempted to forsake each other.
Let us always remember that in each other we have
the most beautiful woman, the most beautiful man,
the strongest one, the sacred one in whose arms
we are repaired.

May we remain young in this relationship.
May we grow wise in this relationship.
Bring us what You desire for us,
and show us how You would have us be.

Thank you, dear God,
you who are the cement between us.
Thank You for this love.

Amen.

Marianne Williamson

How Do I Love Thee?

Whoso loves, believes the impossible.

Elizabeth Barrett Browning

Elizabeth Barrett and Robert Browning were two gifted poets destined to produce some of the most fascinating correspondence in English literature. Robert Browning had never set eyes on Elizabeth Barrett, and they knew nothing of each other beyond their published works. Both were well known in their own right and admired and respected each other's works. This admiration served as a catalyst when Robert wrote Elizabeth a fan letter on January 10, 1845:

> *I love your verses with all my heart, dear Miss Barrett, — and this is no offhand complimentary letter that I shall write, whatever else, no prompt matter-of-course recognition of your genius, and there a graceful and natural end of the thing. Since that day last week when I first read your poems, I quite laugh to remember how I have been turning and turning again in my mind what I should be able to tell you of*

their effect upon me, for in the first flush of delight I thought I would this once get out of my habit of purely passive enjoyment, when I do really enjoy, and thoroughly justify my admiration—perhaps even, as a loyal fellow-craftsman should, try and find fault and do you some little good to be proud of hereafter! —but nothing comes of it all—so into me has gone, and part of me has it become ...in this addressing myself to you—your own self, and for the first time, my feeling rises altogether. I do, as I say, love these books with all my heart—and I love you too.

Elizabeth was then thirty-nine, in poor health, and seldom left the house. She was dominated by her father who forbade any of his children to marry.

Because of her father's objections, they corresponded in secrecy. Their correspondence was so prolific that it fills two thick volumes. Elizabeth recorded their courtship, starting from their initial contact, in her famous *Sonnets from the Portuguese*. They encompass all the human emotions including happiness, regret, confidence and always love.

In May 1845, Elizabeth finally allowed Robert to visit her. They then met secretly once a week. In September she wrote, "You have touched me more profoundly than I thought even you could have touched me... Henceforward I am yours for everything but to do you harm."

They continued to meet for another year and corresponded almost every day, sometimes twice a day. After refusing his overtures, she was finally won over by his letters and visits, and they became lovers.

Robert urged her to marry him and move to Italy.

Elizabeth was reluctant but after much thought agreed. Knowing that her father would object to her marrying, Robert and Elizabeth married in secret on September 12, 1846, and a week later they left England for Italy, first to Pisa, then Florence, then to their eventual home, Casa Guidi.

She never saw her father again, and her father never forgave her. All the letters she wrote him were returned unopened.

Were it not for this relationship, the world would probably never be able to enjoy words such as these:

How do I love thee? Let me count the ways.
I love thee to the depth and breadth and height
My soul can reach, when feeling out of sight
For the ends of Being and ideal Grace.
I love thee to the level of everyday's
Most quiet need, by sun and candle-light.
I love thee freely, as men strive for Right;
I love thee purely, as they turn from Praise.
I love thee with the passion put to use
In my old griefs, and with my childhood's faith.
I love thee with a love I seemed to lose
With my lost saints—I love thee with the breadth,
Smiles, tears, of all my life! —and, if God choose,
I shall but love thee better after death.

Lilian Kew

Till Death Us Do Part

Many lovers vow to be together forever, in life and in death, but I don't believe I've heard of anyone whose loyalty and devotion matched that of Mrs. Isidor Straus.

The year was 1912. Mrs. Straus and her husband were passengers on the *Titanic* during its fateful voyage. Not many women went down with the ship, but Mrs. Straus was one of the few women who did not survive for one simple reason: She could not bear to leave her husband.

This is how Mabel Bird, Mrs. Straus's maid, who survived the disaster, told the story after she was rescued:

"When the *Titanic* began to sink, panicked women and children were the first ones loaded into lifeboats. Mr. and Mrs. Straus were calm and comforting to the passengers, and helped many of them into the boats.

"If it had not been for them," Mabel stated, "I would have drowned. I was in the fourth or fifth lifeboat. Mrs. Straus made me get into the boat, and put some heavy wraps on me."

Then, Mr. Straus begged his wife to get into the lifeboat with her maid and the others. Mrs. Straus started to get in. She had one foot on the gunwale, but then suddenly, she changed her mind, turned away and stepped back onto the sinking ship.

"Please, dear, get into the boat!" her husband pleaded.

Mrs. Straus looked deep into the eyes of the man with whom she'd spent most of her life, the man who had been her best friend, her heart's true companion and always a comfort to her soul. She grabbed his arm and drew his trembling body close to hers.

"No," Mrs. Straus is said to have replied defiantly. "I will not get into the boat. We have been together through a great many years. We are old now. I will not leave you. Where you go, I will go."

And that is where they were last seen, standing arm in arm on the deck, this devoted wife clinging courageously to her husband, this loving husband clinging protectively to his wife, as the ship sank. Together forever...

Barbara De Angelis, Ph. D.

The Well Wisher

Alone now much of the time and grateful that at least one of her eyes is still useful, the wife reads a lot, mostly the books of other women telling stories with which she can empathize. Turning the pages with pen in hand, she underlines the good parts. Earlier she had saved such fragments to share with her husband.

She continues to do this out of habit long established. A son or daughter who comes to visit can expect to be confronted with columns torn from op-ed pages or an insistent "Listen to this..." as their mother quotes from her latest book or magazine.

Some quotations, however, are too private, and not for sharing, and must be stored in a notebook. An example? These lines from Elizabeth Jolley's *Cabin Fever* in which a woman observes, "I experience again the deep-felt wish to once again be part of a married couple, to sit by the fire in winter with the man who is my husband. So intense is this desire that if I write the word "husband" on a piece of paper, my eyes fill with tears. The word "wife" is even worse." This quotation is not something she would read to one of her children. Why are these lines painful to her?

We can start with the first picture in a worn wedding album. There they are, turning from the altar, facing with uncertain smiles a church filled with relatives and friends. The bride was not wearing glasses that day. Thus everything was to her a blur of candlelight, banked poinsettias and faces presumed to be friendly.

They walked to the back of the church and stood at the door as those assembled filed past them. From colleagues and old schoolmates came cheerful expressions of good will clothed in clumsy jokes. Some of their relatives however, were not pleased with this turn of events. One mother had already been removed from the scene, and sat in a car sobbing. The other one stood there surrounded by sympathizers offering condolences. Both of these good women would have assured you that they wanted only the best for their children, had worked and slaved to ensure it, but "the best" they defined in their own way in those hard times long ago, and that meant staying at home to help support the family, not leaving to get married.

The last person to approach the couple was a short sturdy woman who smiled as she took their hands in hers and congratulated them not by name, but as "wife" and "husband."

"I'm Aunt Esther Gubbins," she explained. "I'm here to tell you that you are going to live a good life and be happy. You will work hard and love each other." She said the words slowly, carefully, looking at each of them in turn. And then quickly for such a stout and elderly person, she was gone. And then, they were off, in a borrowed 1938 Buick. With money lent by the groom's brother they could afford a few days at a state park lodge. Sitting there the next evening before a great oak fire, they reviewed the events of their wedding day, beginning with his having to be sewed into a too-large rented shirt and squeezed into a too-narrow rented morning coat. They remembered the good wishes of their friends, the ill-concealed anguish of their mothers, and finally, the strange message conveyed by the woman who identified herself as "Aunt Esther Gubbins." "Who is Aunt Esther Gubbins?" the wife wanted to know. "Is she your mother's sister or your father's?" "Isn't she your aunt?" the husband asked. "I never saw her before that moment." They wondered about her. Someone who had come to the wrong church or at the wrong time, mistaking them for two other persons? Or was she an old lady who just liked to cry at weddings and looked for announcements in church bulletins?

With the passage of time and the accumulation of grandchildren in numbers that would today be regarded as excessive, their mothers were reconciled and loving. One made piles of play clothes for the children, using seersucker remnants from her own sturdy house dresses. The other crocheted and knitted bonnets, mittens, sweaters, and scarves. The fathers had always liked one another. They talked politics and told stories of their own growing up as immigrants in this hostile city. The lives of this couple were unremarkable. The husband could be described as taciturn, undemonstrative. The wife seemed more exuberant, outgoing, one would say. Oddly, neither ever seemed to ask, in those times of great career specialization, "Who's job is this?" or to assert "This is not my job!" Both acted to fill needs as time and opportunity allowed: doing research for a course one of them was taking or a speech he had to make, groping in the medicine chest for ear-drops in the middle of the night to sooth a crying child, tossing on one more load of whites from the perpetual pile at the base of the clothes chute.

Coming in from a hard day's work, he might stand at the door and announce. "Wife, I am home!" And she, restraining the impulse to let loose a string of well-founded complaints, would call from some corner of the house. "Husband I am glad!"

Their children were a source of great pleasure to them. Average? Not to their parents, who loved them. Extravagantly? Only if you believe love should be cautiously measured out and children will be spoiled if they get too much of it.

Once in a while, usually around the time of their anniversary, they would dredge up their old argument about Aunt Esther Gubbins, an argument that reflected the distance between practical and the imaginative, the pragmatist and the romantic. He would insist that the Gubbins person had been only accidentally present at their wedding. But she knew that Aunt Esther, since she was never identified by anyone who was asked about her and was unknown in this close-knit church community, was not there just to get out of the cold and cry at a wedding. She was there on a mission. The children took sides with enthusiasm: the earth bound against fantasists.

Now, he was gone and she was alone. Thinking back on her life, the wife asks herself if one of those tea kettles or sauce pans she has been known to burn dry while she is preoccupied should cause the house to burn down, what would she run back to save? Her mother's cameo, pictures of her husband surrounded by their grandchildren, the vault key, forty-seven dollars hidden in an old sugar bowl?

No. It would be a frayed, yellowing back of an envelope she had kept for a long time. A woman who often does not know where things are and spends a lot of time looking for them, she knows exactly where this item can be found: under a pile of Madeira napkins used on celebratory occasions. The husband had fallen asleep in his chair one evening, nodding over a fat spy novel he was reading. She wrote him a note on the back of the envelope and left it on his book. "Husband, I have gone next door to help Mrs. Norton figure out her Medicare reimbursements."

The next morning, she saw that he had written below her message to him: "Wife, I missed you. You thought I was asleep, but I was just resting my eyes and thinking about that woman who talked to us in church a long time ago. It has always seemed to me that she was the wrong shape for a heavenly messenger, but anyway, it's time to stop wondering whether she came from heaven or the next parish. What matters is this: Whoever she was, Aunt Esther Gubbins was right."

Katharine Byrne

Love Unspoken

Just home from a four-day stay in the hospital, I insist that washing my hair is an immediate necessity. It really isn't. A warm and steamy bathroom seems to be the perfect place for me to hide from the fear twisting around my heart.

I have postponed the inevitable moment all the way through undressing, and I have postponed it through sinking into the warm soapy water. But I can postpone it no longer. So I allow my gaze to slowly and cautiously drift downward. To the empty space where my left breast used to be.

It is bruised ... green and yellow and filled with black stitches covered with dried blood. It is such an indignity, so brutally ugly.

Quickly I concoct exotic mental plans to keep my husband, Jim, from ever again seeing me naked. Mutual passion has been such a strength in our marriage. But now, all of that seems over. How could I entice him with a lopsided and mutilated figure? I am only forty-three years old, and I am so deeply ashamed of my body for this betrayal. I lie back in the bath, waves of sadness washing over me.

The bathroom door swings open and Jim walks straight through my cloud of self-pity. Not saying a word, he leans over to slowly place his lips onto each of my eyelids. He knows this is my most favorite of our private "I love you" traditions. Still silent and without hesitation, he bends further down. I brace myself for the barely hidden revulsion.

Jim looks directly at my wound and gently kisses the prickly stitches. Once. Then twice. Three times. He stands up and smiles lovingly at me. Then he blows me a special airmail kiss, my second most favorite tradition, and softly closes the door behind him.

My warm, grateful tears roll down my cheeks and drop gently into the bathwater. The bruise on my chest is still there. But the one on my heart is gone.

Margie Parker

Inseparable

Love reckons hours for months, and days for years; and every little absence is an age.

John Dryden

In the end, when the statistics of their love affair were tallied, this amazing detail emerged: Paul and Linda McCartney spent nearly every night together.

In thirty years they were apart only one day. Otherwise, Linda traveled with the Beatles and Paul's other bands. He joined her on tours to promote her photography and cookbooks.

At home or away, they slept beneath the same roof, mingling breath and sweat and memory.

A few nights before I learned that Linda McCartney had died, I sat in a strange city, sharing dinner with two dozen other journalists.

Most of us had flown solo to the conference, leaving family at home.

At dinner, we made mostly small talk, the best strangers can do. I felt artificial, not at all myself, onstage.

But the man beside me seemed real. As we talked, he glanced often toward his wife, who sat across the table and down a ways, engaged in her own conversation.

In his youth, he told me, he hopscotched the world, hungry for adventure, covering war and cataclysm. Two marriages failed. He settled down and married again—then spent last year in South Africa.

His wife couldn't be with him except for brief visits. She has a thriving career here.

Now, on the brink of sixty, he'd love to return to South Africa. But a new sensation holds him back.

He told me: "I want to be with her. I want to be with her every night."

I gulped and nodded and said, "Life is short."

Funny: When you're young, you say "Life is short" to justify your excursions, geographic or emotional. When you're older, you say the same thing to justify staying home with the one you love.

That kind of relationship sounds stifling to some people. They want space. They fear being engulfed or getting lost in some rigid twosome.

Early in my marriage, I felt that way. Our work often separated us. He flew off. I flew off. It felt invigorating, and when it wasn't lonely, it seemed healthy. We even came up with a good metaphor: We traveled through life in different boats that moored, whenever they could, in the same harbor.

Now, we want nothing more than to tie our little dinghies to the same buoy, to rock gently together through each night.

Our friends report the same change of heart.

What happened?

For one thing, you realize that sharing a day's details by

phone is never as good as sharing a day. Side by side, life happens to you simultaneously. You carry the same memories, whose details blend each time you retell them.

Apart, you make separate memories. No matter how important, they're just stories to the one who wasn't there.

Plus, when you look back, you count too many weeks and months squandered in foolish places for insignificant reasons. And when you look ahead, you don't have to squint anymore to see that the end is nigh, more nigh all the time.

In middle age, you sometimes feel you have only days left to live.

When I was a child, my friends and I played a little game pretending that a nuclear bomb was headed our way. We had ten minutes to live. What would we do? Where would we go? Whose hand would we want to be holding when the end came?

Paul and Linda McCartney figured this out early, then hung on for thirty years. In the music, the laughter and the good times, I suspect they forgot they would ever have to let go.

Susan Ager

4

UNDERS-
TANDING
EACH OTHER

There is nothing you can do, achieve or buy that will outshine the peace, joy and happiness of being in communion with the partner you love.

Drs. Evelyn and Paul Moschetta

I'll See You in My Dreams

One word frees us of all the weight and pain of life: The word is "love".

Sophocles

Every night, by the time you climb into bed, the day has generally taken such a bite out of both of you that the chances of feeling loving and affectionate can be pretty remote. To combat this, my wife and I have a rule:

No discussing "Things We Have to Do" or "Unpleasant Business" once we get into bed. Unless it's really important. Or you meant to say it before and didn't get a chance. Or you just feel like saying it for no real reason. (We're nothing if not flexible.)

Originally the plan was, no discussion of unpleasantries *while getting ready for bed*, but that's too hard. There's something about putting a toothbrush in your mouth that makes people want to talk.

Consequently, even the most important exchanges take place between rinsing and spitting.

"I saw that doctor today ..." Spit.

"Yeah?"Swish,swish,spit.

"Yeah."Little spit. "He said it's nothing."Big spit.

"Well,I say"—little dribble—"we get a second opinion." Gargle,gargle,cchhwip,pttooey.

(Incidentally,*Cchhwip Pttooey* is not only the sound of someone spitting;but,interestingly enough,the Minister of the Interior of Sri Lanka.)

Every night,you brush and talk and spit and catch up,racing to beat that Conversation Curfew.

See,you don't want to drag the world into bed with you, because there's enough going on there already. Beds are complex, multipurpose arenas, and it's important that the two parties specify which activity they're undertaking.

"Are we talking,or are we reading?"

"Are we sleeping,or are we fooling around?"

You have to clarify.

"Are we not talking because we're mad,or because we both just don't feel like talking?"

"Are we thinking *ambitious* fooling around or *let's just do what we've got to do,and not kill ourselves*?"

The good thing is, when you're together forever, there's less pressure to make any given night magical. You always know you have another shot tomorrow. And the next night.

That's the whole beauty of Forever—nothing but tomorrows.

Of course,if you cash in the Tomorrow Chip too often, you break the bank. One day you roll over, notice each other,and say,"Hey,we used to do something here involving rubbing and touching—any idea what it was? No recollection at all? Hmm ...I know I enjoyed it,I remember that."

So you negotiate,you clarify,and settle in. You find your position, you fix your pillows, and arrange your mutual blanket.

That blanket, essentially, *is* your relationship: one big cover concealing the fact that two people are inside, squirming around each other trying to get comfortable.

How you handle that blanket is crucial.

Sometimes I wake up and I have *no* blanket. There's nothing there to handle. The woman of my dreams, who is sleeping very cozily, has somehow accumulated the bulk of *what's at least half mine*.

I tug at it gingerly. She stirs, and seemingly unaware, she tightens her grasp and rolls farther away, taking with her another good foot and a half of blanket. I watch her and calculate my options. I decide it's not worth waking her up or being spiteful, so I try to make do without.

I stare at the ceiling and count the little paint bumps, hoping I can bore myself back to sleep. Within seconds, my brain comes up with five different parts of the house that need painting and fixing, and then I think about how the guy at the hardware store who was so helpful doesn't work there anymore and how the new guy is really unctuous, and I should probably find someplace else. It's 3:25 in the morning and I'm looking for new hardware stores.

Now I'm more irritated and much more awake. I look over and see my bride dreaming blissfully, secure, cradled and warmed by what is now over 90 percent of the blanket. Despite my affection, I resent her deeply.

I sit up. I look at her. I watch her sleep. I think to myself, "How can this be? After all the negotiating and maneuvering and tap dancing we've done, how is it that this person, who, by my own initiative, will be placing her head twelve inches away from *my* head for the rest of my life, is getting such a better end of the bargain? It just doesn't seem right. Will we never get better at this? Must one of us always be less content than the other?"

I pull up the pathetically small segment of blanket left available to me and scoot up next to the woman of my dreams, partly because I hope that her sleep will rub off on me, and partly because I figure she's got to be warmer than I am.

And as I hold her close against me, it dawns on me: *Now* I remember. *This* is why we go through all of *that*. Because holding The One Who Fits in your arms simply feels this good, and nothing else really does. And to earn *this*, you must swat away all that stands in its way.

At this point, my wife senses I'm staring at her and opens one eye.

"What," she says.

I say, "What do you mean 'what'?"

"What are you doing?"

"Nothing."

"What are you looking at me for?"

"I wasn't looking...I was just thinking...are you really going to be right there every night?"

"Yes."

"Forever?"

"Mm hmm."

"You're saying, that of all the people in the world, the one to whom you will donate your Naked Self, night after night, is *me*?"

"Uh-huh."

If I let it go there, it would have been a nice moment.

"And the reason would be what—because I'm *that* appealing?"

Now she opens both eyes, props herself up on her elbow,

and before she can say anything, I say, "I went too far, I see that now. You just go back to sleep, and I'll say nothing."

She slides toward me, and we find homes for our arms and legs. Before long, we're sleeping.

And in the morning, the dance continues.

Paul Reiser

The Scorecard

To love is to place our happiness in the happiness of another.

Gottfried Wilhelm Van Lubreitz

As the movie came to an end the room filled with chatter. The warm fire, twinkling Christmas lights and laughter from family brought a contented smile to my face. The minute Mom said, "Who wants ..." the room emptied quicker than the stands at a losing football game.

My boyfriend Todd and I were the only ones left. With a bewildered look on his face he asked me what just happened. Catching the laughter on my mom's face, I said to Todd, "We are going to go put gas in my mom's car."

He quickly replied, "It's freezing out there, and it's almost 11:30 P.M."

Smiling, I said, "Then you had better put on your coat and gloves."

After hurriedly chipping the frost off the windshield, we bundled into the car. On the way to the gas station, Todd asked me to explain why in the world we were going to get my mom gas so late at night. Chuckling, I said, "When my siblings and I come home for the holidays, we help my dad get gas for my mom. It has turned into a game with all of us. We can tell when my mom is going to ask and the last one in the room has to go."

"You have got to be kidding me!" Todd responded.

"There is no getting out of it," I said.

While pumping the gas, we clapped our hands and jumped around to stay warm. "I still don't get it. Why doesn't your mom put the gas in the car herself?" Todd asked.

With mirth in my eyes, I said, "I know it sounds insane, but let me explain. My mom has not pumped gas in over two decades. My dad always pumps gas for her." With a confused look, Todd asked if my dad was ever annoyed with having to pump gas for his wife all the time. Shaking my head, I simply said, "No, he has never complained."

"That's crazy," Todd quickly replied.

"No, not really," I explained patiently. "When I came home for the holidays my sophomore year of college, I thought I knew everything. I was on this big female independence kick. One evening, my mom and I were wrapping presents, and I told her that when I got married, my husband was going to help clean, do laundry, cook, the whole bit. Then I asked her if she ever got tired of doing the laundry and dishes. She calmly told me it did not bother her. This was difficult for me to believe. I began to give her a lecture about this being the '90s, and equality between the sexes.

"Mom listened patiently. Then after setting the ribbon aside, she looked me square in the eyes. 'Someday, dear, you will understand.'

"This only irritated me more. I didn't understand one bit. And so I demanded more of an explanation. Mom smiled, and began to explain:

" 'In a marriage, there are some things you like to do and some things you don't. So, together, you figure out what little things you are willing to do for each other. You share the responsibilities. I really don't mind doing the laundry. Sure, it takes some time, but it is something I do for your dad. On the other hand, I do not like to pump gas. The smell of the fumes bothers me. And I don't like to stand out in the freezing cold. So, your dad always puts gas in my car. Your dad grocery shops, and I cook. Your dad mows the grass, and I clean. I could go on and on.'

" 'You see,' my mother continued, 'in marriage, there is no scorecard. You do little things for each other to make the other's life easier. If you think of it as helping the person you love, you don't become annoyed with doing the laundry or cooking, or any task, because you're doing it out of love.'

"Over the years, I have often reflected on what my mom said. She has a great perspective on marriage. I like how my mom and dad take care of each other. And you know what? One day, when I'm married, I don't want to have a scorecard either."

Todd was unusually quiet the rest of the way home. After he shut off the engine, he turned to me and took my hands in his with a warm smile and a twinkle in his eye.

"Anytime you want," he said in a soft voice, "I'll pump gas for you."

Marguerite Murer

Getting Connected

God is in the details.

Ludwig Mies van der Rohe

My wife Lisa and I were struggling to put out the small weekly newspaper we had dedicated ourselves to producing in Guthrie, Oklahoma. I wrote and Lisa sold ads. Many nights we would work well past midnight as the rest of the town and our children slept.

On one such night, we crawled into bed only to crawl back out a few hours later. I ate my cereal, drank a large soda, then headed toward Oklahoma City and the printer. Lisa matched our five children to socks and sent the older three off to school with lunch bags in hand. I was so tired I had no business driving. Lisa was so tired she had no business doing anything.

"It's seventy degrees, and the sun is shining. Another beautiful day," the disc jockey said cheerily on the car radio. I ignored him.

What I couldn't ignore was the need created by the large soft drink. I realized I'd never make it to the city, so I pulled into the rest stop on the interstate just a few miles from our house.

In her exhausted state, meanwhile, Lisa was practicing an all-too-familiar art form: calling utility companies, explaining why the payment was late and begging for one more day of hot water and air conditioning. She looked up the number and dialed the electric company.

As I stepped from the car at the rest stop. I heard the public pay phone ringing. I was the only person there, but I still looked all around. "Somebody answer the phone," I shouted just like at home.

It had to be the wrongest of wrong numbers, I thought. Then I heard myself say, "Why not?" I walked to the phone and picked up the receiver.

"Hello?" I said.

Silence. Followed by a shriek.

"Thom! What on earth are you doing at the electric company?"

"Lisa? What on earth are you doing calling the pay phone at a rest stop?"

We went through "I can't believe this" all the way to "this is downright spooky." I expected Rod Serling to come walking past to the *Twilight Zone* theme.

We stayed on the phone, and our exclamations changed to conversation. An unhurried, real conversation, without interruption, our first in a long time. We even talked about the electric bill. I told her to get some sleep, and she told me to wear my seat belt and lay off soda.

Still, I didn't want to hang up. We'd shared a wondrous experience. Even though the numbers of the electric company and the pay phone differed by only one digit, that I was there when Lisa called was so far beyond probability we could only suppose God knew we both needed, more than anything else that morning, each other's voices. He connected us.

That call was the beginning of a subtle change in our family. We both wondered how we had become so devoted to our work that we could leave our children with a stranger to put them to bed. How could I sit across the breakfast table and never say good morning?

Two years later, we were out of the business that had so dominated our lives, and I had a new job with the telephone company. Now tell me God doesn't have a sense of humor.

Thom Hunter

Reverse Roles

Mary was married to a male chauvinist. They both worked full time, but he never did anything around the house and certainly not any housework. *That*, he declared, was woman's work.

But one evening Mary arrived home from work to find the children bathed, a load of wash in the washing machine and another in the dryer, dinner on the stove and a beautifully set table, complete with flowers.

She was astonished, and she immediately wanted to know what was going on. It turned out that Charley, her husband, had read a magazine article that suggested working wives would be more romantically inclined if they weren't so tired from having to do all the housework in addition to holding down a full-time job.

The next day, she couldn't wait to tell her friends in the office. "How did it work out?" they asked.

"Well, it was a great dinner," Mary said. "Charley even cleaned up, helped the kids with their homework, folded the laundry and put everything away."

"But what about afterward?" her friends wanted to know.

"It didn't work out," Mary said. "Charley was too tired."

The Best of Bits & Pieces

"I brought you your slippers. You'll feel more comfortable doing the dishes."

Reprinted by permission of Goddard Sherman.

A Tight Situation

Sometimes funny memories are the most special way to remember a beloved spouse. It helps take away some of the feeling of loss. Before he passed away, my husband loved to share this story with our friends. Now, it makes me smile to share this story with you.

Our neighbor's son was getting married in 1971 at an out-of-town Catholic church, and my husband and I were invited. We immediately rushed out to the local department store, and I bought a nice pink linen dress with a jacket and all those cute dyed-to-match accessories. The dress was a little tight, but I had a month before the June 30 wedding and I would lose a few pounds.

June 29 came and, of course, I had not lost a single pound; in fact, I had gained two. But, I figured a nice new girdle would cure everything. So on our way out of the city, we stopped once again at the store. I ran in and told the clerk I needed a size large panty girdle.

The clerk found the box with the described girdle, marked "LG", and asked if I would like to try it on. "Oh, no, a large will fit just right. I won't need to try it on."

The next morning was one of those ninety-degree days, so I waited to get dressed until about forty-five minutes before time to go. I popped open the girdle box only to find a new,

$49.95 satin-paneled girdle in a size small. Since it was too late to find another one and the dress wouldn't fit right without a girdle, a fight broke out in the hotel room between me and the girdle. Have you ever tried to shake twenty pounds of potatoes into a five-pound sack? Finally, my husband, laughing like crazy, got hold of each side and shook me down into it. Once snug in my girdle, I put on all of the pink accessories, which did not go very well with my purple face, and I was ready to go.

All the way to the church my husband kept asking, "Are you all right? You look funny!" Then he would laugh. Men just do not appreciate what women go through to look good!

As we eased into the pew at the church, he asked if I could make it. Now, he was getting worried because I was breathing funny. I told him that I would be fine. Since we are Southern Baptist, and one of our wedding ceremonies takes thirty minutes or less, I assumed that this ceremony wouldn't last very long.

Seated in the pew with us were two little old ladies, who politely introduced themselves. Then, one of them said, "Isn't it just lovely, they are having a high mass."

"Oh, yes, lovely," I said, then turned to my husband and asked, "What is a high mass?" He shrugged his shoulders.

Unfortunately, I learned that this particular mass would last one hour, twenty-two minutes and eight-and-one-half seconds—the priest blessed everything except my girdle!

Over on the left side of the church, the bride's mother was crying and over on our side, I was crying. One of the little old ladies elbowed the other and said, "Oh, look, she's so touched."

They were right—I have never been so touched in my life! My ankles were swelling, my knees were blue and my thighs had lost all feeling. My husband was fanning me with my pink accessories, asking questions and trying to comfort me.

As soon as the priest pronounced them married, and the wedding party made their way back up the aisle to exit the church, I bolted into position as the fifth "bridesmaid" with my husband right behind me, still asking me questions: "Are you okay?" "Can I help?" "Can you breathe?"

"Please, just get me out of here!" I gasped.

We hop-danced to our car across the parking lot, and once there he opened the front and back passenger doors against the next car. Right there, before God, mankind and the wedding party, I squeezed my bruised and battered body out of that girdle! Then, to my horror just as I lifted my foot to pull the elastic torture chamber off my body once and for all, the dumb girdle catapulted out of my hand and landed under the car next to ours. My husband was laughing so hard, he couldn't even bend over to try and retrieve it, and I was too miserable to care. So we just drove away.

Over the years, he and I had often wondered what the parishioners of that fancy uptown church thought the next morning when they found an overly stretched $49.95 satin-paneled, size small girdle in their parking lot.

Barbara D. Starkey

The Richest Woman in the World

I just spent four days with a girlfriend who is married to a very wealthy man. He gave her a $35,000 ruby ring as an engagement present. He gave her a $25,000 emerald necklace for Mother's Day. He gave her $250,000 to redecorate their enormous home on five acres of land. Her bathroom cost $120,000 to build. Even her dog eats from a silver-plated dish engraved with his name.

Her husband has taken her all over the world—Tahiti for sun, Paris for clothes, London for the theater, Australia for adventure. There is nowhere she cannot go, nothing she cannot buy, nothing she cannot have—except for one thing: He does not love her the way she wants to be loved.

We sat in her study late last night, my friend and I, talking as only women who have known each other since they were just girls can talk. We talked about our bodies, changing with each passing year, hers now rounded with the new life she was carrying inside. We talked about what we used to believe in and our search for new meaning. And we talked about our men—her wealthy, successful financier, my hard-working, struggling artist.

"Are you happy?" I asked her. She sat quietly for a moment, toying with the three-carat diamond wedding ring on her finger. Then, slowly, almost in a whisper, she began to explain. She appreciated all of her wealth, but she would trade it in a minute for a certain quality of love she didn't feel with her husband. She loved him intellectually more than she *felt* her love for him. She did not respect many of his values in life, and this turned her off to him sexually. Although he was fully committed to her, and took care of her, he did not give her the experience of being loved from moment to moment — the affection, the tenderness, the words lovers use, the listening, the sensitivity, the nurturing, the respect, the willingness to participate with her in creating the relationship each day.

As I listened to my friend, I came to realize more than ever before that the love of my true companion makes me rich beyond anything material a man could ever give to me. This was not the first time I have deeply felt this, but once again, it was a reminder of my great good fortune.

And I thought about the drawerful of cards and love notes written by him, and the three latest delightful additions in my purse. I thought about him touching me, grasping my hand protectively as we cross the street, stroking my hair as I lie in his lap, grabbing me and gobbling up my neck, kissing me all over my face when I correctly guess his charades. I thought about the adventures our minds go on together, exploring ideas and concepts, understanding our past, glimpsing our future. I thought about our trust, and our respect, and our hunger for life and learning.

And in that moment, I saw that my friend envied me and my relationship. She, who sat in her luxurious home, wrapped in jewels and splendor, envied our vitality, our playfulness, our passion, our commitment — yes, our commitment.

For in that moment, I saw that what we have that is

greater than anything else between us is commitment: to loving one another fully, completely, as deeply as we know how for as long as we can.

It is not a commitment that has been declared to others, or perhaps, even out loud between ourselves.

It is not symbolized by a diamond or even a simple band of gold. It is not defined by time, or even the space in which we live apart or together.

Rather, it is a living commitment, reaffirmed each time we reach out to one another in pure joy, each time we tell the truth, each time one of us is there to support or comfort the other, each time we share a newly uncovered insight or emotion.

It is a commitment continually revealed in each new level of trust, each new layer of vulnerability, each new depth of love.

It is a commitment continually rediscovered as each day we each rediscover who we are and how much love our hearts are capable of giving.

It is a commitment that is a true marriage of spirit—whose ceremony of union is found in each and every moment we love one another, whose anniversary is found in each and every day in which love grows.

Today, when I arrived home, I found a large check waiting for me, money I hadn't expected. And I laughed at the meaningless numbers all lined up in a row.

For last night, after talking with my friend, I learned the difference between having money and truly being wealthy. And I knew that I was already the richest woman in the world.

Barbara De Angelis, Ph. D.

On Marriage

You were born together, and together you shall be forevermore.

You shall be together when the white wings of death scatter your days.

Aye, you shall be together even in the silent memory of God.

But let there be spaces in your togetherness,

and let the winds of the heavens dance between you.

Love one another, but make not a bond of love:

Let it rather be a moving sea between the shores of your souls.

Fill each other's cup but drink not from one cup.

Give one another of your bread but eat not of the same loaf.

Sing and dance together and be joyous, but let each one of you be alone,

even as the strings of a lute are alone though they quiver with the same music.

Give your hearts, but not into each other's keeping.

For only the hand of Life can contain your hearts.

And stand together yet not too near together:

For the pillars of the temple stand apart,

and the oak tree and the cypress grow not in each other's shadow.

Kahlil Gibran

The Mayonnaise War

Back when I was a new Christian, I used to brag that the divorce rate among active Christians was only one out of a thousand marriages.

Sadly, that argument bit the dust long ago.

In fact, as a bookseller and book reviewer, I'm noticing more and more titles on marital problems among Christians. After all, the vow was "for better or for worse," and as I look back on my own marriage, I see how many pitfalls have come from mistaken expectations.

My wife thought she was marrying Ward Cleaver, and I assumed every new wife stepped out of a *Good Housekeeping* advertisement, a can of Pledge in one hand, the other busily stirring the stroganoff and a seal of approval on her forehead.

Surprise—we were both wrong. I made that discovery the first night I opened the fridge to fix a sandwich.

"Hey, Honey ...where's the Best Foods Mayonnaise?"

Silence. And then, "Darling ...I don't use Best Foods, I use Kraft Miracle Whip."

Silence again.

Over the next several days, we discovered she liked Crest, I brushed with whatever was on sale. I liked green olives, she hated them and would only eat black ones. When I, shivering, turned up the furnace and the electric blanket, she was right behind me turning them down. Remembering her childhood, she liked to take Sunday afternoon drives—to which I would respond. "Yes, but that was when gas was twenty-nine cents a gallon. Let's watch an old movie instead."

The worst discovery of all was that she was a morning person, popping out of bed like a piece of toast, while I awoke with pajamas nailed to the mattress. "If God meant man to see the sunrise," I explained, "he'd have scheduled it for much later in the day."

The night we realized we *both* liked Ivory soap, we celebrated.

I guess that we discovered no disagreement is so small it can't evolve into a major problem, and that two monologues do not equal a dialogue. But most of all, we learned we no longer belonged to the separate universes we once did as singles. Our task was now to forge a new universe, one in which we would inhabit together.

After all these years, I'm still a night person, and my wife is still a morning glory. As for Ward Cleaver, she simply has to face it. I'm probably always going to be more like the Beav. And I've come to realize she's more likely to step out of the pages of the *National Enquirer* than *Good Housekeeping*. But we love each other—and as a result, she's come to like grits for breakfast (or any other time), while I finally understand that the garbage does not take itself out.

We now have separate controls for the electric blanket. I put on a sweater when I'm cold. And in the refrigerator, side by side like a pair of contented lovebirds, sits a jar each of Best Foods Mayonnaise and Kraft Miracle Whip.

Nick Harrison

Reprinted with permission of King Features Syndicate.

Behind Every Great Man Is a Great Woman

Thomas Wheeler, CEO of the Massachusetts Mutual Life Insurance Company, and his wife were driving along an interstate highway when he noticed that their car was low on gas. Wheeler got off the highway at the next exit and soon found a rundown gas station with just one gas pump. He asked the lone attendant to fill the tank and check the oil, then went for a little walk around the station to stretch his legs.

As he was returning to the car, he noticed that the attendant and his wife were engaged in an animated conversation. The conversation stopped as he paid the attendant. But as he was getting back into the car, he saw the attendant wave and heard him say, "It was great talking to you."

As they drove out of the station, Wheeler asked his wife if she knew the man. She readily admitted she did. They had gone to high school together and had dated steadily for about a year.

"Boy, were you lucky that I came along," bragged Wheeler. "If you had married him, you'd be the wife of a gas station attendant instead of the wife of a chief executive officer."

"My dear," replied his wife, "if I had married him, he'd be the chief executive officer and you'd be the gas station attendant."

The Best of Bits & Pieces

An Affair to Remember

The clock radio was playing a gentle tune, and I woke up to another day of infinite wonder and promise.

"Morning, sweetie," I said, my head still snuggled in my pillow.

"Who's Angela?" my wife asked in the tone Mike Wallace uses when cameras are chasing some poor jerk down a sidewalk in Newark, New Jersey.

A million years of evolution have given married suburban guys a kind of sixth sense that tells them when to be absolutely truthful, answering all questions fully and without reservation. "I don't know any Angela," I said.

"Oh, I know you don't," Kathleen said, sitting up and slamming her hand on the alarm button. "This is so ridiculous. It's just that I had this dream last night where you left the kids and me and ran off with some Angela woman. I've been awake for three hours getting madder and madder."

"Silly girl," I said, snuggling deeper into the blankets. "I promise I didn't run off with anybody. Not last night or any other night. And especially not with any Angela."

Kathleen threw back the blankets with considerably more force than the circumstances required and got out of bed.

"It was just a dream," I said, wishing desperately for two more minutes of unconsciousness. "I don't know an Angela.

I'm here with you and our children. I'm not leaving. Never, never, never."

The shower door banged shut, and I drifted off. Suddenly a wet towel hit me in the face.

"Sorry, hon, I was aiming for the hamper," Kathleen said. "Anyway, you and Angela were living together in one of those luxury high-rise condos downtown."

"Ha. See how crazy that is? Child support would wipe me out. I couldn't afford to live under a bridge if I left you. Which I have no plans to do."

"Angela's a surgeon," she said as if she were talking to a complete idiot, "With an international reputation. She's filthy rich. Or don't you realize that either? Oh, of course you don't. Just a dream."

"Listen, I know dreams can seem pretty realistic sometimes. But you're the woman of my dreams. Okay? What kind of surgeon?"

From the bathroom came the unmistakable sound of toiletries being destroyed.

"You want to know what really got me?" she said. "The kids. The kids went to visit one weekend, and you know what that — you know — Angela did? She made teddy bear pancakes. With little raisin eyes. The children talked about those for days: 'How come you never make us teddy bear pancakes, Mom?'"

"Teddy bear pancakes? That sounds kind a cute. They'd probably be pretty easy ..."

"Oooooh," Kathleen said. "This is so dumb. How can anybody get upset over a stupid dream about your husband running off with a world-famous surgeon who can sit down at a piano with the kids and play all the television theme songs by ear and knows all the verses and can put your daughter's hair up in a perfect French braid and show your boy how to play 'stretch' with a jackknife and teach aerobics?"

"Kathleen, I couldn't love a surgeon. Surgeons are notoriously self-centered and egotistical. But maybe Angela was different."

"Angela works among the poor," Kathleen said. "Here's that tennis shoe you've been looking for. Oops, are you all right?"

"George Bush gave her some kind of plaque. I saw it on TV. In my dream. There she was with those cheekbones and that mane of black hair. 'Others deserve this far more than I do, Mr. President.' I just about threw up."

The tennis shoe bruise probably wouldn't show unless I went swimming or something.

"What with teddy bear pancakes, humanitarianism and piano lessons. Angela couldn't have much time left over for a guy," I said. "I mean, a guy like me."

"Oh no. The kids told me how she'd spend hours rubbing your shoulders and sometimes she'd sit at your feet on that spotless white carpet — 'It's like snow, Mom' — and stare up at you, laughing at every stupid little thing you said. Darn! Your watch fell in the sink. Sorry, sweetie."

"I think you're being a little hard on Angela," I said. "She sounds like a pretty nice person who's only trying to make a life for herself."

"She's a vicious little home wrecker, and if you ever so much as look at her again, you'll need more than a world-renowned surgeon to put you back together again!"

Later that day I sent flowers to Kathleen's office. It's just a start, of course. When somebody like Angela comes into your life, it takes a while to patch things up.

Patrick O'Neill

Coming Home

I've always considered myself a strong, independent female. But I didn't know the gut ache of aloneness until we moved to America.

It had been a big decision for my husband, two children, and me to pull up roots in Toronto, Canada, and emigrate. But Doug had a job offer he couldn't refuse—chief financial officer for a major company in northern Virginia. He'd signed on January first, and I was to follow as soon as possible.

We had two shocks in quick succession. The first was that within two weeks after Doug came on board, his new company entered into major merger talks with a competitor. That meant my husband accompanied the president all over the United States for the negotiations. His weekends were spent in New York or Wisconsin rather than at home with us. But in Canada, cushioned by old friends and some family, Doug's absences were not so bad.

Of course, I missed his smile, his jokes, his loving support. Of course, the kids went out of their skulls when he came home. But, caught up in the move and in good-byes, we were too busy to be lonely.

Once we got to Virginia, however, loneliness struck like a runaway train.

Then came the second shock. I'd been given rapturous

accounts of the mildness of the weather compared to the snow-cold misery of the Toronto winters. Never believe propaganda, no matter how benign.

We arrived in March, during an ice storm that raged for five days, and Doug couldn't be home to welcome us. He was in New York.

So, here I was—up to my ying-yang in boxes, house-bound kids and a sick dog. I couldn't find anything. The electricity kept going out. Thank God, the Domino's Pizza guy managed to slog through the storm so I could feed the children. Even the dog had extra-cheese deep-dish that night. I saved the pepperoni for breakfast.

The phone rang at five o'clock. I dug through wadded-up paper and piles of cardboard until I fished it out from behind my oh-so-empty canisters. "Hello?"

"Cath?"

"Yes, Doug, it's me. You were expecting maybe Michelle Pfeiffer?"

"A guy can hope, can't he?"

"Ha ha."

"You're in a good mood."

"Peachy."

"I just wanted to check in with you real quick, Cath, and see how your day's been, and how the kids are."

"Great," I answered ...*if you consider two nutsy children, one dying dog, an ice rink for a driveway and no heat great.* "The man brought the wood this morning."

"At least you can have a fire."

"Yep."

"I wish I were home. I hate being away from you, and I'm sorry you have to shoulder all the burden of the move."

My heart thawed. I knew he meant every word. "We miss

you, too. Like crazy. But Doug, we both have jobs to do."

"I know. I know. Just a sec, someone's at the door." I waited, hearing snatches of conversation before my husband picked up the phone again. "Listen, honey, the limo's here. We're going out to Montrachet for dinner. I'll call you when I get back. I love you."

"Yeah. Love you, too."

The Phone dangled from my fingers, and I caught a glimpse of my reflection in the black expanse of naked window over the kitchen sink. My short brown hair clung to my neck in greasy strings. I'd been wearing the same jeans and sweatshirt for two days. Dark smudges underlined my eyes, and my cheeks and lips were screaming for color. Try as I might, I could find neither hide nor hair of the girl Doug had fallen for—at first sight, he always said—so many years before.

I kicked at the Domino's box crumpled on the floor. No wonder I hardly saw my husband anymore. How could I compete with Montrachet and limousines?

Within minutes, the phone rang again. "Hello?" I mumbled, barely gathering the strength to be civil. If this was the power company calling with another excuse, I was going to lose it.

"Cath? It's Doug. I'm coming home."

Please, please. "You can't—the biggest ice storm of the century is raging out there."

"I can't take being away from you another day. And I've got to see the kids, I'll go crazy if I don't."

"But the merger talks ... the negotiations." It would be business suicide for Doug to leave now. He hadn't established himself yet.

"I heard your voice, Cath. You sound like I flee. I'm

coming home."

"I'm so glad," the last word ended in a squeaky sob. I swallowed hard and tried again. "I'll keep the fire burning."

"I know you will. I'll be home by seven."

At 6:30 both kids and I were groomed and ready for Doug. The fire was lit, and our new home was beautiful, painted in the delightful colors of anticipation.

Three hours later, I tucked two very disappointed little souls into bed, and settled by the fire to listen to the storm rage. *Why didn't I tell him to stay in New York? Why had I let him travel in this?*

At ten o'clock the phone rang, and I made a dive for it.

"I'm on the ground," Doug said. "Almost home, honey. See you in half an hour."

I threw two big logs on the fire. Was it my imagination, or had the wind picked up, howling like a banshee around the house? Were ice pellets truly trying to break our windows? My last fingernail was chewed to the quick, and I started in on the pencil I clutched.

By eleven my weary body didn't care that my heart was scared to death. I found myself dozing and starting, dozing and starting until finally I fell asleep.

The next thing I knew, a pair of cold arms was wrapped around me. I felt the scratchy weave of a Fair Isle sweater against my cheek, and the sweet familiar scent of Drakkar Noir cut into my nightmares. I pushed my face deeper into the rough, wool haven of my husband's chest and inhaled deeply. We didn't move for a long time.

"I had to put the kids to bed," I whispered finally.

"Come on." Doug smiled and led me upstairs.

Mark and Jane were dead to the world. I watched my husband bend over each in turn. He rested his face ever so lightly against their cheeks and inhaled deeply.

"I love their smell. I'd almost forgotten it," he said, a little sheepishly.

We went downstairs again. The former owners had left a bright white light on the landing. For the first time, I took a good look at Doug's face. He's only forty but in the wee hours of this morning, fatigue had fashioned his cheeks into sunken hollows. He looked like he'd been dragged through a knothole.

He was the most gorgeous sight I'd ever seen.

We didn't do anything grand the rest of the night—no storybook lovemaking on a bearskin rug. In our house it would more likely have been a pizza box anyway. I rummaged a blanket and pillows from some carton, and we snuggled together in front of the fire, not saying much. In fact, words were inadequate and unnecessary.

He left at 5:30 in the morning, and I stayed awake. All I thought about was my husband, and the efforts he'd made for only a few hours with us.

And I knew I was loved. And it was enough.

Cathy Grant
As told to Samantha Glen and Mary Pesaresi

5

OVERCOMING OBSTACLES

Your heart is not living until it has experienced pain... The pain of love breaks open the heart, even if it is as hard as a rock.

Hazrat Inayat Khan

Where Love Lands

It's only when we truly know and understand that we have a limited time on earth—and that we have no way of knowing when our time is up—that we will begin to live each day to the fullest, as if it was the only one we had.

Elisabeth Kübler-Ross

No one knows where love's wings will land. At times, it turns up in the most unusual spots. There was nothing more surprising than when it descended upon a rehabilitation hospital in a Los Angeles suburb—a hospital where most of the patients can no longer move of their own accord.

When the staff heard the news, some of the nurses began to cry. The administrator was in shock, but from then on, Harry MacNarama would bless it as one of the greatest days in his entire life.

Now the trouble was, how were they going to make the wedding dress? He knew his staff would find a way, and when one of his nurses volunteered, Harry was relieved. He wanted this to be the finest day in the lives of two of his patients—Juana and Michael.

Michael, strapped in his wheelchair and breathing through his ventilator, appeared at Harry's office door one morning.

"Harry, I want to get married," Michael announced.

"Married?" Harry's mouth dropped open. How serious was this? "To who?" Harry asked.

"To Juana," Michael said. "We're in love."

Love. Love had found its way through the hospital doors, over two bodies that refused to work for their owners and penetrated their hearts—despite the fact that the two patients were unable to feed or cloth themselves, required ventilators just to breath and could never walk again. Michael had spinal muscular atrophy; Juana had multiple sclerosis.

Just how serious this marriage idea was, became quite apparent when Michael pulled out the engagement ring and beamed as he hadn't done in years. In fact, the staff had never seen a kinder, sweeter Michael, who had been one of the angriest men Harry's employees had ever worked with.

The reason for Michael's anger was understandable. For twenty-five years, he had lived his life at a medical center where his mother had placed him at age nine and visited him several times a week until she died. He was always a raspy sort of guy, who cussed out his nurses routinely, but at least he felt he had family at the hospital. The patients were his friends.

He also was very close with seventy-year-old Betty Vogle, a volunteer who wound her way into Michael's heart—not such an easy task—by doing his laundry and being there for him whenever she could.

There even had been a girl once who went about in a squeaky wheelchair who he was sure had eyed him. But she hadn't stayed long at the center. And after spending more than half his life there, now Michael wasn't going to get to stay either.

The center was closing, and Michael was shipped to live at the rehabilitation hospital, far from his friends and worse, far from Betty.

That's when Michael turned into a recluse. He wouldn't come out from his room. He left it dark. His sister, a red-headed woman who sparkled with life, grew increasingly concerned. So did Betty, who drove more than two hours to see him. But Michael's spirits sagged so low, no one could reach him.

And then, one day, he was lying in bed when he heard a familiar creaking sound coming down the hall. It sounded like that same, ancient, squeaking wheelchair that girl, Juana, had used at the center where he used to live.

The squeaking stopped at his door, and Juana peered in and asked him to come outdoors with her. He was intrigued and from the moment he met Juana again, it was as though she breathed life back into him.

He was staring at the clouds and blue skies again. He began to participate in the hospital's recreation programs. He spent hours talking with Juana. His room was sunny and light. And then he asked Juana, who'd been living in a wheelchair since age twenty-four, if she would marry him.

Juana had already had a tough life. She was pulled out of school before finishing the third grade, because she collapsed and fell a lot. Her mother, thinking she was lazy, slapped her around. She lived in terror that her mother wouldn't want her anymore, so on the occasions when she was well enough, she cleaned house "like a little maid".

Before the age of twenty-four, like Michael, she had a tracheotomy just to breathe and that was when she was officially diagnosed with multiple sclerosis. By the time she was thirty, she had moved into a hospital with round-the-clock care.

So when Michael asked her the big question, she didn't think she could handle the pain if he was teasing.

"He told me he loved me, and I was so scared," she said. "I thought he was playing a game with me. But he told me it was true. He told me he loved me."

On Valentine's Day, Juana wore a wedding dress made of white satin, dotted with pearl beads and cut loose enough to drape around a wheelchair and a ventilator. Juana was rolled to the front of the room, assisted by Harry, who proudly gave the bride away. Her face streamed with tears.

Michael wore a crisp white shirt, black jacket and a bow tie that fit neatly over his tracheotomy. He beamed with pleasure.

Nurses filled the doorways. Patients filled the room. An overflow of hospital employees spilled into the halls. Sobs echoed in every corner of the room. In the hospital's history, no two people—living their lives bound to wheelchairs—had ever married.

Janet Yamaguchi, the hospital's recreation leader, had planned everything. Employees had donated their own money to buy the red and white balloons, matching flowers, and an archway dotted with leaves. Janet had the hospital chef make a three-tiered, lemon-filled wedding cake. A marketing consultant hired a photographer.

Janet negotiated with family members. It was one of the most trying and satisfying times of her life to watch the couple get married.

She thought of everything.

The final touch—the kiss—could not be completed. Janet

used a white satin rope to tie the couple's wheelchairs to symbolize the romantic moment.

After the ceremony, the minister slipped out trying to hold back her tears. "I've performed thousands of weddings, but this is the most wonderful one I've done so far," the minister said. "These people have passed the barriers and showed pure love."

That evening, Michael and Juana rolled into their own room for the first time together. The hospital staff showed up with a honeymoon dinner and gave them two glasses of sparkling cider for a private toast. Michael and Juana knew they had moved many people with their love, and they had been given the greatest gift of all. They had the gift of love. And it's never known where it will land.

Diana Chapman

Derian's Gift of Love

Ah, surely nothing dies but something mourns.

Lord Byron

Our son Derian was given a clean bill of health the first twenty-four hours of his life. However, just before we were to leave the hospital, he turned blue. He needed heart surgery immediately. From the instant the seriousness of Derian's condition was explained to us, our lives took a different direction. We changed because we had no choice.

We held our helpless newborn in our arms, as we waited for the surgeon to come and open up his chest. We were drowning in a sea of confusion, terror, despair and anger. We held hands as we gave him the last of a series of kisses, each kiss drenched with the hope that we would be able to kiss him "hello" following a successful surgery. The team then came and carefully took him from our arms, promising to take good care of him. Our hearts ached as we watched Derian leave with strangers dressed in blue scrubs. We clung to each other with tears and a strong grip.

At that moment, our relationship changed. We had never

really needed to need each other before now. No one else could feel the way we felt about our child. No one else would face the struggle the same way we would. No one else could feel the same pain and fear we felt. We were determined to raise this child. We grew into a connected force, a solid bond—Derian's parents. It was strange though, that even with death looking over our shoulders and shadowing our little son, we never had enough courage to pray to the same God together and beg for his life.

Derian was a fighter and made it through the surgery. However a few days later, he had a full cardiac arrest. Then the night before he was to leave the hospital, he needed another heart surgery. Our first thirty-six days of parenting were spent in the hospital.

Life started moving like a roller coaster — fast, wild and out of control as time moved on. Three months after we brought Derian home, I found out I was pregnant again. I had often heard God never gives you more than you can handle, but at this point, I was sure I was on overload.

I couldn't believe God thought I could handle another baby so soon. A short time before I was to deliver our second child, Derian required another heart surgery. Once again, he fought his way through surgery and to a successful recovery.

Our son Connor was born in September. I had taken a leave from teaching and had planned on returning the second trimester that school year. One month before I was to return back to school, we took Derian to the cardiologist for a checkup. He told us Derian would need to have yet another heart surgery the following month. His words stung, as we had been told he would not need any more surgery. This would be his fourth heart surgery in his seventeen-month life.

We were completely caught offguard by this. We had financially planned for a three-month maternity leave, but now I would need to take another month off, unpaid. I had no sick days left. How were we going to afford this? How were we going to care for a newborn and Derian at the same time? How many surgeries could his little heart take? And always the underlying question of him being able to fight through it. We were scared. Our reality kept ripping us out of the mainstream of life. We were sinking with responsibility and despair.

By this time, Christmas was marching its way through December. We tried to join in the festivities but knowing Derian was going in for surgery in January took the merry out of Christmas. Holidays had always been an important part of life for us so Robb couldn't let Christmas pass without doing a few traditional things. When he was invited to a Christmas party after work, he jumped at the chance if only to feel the presence of "normalcy" once again. I was glad he was going. I wanted him to be free from worry for just a little while.

I got Derian and Connor down to sleep relatively easily that night and was just preparing for bed myself when Robb came home. He was unusually pale, his eyes had a startled look and he was trembling. I was almost afraid to hear what happened.

He said in a deep, serious tone, "Patsy, I need to talk to you. A strange thing happened to me on the way home. As I was driving, I was talking to God."

I held my breath. Robb and I had never spoken to each other about God before. The air between us felt very still, very reverent. I listened intently as he continued.

"Patsy, I told God that if he needed to take someone from

our family, it should be me, rather than Derian." My husband's eyes turned red, and I could see tears running down his face.

"Then I felt the deep heat of a hand resting on my shoulder and heard the soft, quiet whisper of an angel say, 'Derian's going to be okay—don't worry.'"

I was stunned with the force of what Robb was saying to me. For a moment, I just stared at him. Then we fell into a peace-filled embrace.

This was the most important moment in our marriage. His willingness to share his spiritual encounter with me was the most intimate experience I have ever had. He allowed me to walk in his soul, and what a soul it was. The depth of his love for our son moved me in a profound way. I have never looked at him the same again.

Our son did make it through that surgery. During the year following this ordeal, my relationship with Robb reached a new level of closeness, a new depth of love. Our shared faith had created not only more emotional intimacy, but new spiritual intimacy. It strengthened, united and prepared us. We believe Robb's angel led us to this higher level in our marriage because all too soon we had a new reality to face—Derian's fifth surgery.

This time, our baby did not make it through. Soon after the surgery, he died.

As devastating as it was to lose this child, Robb and I remain united in our relationship. It was as though Derian gave us a gift of deeper love for one another. Despite the pain, together we still believe in prayer, miracles, a mighty God—and most of all, the divine guidance we now receive from a little angel named Derian.

Patsy Keech

Engraved in His Heart

It was right before Christmas. My husband, Dan, and a buddy of his, Mike, had gone to a canyon near our home in Southern California to see if the vegetation, scorched by fires a few months earlier, was growing back. Dan and Mike were both members of the California Native Plant Society. They were real "plant hounds", always exploring the nearby canyons and hills to see what kind of plants they could find and photograph.

That day, after Mike left, Dan decided to do a little "solo research" by hiking up into Laguna Canyon, a more remote section of the area that was not often explored. He had walked into the canyon a few miles, gotten some pictures and was starting to make his way back to his truck, when he stepped on a water-soaked patch of ground that gave way. He fell thirty-five feet down the rough slope, hitting a number of trees, before he landed on a ledge. He could tell right away that something was terribly wrong with his left leg. It lied across his other leg at an "impossible angle".

Stunned by the fall, it took Dan a little while to realize that he was too crippled to walk. Then Dan knew he was in serious trouble. Night would fall soon and not a soul knew where he was. He had to get to a main trail or he might die out there before anyone could find him. He braced the broken leg against the other leg and, resting his weight on his hands, began inching his way down the canyon.

Making slow and painful progress, Dan stopped often to rest and call for help. The only response was the eerie sound of his own voice echoing off the walls of the canyon. As the sun set, the temperature began to drop. It was cold in the hills at night and Dan knew that if he stopped for too long, he would probably lose consciousness. It was increasingly hard, but Dan forced himself after each pause to keep hauling his sore body forward on his aching hands. He continued this awful journey for another twelve hours.

Finally, his strength and determination gave out. He was utterly exhausted and couldn't move another inch. Although it seemed futile, he summoned up a last burst of strength and shouted for help.

He was astounded when he heard a voice return his call. A real voice, not another mocking and empty echo. It was Dan's stepson—my son, Jeb. He and I were out with the police and the paramedics who were searching for Dan.

Earlier, when Dan didn't come home, I had gotten worried and called Mike. At first, Mike tried to find Dan himself, driving from canyon to canyon looking for Dan's truck. Finally, he called the police and reported Dan missing.

I'd kept calm and strong until the moment Jeb said he'd heard Dan's voice. Then I dissolved into tears, finally feeling the fear and dread I'd been pushing aside for hours. It took over two hours for the rescue team to bring Daniel down the ravine. Then the paramedics trundled him away on a stretcher and when I got to see him at the hospital, my tears started anew. The thought of how close I came to losing this wonderful man undid me. It was only when I felt Dan's arms around me that I finally stopped sobbing.

As I sat next to his hospital bed, my eyes fastened to the face I had been so afraid I would never see again, Dan told me his story. Immediately after his slide down the canyon, when he realized the seriousness of his predicament, Dan said that he thought of me and how much he would miss me if he didn't make it back. As he lay at the bottom of the rough cliff, he groped around until he found a suitable rock. Using the rock, which was sharply pointed, he managed to carve a message to me in a large rock near where he lay. If the worst should happen, he hoped I would eventually see the rock and know that I had been with him always, held close in his heart.

I started weeping all over again. I knew how deeply I loved my husband, but I was unprepared for this, the depth of his love for me.

For somewhere deep in the wooded hills of Laguna Canyon, there is a large rock with a heart carved on its side. And in this heart are carved the words: Elizabeth, I love you.

Elizabeth Songster

A Moment of Comfort

Wherever you are, I am there also.

Beethoven

Michele Kaplanak's husband, Ed, is a construction worker who once, due to the scarcity of local employment, was forced to take a job on a large dam project more than three hundred miles from their home.

"It was the longest six months I've ever spent," Michele said. "Ed could get home only on weekends. He would not arrive until after midnight on Friday, and he would have to be back on the road right after the noon meal on Sunday. For those six months, we lived only on Saturdays."

She remembered one dreary fall day when she was particularly lonely. The clouds hung low in the sky and drizzled on the leaves at sporadic intervals.

"It was the kind of day to share with someone you love," she said. "It was the kind of day to cuddle by an open fireplace."

She felt lonely and depressed, but she pulled on a heavy sweater and sat in her chilly house, pasting premium stamps in books.

"That night my bed felt as cold and damp and lonely as a

grave,"Michele said. "My only consolation was that it was Thursday night, and Ed would be home that next evening. I lay shivering between the sheets, cursing the job situation that had taken my husband so far away from me."

Then she thought she felt a slight pressure on Ed's side of the bed.

"I turned over and saw nothing, but it seemed to me that I could feel a kind of warmth coming from Ed's pillow."

She ran her hand along the inside of the sheets.

"For a crazy minute there, I feared that I might be losing my grip on reality," Michele said. "Ed's side of the bed most definitely felt warm, like he had been sleeping there and had just gotten up."

Michele lay on her side of the bed for a few moments longer, then, once again, she slid her hand over the sheet.

"There could be no mistaking it! The bed on Ed's side was as warm as toast," she reported.

It had been a lonely day for Michele. She had no interest in attempting to theorize why that side of the bed should be so warm when no one was sleeping there.

"Without another moment's hesitation, I slid over into the blessed pocket of warmth and comfort and fell fast asleep almost at once."

Michele really did not think of the strange incident again until three days later, when she and her husband were eating their farewell Sunday meal. Ed's response to her curious story was hardly what she had expected.

"He stared at me for a few moments in complete silence, as if uncertain how next to proceed. Then he spoke to me in slow, measured sentences and told me a most amazing story."

That Thursday night, Ed Kaplanak had been lying in the

construction workers' bunkhouse, trying to come to terms with his loneliness.

"I really felt like chucking it all that night," he told Michele. "Job or no job, I just wanted to come home to you right then."

That night, as he lay there surrounded by his snoring bunkmates, Ed's entire being seemed suffused with personal anguish. He wanted so much to be in his own clean bed to be able to feel Michele sleeping next to him.

"I decided to experiment," he told Michele. "I wanted to see if it were possible to will myself home over those three hundred miles. I rested my hands behind my head and summoned every ounce of concentration that I had inside my brain. I thought of nothing but you and home. I kept telling myself that it was possible to project my spirit to you. I have always believed that we were destined to be together and that all things would be possible for us—even this.

"There was a kind of rushing sensation, and I stood beside our bed, looking down at you. You were just lying there, looking kind of sad, not yet sleeping. I slipped into bed beside you, and you moved your hand over me. A few minutes later, you did it again. I thought that you knew I was there, because you rolled over and snuggled up next to me. I put my arm around you and we both went right to sleep."

Michele said that although Ed awakened back in the bunkhouse and she awakened alone in their bed back home, they will always wonder if Ed really did come home that night—or if their deep love enabled them to share a vivid dream so that they could experience a moment of comfort when they were both longing so terribly for one another.

Brad Steiger

New Sneakers

Blessed is the influence of one true, loving human soul on another.

George Eliot

I had no idea where we were going or what we were doing. We were just walking. I was thinking back on all the abuse that I had suffered at the hands of my husband. In those few years, I had been beaten, broken, shot, stabbed and raped. I finally drew up enough courage and strength to leave him. I took my two little girls, Kodie and Kadie, with me. This was our third week on the streets. I tried getting a job, but I could not afford day care. I wanted to work, but I didn't know what to do with the girls. They were still babies at two and four. I was lost.

I went to a couple of local missions, but they turned us away. I had not grabbed the children's birth certificates when I left. There was no way I was going back to that house. Ever!

A local Kentucky Fried Chicken threw away chicken that had sat in the warmer too long. I talked to the manager and asked him if I might have it for my girls. He said I'd have to wait until he put the chicken in the Dumpster. Hunger is not proud. A cashier had overheard us talking, and she said it would be left on top of the Dumpster for us. I thanked her. We ate like that for a couple of days.

One day, while walking with the girls, I stopped in at a local pizzeria to find out if I could get a cup of water for the baby. And then I saw him—muscular, handsome and Italian. He was the most beautiful man I had ever laid eyes on! I knew that I looked terrible, but still, he gave us a friendly smile. I asked him if we could have some water, and he said to have a seat while he got it.

He brought over the water and started talking about how hard it was to raise a family in this city. He left for a moment to answer the phone, and when he came back, he brought a lot of food with him. More food than I had seen in the whole month! I was so embarrassed. I told him that I didn't have any money to pay for it. "It's on the house," he said. "Only pretty ladies like you get this kind of treatment though." I thought he must be crazy!

We sat there for a while, making small talk. Then, he began asking questions that made me nervous. "How'd you get all those bruises on your face? Why don't you have a coat on?" Things like that. I answered as calmly as I could. He listened thoughtfully. Then, he wrapped up the food and put it in the pocket of the stroller. I washed the girls up in the washroom, and I tried to clean myself up a little bit. I looked awful. We were not dirty though, just disheveled. On the way out, we thanked him and he said to come back anytime we wanted. I didn't want to wear out our welcome though. Winter was coming fast, and I either had to come up with a solution about a job, or figure out how I could get to Georgia to be with family. We left and started looking for a place to sleep for the night.

A little while later, as we wandered aimlessly, the baby spit up. I had seen the man put some napkins in with the food, and when I went to look for one, I found nine dollars folded up in a little wad. *Maybe he accidentally put the money in there when he gave me the food*, I thought. But I knew I couldn't accept it. So I turned around and started back to the restaurant.

There he was again. I told him that I had found this money, and I wanted to return it. "I put it there on purpose," he said kindly. "I'm sorry I didn't have more on me."

Why was he doing this? An angel. That was my first thought. All I could do was to stammer another embarrassed thank-you. "Bring the girls in tomorrow for lunch," he responded. I was stumped! Why was he being so nice to us? But with no other hope, I agreed, said good-bye, and we started out again.

About halfway down the street, I could feel that we were being followed. It made me nervous because I had two children to protect. Quickly, I ducked into an alley with the kids and tried to keep the baby quiet. She wanted to make noise though, and there was no hushing her. I felt someone approaching and held my breath.

It was the man from the restaurant!

"I know you don't have any place to stay," he said.

"How do you know that?" My heart was racing. Was he going to turn my children in to the state?

"I can tell by your shoes."

I looked down at my feet. My sneakers had little happy faces all over them, but were a little worse for wear. They were full of holes and were held together with threads.

My face turned bright red. "Well," I stammered, "I just

like wearing comfortable shoes."

"Look," he began, "would you like a warm place to clean up and spend the night?"

I hesitated. I didn't know this guy at all! Sure, I loved the way his brown eyes warmed my heart, but that was not enough to base a "go into a stranger's house" decision on.

"Thank you," I said quietly, "but no."

He pointed to the apartment above us.

"If you change your mind, all you have to do is come up and knock on the door."

I thanked him again and watched him walk away.

It was time to get the girls comfortable for the night—as comfortable as you can be when you are sleeping on the street. As I sat down next to the stroller, I saw a shadow in the window above us. It was him. He sat there for hours. Just watching over us.

Finally, I fell into a restless sleep. Exhausted from my ordeal, I hadn't even noticed that it had started to rain, and so at first, I didn't even realize that he was standing there above me. It was three in the morning.

"Please," he said, "bring the girls upstairs. I don't want anyone getting sick."

"I can't," I responded.

"All right," he retorted. "I guess I will just have to spend the night here with you." And with that, he sat down on the ground.

I gave in. "No sense in all of us getting wet," I mumbled. I let him carry the stroller up the stairs, with one child still in it. He offered me and the girls his bed any made a place for himself on the couch.

"Are you sure about this?" I asked timidly.

"Look, just try and get some sleep, okay?" And with that,

he bade me good night. But I couldn't sleep at all. I wasn't scared of this gentle man anymore. I was ...nervous.

The next day, he went out and got the kids some new clothes and toys, and brought me some new sneakers. That was almost six years ago. We are still together, and we also have two little boys. I thank God for sending us Johnnie Trabucco. We now have a stable home and a loving environment. There is no more hurt.

Kim Lonette Trabucco

Married to a Stranger

In wedding portraits on the walls of their Las Vegas, New Mexico, living room, Kim and Krickitt Carpenter look like any young newlyweds — deeply in love and filled with hope for their new life together. But Krickitt admits it causes her some pain now to look at the pictures or to see herself in the wedding video, walking down the aisle in her lacy white gown. "I would almost rather not watch it," she says. "It makes me miss the girl in the picture more and more."

In a sense, that Krickitt is gone, lost forever. Less than ten weeks after the September 1993 ceremony, the Carpenters were in a nightmarish auto accident that badly injured them both and left Krickitt comatose. Though doctors initially doubted she would survive, she rallied, regaining consciousness and, eventually, most of her physical abilities. But the trauma to her brain caused retrograde amnesia, erasing virtually her entire memory of the previous eighteen months — including any recollection of the man she had fallen in love with and married. "The last two years have been based on a story I'm told," says Krickitt, twenty-six, "because I don't remember any of it."

Krickitt Pappas was a sales representative for an Anaheim, California, sportswear company when Kim, then baseball coach and assistant athletic director at New Mexico

Highlands University in Las Vegas, phoned in September 1992 to order some team jackets. While chatting, they discovered mutual interests—both were devout Christians, and Krickitt's father had also coached baseball. One call led to another, and by January, Kim, now thirty, recalls, "we were probably talking five hours a week." The following April, he invited her to visit New Mexico for a weekend. "She got off the plane—I'll never forget," he says. "It was like I'd always known her." Over the next few months, they spent nearly every weekend together. In June, he showed up unannounced at her apartment with flowers and a ring. "I asked if she'd become my lifetime buddy," he says.

They seemed a good fit. Kim, who had played college baseball and golf at Highlands, was one of three sons of Danny Carpenter, a retired printing firm owner, and his wife Maureen. Krickitt (born Kristian and nicknamed as a baby by an aunt) was a two-time Academic All-American gymnast at Cal State, Fullerton. She grew up in Phoenix, the daughter of Gus and Mary Pappas, former school-teachers and coaches who also have a son, Jamey. Krickitt and Kim married that fall and moved into an apartment in Las Vegas (128 miles northeast of Albuquerque), where Krickitt found work as a hospital fitness instructor.

They were just settling into married life when, on November 24, they set out to visit her parents in Phoenix. Krickitt—with Kim lying in the backseat and a friend in the passenger seat—was driving west on Interstate 40 and had to swerve to avoid hitting a slow-moving truck. A pickup following them smashed into the Carpenters' car. Their Ford Escort flipped over on its roof and went into a sickening skid. "I can remember every split second of that wreck," says Kim. "I screamed and screamed and screamed for Krickitt and got no answer. "Kim suffered a punctured lung, a bruise on his heart, a concussion and a broken hand. Milan Rasic, the friend, had a separated shoulder. But worst off was Krickitt, who had suffered a terrible skull fracture when the roof of the car caved in around her head. Unconscious and fastened by a seat belt, she hung upside down for thirty minutes before rescuers arrived, then forty more minutes before they could free her. Emergency medic D. J. Combs recalls that her pupils were fixed in a rightward gaze: "She had what we call 'doll's eyes.'"

"It was pretty bleak initially," says emergency-room doctor Alan Beamsley, who was at the Gallup, New Mexico, hospital where Krickitt arrived nearly ninety minutes after the accident. "We were scared for her." A doctor brought Kim an envelope containing Krickitt's rings and watch. "He said, 'I'm very sorry, Mr. Carpenter,'" Kim recalls. "I thought she'd died." Despite doctors' advice, he refused treatment for himself to stay by his wife's side. "I didn't recognize her, she was so messed up," he says, "I grabbed her hand and said, 'We're gonna get through this."

When a helicopter arrived to take Krickitt the 140 miles to the University of New Mexico hospital in Albuquerque, there was no room for Kim. Emergency medic Combs remembers his plea: "If my wife's going to die, I want to be there." By the time Kim reached Albuquerque five hours later, Krickitt was in a coma. The next morning, Thanksgiving, her parents flew in from Phoenix. Though doctors held out little hope, Kim recalls, "we went to the chapel and started praying." That day, the swelling started to subside and her dangerously low blood pressure slowly began to rise. In five days, she went off life support and ten days after the accident, emerging from her coma, she was transferred to

Phoenix's Barrow Neurological Institute.

Three weeks after the accident, when a nurse asked her what year it was, Krickitt responded: "1969." She was able to name her parents. But when the nurse asked, "Who's your husband?" she replied, "I'm not married." Tests soon showed that she had maintained most of her long-term memory. As for her husband, he was a complete stranger—she felt nothing for him. "I don't have a visual memory in my head, and I have no memory in my heart," she says now.

Kim remembers comforting himself by saying, "This isn't my wife; my wife is in this body, trapped and trying to get out." He worked to encourage her rehabilitation. But Krickitt found his presence and pep talks annoying. "I think she resented his pushing because at that point she wasn't Krickitt," says her mother, Mary, adding that the process of reteaching her daughter the most basic tasks "was like raising her again." Facing medical bills in excess of two hundred thousand dollars and relentless bill collectors, Kim returned to his Las Vegas job with serious doubts about the future. "I honestly didn't think our marriage would work," says Kim, but he wouldn't give up. "I made a vow before God," he explains, " 'until death do you part.' "

Making steady progress, Krickitt traveled with her mother to visit Kim, then returned on her own to see him again. "I figured, if I fell in love with this guy before, I guess I just need to meet him again," says Krickitt. Almost five months after the crash, she moved back in with him, but their life together was difficult. Her injuries had caused deep emotional swings and left her quick-tempered. And she was baffled by her reentry into marriage. "I remember asking, 'How did I do the wife thing? Did I cook for you? Did I bring you lunch?' " Her neurological problems posed other difficulties.

She was unable to drive and couldn't remember directions. She tired easily, and her emotions were jumbled—she would laugh when she meant to cry and cry when she meant to laugh. Says Kim: "I was thinking, 'Man, I'm living with someone with two different personalities.'"

She has slowly regained control of her life, returning to work in August 1994, but a new personality emerged—a blend of her old self with new, more outgoing traits. (She is likely to have chronic lingering effects, including short-term memory lapses and occasional clumsiness.) And it was difficult to make the marriage work again. Mike Hill, a therapist the couple started seeing in fall 1994, pinpointed the problem, saying, "There wasn't that emotional attachment that comes through the early part of the relationship. You need to establish some memories of your own." So Kim and Krickitt began dating again—chatting over pizza, shopping, jet skiing at a nearby lake. "I got to know my husband again," says Krickitt. "There was a point when I really started to enjoy this companion. I would miss him if he wasn't around."

This year on Valentine's Day, Kim proposed again. Krickitt accepted. "I could've not fallen in love with him again, but the Lord didn't allow that," she says. On May 25, the two again exchanged rings—new ones—and read newly written vows. "Only one thing can surpass forever the painful events we have felt," Kim told her. "That is the love I have for you."

Thomas Fields-Meyer and Michael Haederle

The Wives of Weinsberg

Love is the only gold.

Alfred, Lord Tennyson

It happened in Germany, in the Middle Ages. The year was 1141. Wolf, the Duke of Bavaria, sat trapped inside his castle of Weinsberg. Outside his walls lay the army of Frederick, the duke of Swabia, and his brother, the emperor Konrad.

The siege had lasted long, and the time had come when Wolf knew he must surrender. Messengers rode back and forth, terms were proposed, conditions allowed, arrangements completed. Sadly, Wolf and his officers prepared to give themselves to their bitter enemy.

But the wives of Weinsberg were not ready to lose all. They sent a message to Konrad, asking the emperor to promise safe conduct for all the women in the castle. They also asked if they might come out with as many of their valuables as they could carry in their arms as they left.

The request was freely granted, and soon the castle gates opened. Out came the ladies—but in startling fashion. They carried not gold or jewels. Each one was bending under the weight of her husband, whom she hoped to save from the vengeance of the victorious host.

Konrad, who was really a generous and merciful man, is said to have been brought to tears by the extraordinary performance. He hastened to assure the women of their husband's perfect safety and freedom. Then he invited them all to a banquet and made peace with the Duke of Bavaria on terms much more favorable than expected.

The castle was afterwards known as the Hill of Weibertreue, or woman's fidelity.

Charlotte Yonge

Love Me Tender

The most difficult year of marriage is the one you're in.

Franklin P. Jones

It's raining. Of course. Why would it do anything else on the worst day of my life?

Eighteen-year-old Libby Dalton stared out the window, her elbows propped on the table, her chin buried in her fists. Stacks of boxes cast sporadic ghostly patterns on the wall as the lighting flickered through the rain beating incessantly on the windowpanes.

Within the hour, they'd be leaving home and family to live in some godforsaken place called Levittown, New York.

Was it only a month ago that Johnny burst into the apartment with his great news ...the job offer, the chance to get out of Milford and into something he really wanted? How could she tell him she could not leave her family — her home—her life?

Elizabeth Jane Berens and John Dalton Jr., the blond, blue-eyed cheerleader and the handsome football player, had been sweethearts all through high school: elected homecoming royalty their senior year and labeled in the yearbook as Milford High School's Cutest Couple.

It was the fifties, and life was sweet in small-town America. Elvis Presley was king, and his latest hit, "Love Me Tender", had just hit the airwaves. At the senior prom, Milford's cutest couple slow danced, lost in each other's arms as the band played "their song". Johnny's soft voice crooned the lyrics in her ear, and Libby's heart melted.

"Be careful," her mother warned. "You know what happens to girls who don't behave themselves."

Libby had no intention of being one of the girls talked about in the locker rooms. They would wait.

But on graduation night, without a word to anyone, they ran across the state line and stood before a justice of the peace. They could wait no longer.

On the arm of her new husband, Libby proudly displayed her wedding ring to dismayed parents who saw their dreams—the football scholarship, the college diploma, the long, white dress and veil, vanish like bubbles in the air.

"Are you pregnant?" her mother asked when she got Libby off to one side.

"No," Libby assured her, hurt at the suggestion.

It was fun at first, playing house in the tiny apartment where they never seemed to get enough of each other. Johnny worked full-time as a mechanic at Buckner's garage and attended vo-tech at night, training to be an electrician. Libby waited tables at the local diner. The newness soon wore off, and as they stumbled over each other in the close confines of two rooms, they dreamed and saved for a house of their own.

Now, a year later, Libby was five months pregnant, sick every day and had to give up her job. High school friends quit calling the couple, who no longer had money for dancing and movies. Frequent arguments replaced words of love, as hopes and plans for the future dissolved into the empty frustration of barely getting by. Libby spent her days, and lately her nights, alone in the tiny apartment, suspecting that Johnny might be "fooling around". Nobody works *every* night.

As she returned from another bout of morning sickness, Libby glanced in the mirror at the swollen body and unkempt hair.

Who could blame Johnny for looking around? What is there for him here? A baby coming, a fat, ugly wife and never any money.

Her mother fussed about the pale face and circles under her eyes. "You must take care of yourself, Libby," her mo ther told her. "Think of your husband, think of the baby."

That's all Libby did think about—the baby ...that impersonal lump inside, ruining her figure and making her constantly sick.

Then came the day Johnny told her about the new job in Levittown.

"We'll be moving into a company house," he said, his eyes shining. "It's small, but it's better than this dump."

She nodded and blinked rapidly so he wouldn't see the tears. She couldn't leave Milford.

No one would be coming to say good-bye today... It had been done last night at the farewell party. As Johnny hauled out the last box, she took a final walk through their first home, her footsteps echoing on bare wooden floors. The odor of furniture polish and wax still hung in the air. Faint voices filled the rooms as she remembered the night they waxed those floors, giggling and pushing each other, pausing in the middle to love each other. Two cluttered rooms, now cold and empty. Funny how quickly they became impersonal cubes as though no one had ever lived, or loved, there. She closed the door behind her for the last time and hurried out to the truck.

The weather worsened as they drove, along with her mood.

"It's a big company," Johnny said. "Levitton Manufacturing...electronic parts...a chance to get ahead..."

She nodded briefly, then returned to staring out the window. He finally gave up his attempts at small talk, and they drove on in silence, broken only by the squeaky thumps of windshield wipers.

As they reached the outskirts of Levittown, the rain stopped and the sun shone through broken patches in the clouds.

"A good sign," Johnny said, looking up at the sky.

She nodded silently.

After a few wrong turns, they found their new home, and Libby stared solemnly at the tiny box in the middle of identical boxes, like Monopoly houses lined up on Oriental Avenue.

"Are you ever going to smile again, Lib?"

She climbed out of the cab and scolded herself. *Grow up, Libby. Do you think this is any easier for him*?

She wanted to say she was sorry, but the ever ready tears welled up and she turned away. Without a word, they carried boxes into the house, setting them down wherever they could find room.

"Sit down and rest, Lib," Johnny said. "I'll finish unloading."

She sat on a box and stared out the window. *At least it stopped raining*.

A knock interrupted her thoughts, and she opened the door to a girl about her own age, obviously pregnant, holding a small plate of cookies. "Welcome to the neighborhood," she said. "I'm Susan, but everybody calls me Souie."

They sat on boxes, eating cookies and comparing pregnancies, morning sickness and backaches. Souie was due in two months. Libby in four.

"I can come over tomorrow and help you settle in if you like," Souie said. "It's so good to have someone to talk to."

Amen, thought Libby.

After Souie left, Libby glanced around the room with a new eye. *Maybe some blue curtains in the kitchen...*

The door suddenly sprang open and Johnny ran in, hurriedly digging through the boxes. He pulled out a small radio, plugged it into the wall socket, and suddenly "their song" and the voice of Elvis singing drifted into the kitchen.

They heard the disc jockey's voice over the music, " ...and this request comes from a pair of newcomers in town. Congratulations to John and Libby Dalton on their wedding anniversary."

Johnny had remembered their anniversary. She had forgotten. Tears streamed down her face, and the wall of silence and self-pity she had built around herself crumbled.

He pulled her up to him, and she heard his voice singing soft and sweet in her ear.

Together they danced in between the packing cartons, clinging to each other as if discovering love for the first time. Sunlight filtered through the window in the new house in the new town, and as she felt the first kicks of the new life inside her, Libby Dalton learned the meaning of love.

Jacklyn Lee Lindstrom

Is There Really a Prince Charming ?

Real joy comes not from ease of riches or from the praise of men, but from doing something worthwhile.

W. T. Grenfell

A lot of girls grow up thinking that a Prince Charming roams the skies and the plains just waiting for that special moment to zoom into their lives, snatch them up and carry them away from a world of shrouded gloom to one of white, wedded bliss.

When girls flower into womanhood, they are always a bit shocked to discover they are Cinderella or Snow White, and the man they thought was Prince Charming really turned out to be Prince Clod.

Marianne had lived a life like Cinderella, sweeping parking lots for a dollar at age eight, trying to provide for herself and her baby brothers as her mother lived daily tackling a mental illness. When she had just passed her teen years, she met the man she thought was her Prince Charming.

She met him where she was a waitress, and he enthralled her. A musician with a successful band, he seemed to have the widest, most endearing eyes when he spotted her. And why not? She looked as sweet as Cinderella, blonde-brown curls, emerald green eyes and a face that echoed of innocence and love, which was really the look of an awestruck teenager.

All Marianne could think was: *He loves me. He loves me. He loves me.*

And this was true at the time. With the speed of a stallion, the man grabbed her up in his arms and carried her off to marriage. Everything was perfect as far as Marianne was concerned. She had a nice home and enjoyed watching her husband play in his band. She felt loved and adored for the first time in her life. Move over Snow White. Here she comes. And she was about to have a baby.

She didn't know about the other women.

The two were also ill-fated in another way. They had not only wedded each other, but they wedded their recessive genes. When her first son, Loren, arrived, Marianne knew something was wrong. He didn't respond to sound. For a year, Marianne struggled and consulted with doctors who told her nothing was wrong.

But finally a specialist announced that Loren was deaf and that there was nothing she could do. She sobbed for the first two years of Loren's life while her husband kept saying that their son was just fine.

Doctors assured them that another child wouldn't suffer such misfortune. But when Lance was born, they soon learned the newborn was deaf, too.

The walls of their already strained marriage, which stood on a young girl's fairy-tale dreams, cracked, but they caved in when Marianne grew angry that her husband didn't want to learn to communicate with his two sons.

He left that to her. She learned sign language as quickly as possible. Her husband wasn't interested. When he talked to the boys, he treated them like they were dogs, patting them on the head, barking out a word or two.

She took her sons to her husband's parents' house. His parents ignored the kids.

She took her sons shopping. Clerks gasped when her sons made grunting sounds. And now, she knew about the other women. Sometimes her husband didn't bother to come home. Her friends quit calling her and Marianne felt a biting loneliness.

The stress and the loneliness began to destroy Marianne. She sucked down alcohol like it was water. She fed and clothed her sons, put them to bed, but refused to leave her home. She thought about slashing her wrists.

"Imagine, when your friends and your own family don't bother to want to learn to communicate with your sons," she explained. "You don't have to know sign language. Kindness is a language. We all understand it. When you see a child like this, don't act shocked. Don't gasp and walk away. The message you send to a child is: 'My God, you are a freak.' Reach out your hand and smile."

Smiles, hugs and kisses are what saved Marianne's life. Lance and Loren's eyes were pools of adoration and love—a true love. The type Marianne had never experienced in her life.

It became apparent to Marianne that she could squander her own life away with alcohol and panic attacks, but she couldn't waste her son's lives like this. She buckled down and went back to school to earn a high school degree. She got a job with an insurance firm and saved her pennies.

The better she felt about herself, the prouder she grew of

Loren and Lance. She started bringing them to visit with her coworkers, who showered them with kindness. It was time for her and her boys to leave their house, cut ties with the father and move on with their lives.

One day, her sons came with her to work, and when she walked into the office of the insurance manager, a man named Eric, she found Loren sitting on his lap. Eric looked up at her, and the skies began to tumble. He said these simple words: "I feel like an idiot. I'd love to talk with your son. Do you know where I could go learn sign language?"

Marianne thought she would faint. Not a soul had ever asked her before if they could learn to communicate with her sons. She was shaking inside as she explained to Eric that if he was really interested, she knew where he could learn. It seemed better not to believe him, but he showed quickly he wasn't kidding when he enrolled in the class and began to sign words of hello to her in a few days.

When the kids came in, he took them for walks along the pier near their office. Often she went along and watched Eric, who was becoming a master of sign language, talk and laugh with her boys as no one else had before.

And each time her sons saw Eric they brightened like the sun and stars in the sky. She had never seen them so happy. Her heart twitched as though it were being strummed. She began to fall in love.

She didn't know if Eric felt the same until they left work together one evening and took a stroll out on a pier above the Pacific Ocean. He signed to her that he was in love and wanted to marry. Marianne's heart danced with joy.

The couple moved into a small town and opened up a thriving insurance business. They had two more children, Casey and Katie, neither of whom were born deaf, but both learned sign language before the age of five.

And at the happiest moments of her life, Marianne would wake up in the middle of the night, her ear burning in pain, and begin to sob. Her behavior was inexplicable because she couldn't think of a time when she felt more loved or happy.

Eric would run his hands across her hair, hold her chin and ask her what was wrong. All she could say was: "I don't know. I don't know." He held her for a long while. Weeks went by and Marianne continued to wake up sobbing.

Then, like a lightning bolt, she woke up knowing the answer.

She cried to Eric, her "knight in shining armor", that she wasn't doing enough to help deaf children in the world. She was supposed to help them find their place in society. She was supposed to teach the world how to communicate with these children.

Eric wrapped his arms around her and said: "Let's do it."

Together they formed Hands Across Amrica — "It Starts with You" — an organization that encourages the public to learn sign language and has started making educational videos that use both deaf and hearing children together.

So if you ever have a chance to talk with Marianne and ask her if there is any truth to fairy tales like Cinderella and Snow White, she'll probably say she's learned a lot about such stories in her lifetime.

She's likely to say: "There sure are a lot of Prince Clods out there. But there sure are some Prince Charmings, and there are really a lot of Cinderellas, too."

Diana Chapman

Do You Want Me ?

I rise early on this Friday, as I do every day, to prepare coffee and mix a protein shake. The television news plays quietly in the corner. Flossie, my wife, is still asleep.

Sometime after eight, she begins floating out of slumber. I bring the shake to her bedside, put the straw in her mouth and give her cheek a little pat as she begins to drink. Slowly the liquid recedes.

I sit there holding the glass, thinking about the past eight years. At first, she asked only an occasional incoherent or irrelevant question; otherwise she was normal. I tried for two years to find out what was wrong. She grew agitated, restless, defensive; she was constantly tired and unable to hold a conversation.

At last, a neurologist diagnosed Alzheimer's disease. He said he wasn't sure — but a firm diagnosis could come only from examining brain tissue after death. There was no known cause for his malady. And no known cure.

I enrolled her in a day care center for adults. But she kept wandering off the property. We medicated her to keep her calm. Perhaps from receiving too much of one drug, she suffered a violent seizure that left her immeasurably worse: lethargic, incontinent and unable to speak clearly or care for herself. My anguish gradually became resignation. I gave up any plans of retirement travel, recreation, visits to see the grandchildren—the golden era older people dream about.

The years have passed, and my days have become a routine, demanding, lonely, seemingly without accomplishment to measure. She has gradually dropped in strength and weight, from 125 pounds to 86. I take some time to work with a support group and to attend church, but the daily needs keep me feeding, bathing, diapering, changing beds, cleaning house, fixing meals, dressing and undressing her, whatever else a nurse and homemaker does, morning to night.

Occasionally, a word bubbles up from the muddled processes of Flossie's diseased brain. Sometimes relevant, sometimes the name of a family member, or the name of an object. Just a single word.

On this Friday morning, after she finishes her shake, I give her some apple juice, then massage her arms and caress her forehead and cheeks. Most of the time, her eyes are closed, but today she looks up at me, and suddenly her mouth forms four words in a row.

"Do you want me?"

Perfect enunciation, softly spoken. I want to jump for joy.

"Of course I want you, Flossie!" I say, hugging and kissing her.

And so, after months of total silence, she has put together the most sincere question a human being can ask. She speaks, in a way, for people everywhere: those shackled by sin, addiction, hunger, thirst, mental illness, physical pain... frightened, enervated people afraid of the answer but desperate enough to frame the question anyway.

And, Flossie, I can answer you even more specifically. It may be difficult for you to understand what's happening.

That's why I'm here, to minister God's love to you, to bring you wholeness, comfort and release. Mine are the hands God uses to do his work, just as he uses others' hands in other places. In spite of our shortcomings, we strive to make people free, well and happy, blessing them with hope for the future while bringing protein shakes every morning.

Park York

Love Is a Reason to Live

Evening descends on Belcourt Castle in Newport, Rhode Island. Hundreds of costumed revelers are making merry at a Halloween party. Ghosts dance with goblins as the music plays.

A pretty young woman smiles behind a gold and silver half-mask, but her smile is forced. From across the room she is spotted by someone who thinks he recognizes her. The Fly Knight—a fellow in a medieval knight suit with the head of a fly—says to himself, *I've seen that smile*. He makes his way across the crowded room. "What's your name?" he asks.

"Diana."

"Diana who?" he says.

"Diana Golden."

"Hi, I'm Steve Brosnihan, the cartoonist from Dartmouth."

Steve is already infatuated: He has been so from afar, with this very woman, for many years. For Diana's part, meeting Steve puts her on guard. She knows what Steve does not—that she is dying. The last thing Diana needs right now is to fall in love.

Diana Golden grew up a happy, shy, somewhat klutzy kid in Lincoln, Massachusetts, thirteen miles from Boston. One winter day when she was twelve years old, after a fine day of building snow forts, her right leg collapsed beneath her.

Doctors at the Dana-Farber Cancer Institute in Boston diagnosed bone cancer and said they had to amputate.

Diana asked if she would still be able to ski, a sport she'd always loved. She felt heartened when they said yes.

In a way, Diana gained identity through her illness: She became obsessive about skiing and racing. She started getting noticed as the one-legged ski champion. "I was on the TV show *Zoom* telling other kids: 'Yes, I can!' I liked that, and drove myself to get better and better."

She went to Dartmouth College in New Hampshire, where she trained with the ski team. In the off season she'd do laps at the track on her crutches or hop the steps at the football stadium.

The stadium was adjacent to the baseball field where Steve Brosnihan, a kid from Rhode Island one year ahead of Diana, used to work out as a pitcher. "I admired her so much; she was so vivacious," Steve says. "Sometimes I'd see her crossing the college green, and I'd speed up just to get ahead of her so I could see her smile. But she doesn't remember that."

After graduating from college in 1984, Diana began building the greatest career in the history of disabled sports. It is impossible to overestimate what Diana Golden meant to the handicapped-athletics movement. She was its Babe Ruth, the best in the world.

She was also the most charismatic. His vivacity — which had once caused her parents to bribe her with cash to shut her up during long family ski trips — lent a bright look and sound to the ski circuit. She was smart and funny. Knocked down by a skier on the slopes at Vail, Colorado, she screamed, "Look what you've done to my leg!"

What made Diana Golden such a luminous personality on

the ski tour and then on the speaking circuit was her willingness to be up-front about how she felt and why. She'd say such coolly courageous things as, "Losing a leg? It's nothing. A body part." When she told kids they could fight past illness, she meant it.

In 1988 Diana mounted the podium at the Calgary Olympics to claim the gold medal in the Disabled Giant Slalom. She also won nineteen U. S. and ten World Disabled Championships gold medals. By the time she retired in 1990, she had been honored as one of America's greatest athletes. Not disabled athletes — *athletes*. The Women's Sports Foundation gave her its Flo Hyman Award, which had previously gone to Martina Navratilova, Jackie Joyner-Kersee and Chris Evert.

But suddenly life changed for Diana. A biopsy of her right breast on New Year's Eve 1992 indicated cancer. A week later her doctor recommended a biopsy on the left breast, using the same words about the latest suspicious spots: "It's probably nothing." When told she would need a bilateral mastectomy, she kept a stiff upper lip. "I can still have a baby," she told her friends.

Following surgery, chemotherapy sapped her strength, the thing that had become "the foundation of my identity." Treatments made her sick. Trying to find a way back, she went to the pool to exercise, but she couldn't bring herself to undress. "After all these years of missing a leg, I felt acutely self-conscious," she says.

That night she decided to confront herself, and stood naked before a mirror. She stared hard, trying to come to terms with her scarred self. She wrote down what she felt: "The scars on my chest and my leg were a big deal. They were my marks of life. All of us are scarred by life, it's just that some scars show more clearly than others. Our scars tell us that we have lived."

Her annual gynecological exam followed, and when the doctor once again said, "It's probably nothing," Diana felt she had been hit by a train.

During surgery doctors found a large, potentially malignant growth spread over almost her entire uterus. They acted immediately. Diana awoke to the words, "We had to remove your uterus."

She had trouble breathing; she felt violated. Thus began her descent. After recuperating from surgery, Diana returned to the speaking circuit. But her usual bravado wasn't ringing true to her. Fear was being repressed; anger and regret were creeping in. "It became harder and harder for me to tell people they could overcome anything if they tried."

In 1993 she took an overdose of pills, but quickly realized she didn't want to die. She called a friend and was rushed to the hospital.

Diana was frantically seeking reasons to continue. She invested hope in a puppy that, a month after coming home with her, suffered a seizure and had to be put to sleep. Diana, who was living at the time in Boulder, Colorado, couldn't shake her depression. One day she climbed into her Jeep and drove hard for the Rockies, intending to jump into the Black Canyon of the Gunnison River.

But again life called her back. In the town of Gunnison she phoned a crisis hot line, and she and the counselor concluded that one answer might be another puppy. And so she got herself Midnight Sun, an Alaskan malamute she calls "my light in the night".

But Diana's losses were not over. In March of 1996 she was told she had metastatic breast cancer. It had spread to several vertebrae. Diana decided to move back home to be with her family as she underwent treatment. Then, with thinking to be done, she went to Peaks Island off the coast of Maine. Alone in a rented house in late autumn of the year, she contemplated her roller-coaster life and wrote poetry:

The autumn leaves
doing their butterfly dance toward death.
Such valor they must have
to dance the dance so gracefully.

As all this was happening, Steve knew little of it. He was working in Bristol, Rhode Island, as a newspaper cartoonist. "I just knew Diana had become a famous athlete," he says. "I remembered her, of course, like everyone else who meets her—one-legged, attractive, the smile."

Then one day in 1992, Steve noticed that Diana had given a commencement address in Rhode Island. He wrote and asked her to visit Camp Home in North Scituate, a camp for kids with cancer where he volunteered each summer. She called back and they chatted, but she asked him to set up an appointment with her manager. The manager told Steve that Diana couldn't fit him in.

"I wanted to get in her company but there was no way. I'd been blown off," Steve smiles. "So I gave up. Until Newport."

After meeting Steve that magical Halloween night in 1996, Diana sensed something between them. There was no way she expected such a thing could happen. "We talked and I told him about ...*it*," she says. "I wrote him a letter telling him to be careful. I wanted to make sure I didn't misinterpret his interest or intentions. He said not to worry—he meant everything he was saying."

The following New Year's Eve, Steve and Diana went

dancing with friends at the Park Plaza Hotel in Boston. That was the night he said, "I love you."

The next day Diana and her sister, Meryl, were shopping at a department store. On a whim, Diana went up to the formal dresses section. "I found this beautiful dress and said, 'This is the dress I'm going to marry Steve in.'"

"What are you talking about!" Meryl said. "Has he proposed?"

"I said, 'Not yet.' But I was sure he would." She bought the dress.

Steve proposed to Diana six weeks later, on Valentine's Day, while her chemo drugs were dripping at Dana-Farber. "Chemo days aren't the greatest for Diana," he says, explaining his timing. "So I thought I'd make one of them a little better."

Diana said yes. She and Steve began to plan the big day: August 9, 1997, immediate family only, a simple honeymoon. But a few months later, Diana remembers telling Steve, "I think I'm getting cold foot."

"We're both nervous; it's not something to be scared of," Steve reassured her. "The Diana I know wouldn't run away."

Meanwhile, Steve had been telling his friends about Diana. He made a special trip to see his close friend, Anglican priest Father John Francis, who grilled him 'til two o'clock in the morning about his intentions, then gave Steve his blessing.

"I know it will end with sadness," Steve says, "but I'm as happy as I've ever been. And this right now is more important than whatever sadness might someday come."

At the hospital, a month or so before the wedding, Steve sits on the edge of Diana's bed, holding her hand as the chemo enters a vein. "The tumor markers are better than they've been in a year," he says. Still, Diana's doctor alters the prognosis, which foresees death in one year to—outside chance—five.

These days Diana is able to handle such news, as she has climbed a long way from her nadir of despair. Love has become her foundation and shelter.

Still, Diana says, it's not all perfect. She gets frustrated. "We can have a normal day—maybe we went riding on the tandem bike and it was lovely. But was it enough? I know we only have so many days left—and I want each one to be incredible."

Before she met Steve, Diana had convinced herself that she could live, numbly, until she inevitably died. And then she fell in love, and the needle on the graph started to fluctuate wildly again.

We all know, all of us do, that death is waiting. But few of us feel that death is beckoning. It's a mighty difference, a difference hard to live with. Diana's trying; so is Steve. For not to try is not to love—and not to love is, now, impossible.

Robert R. Sullivan

6

ON FAMILY

The only way you can live forever is to love somebody — then you really leave a gift behind.

Bernie Siegel, M. D.

A Legend of Love

If love does not know how to give and take without restrictions, it is not love, but a transaction.

Emma Goldman

Edward Wellman bade good-bye to his family in the old country headed for a better life in America. Papa handed him the family's savings hidden in a leather satchel. "Times are desperate here," he said, hugging his son goodbye. "You are our hope." Edward boarded the Atlantic freighter offering free transport to young men willing to shovel coal in return for the month-long journey. If Edward struck gold in the Colorado Rockies, the rest of the family could eventually join him.

For months, Edward worked his claim tirelessly, and the small vein of gold provided a moderate but steady income. At the end of each day, as he walked through the door of his two-room cabin, he yearned for the woman he loved to greet him. Leaving Ingrid behind before he could officially court her had been his only regret in accepting this American adventure. Their families had been friends for years and for as long as he could remember, he had secretly hoped to make

Ingrid his wife. Her long, flowing hair and radiant smile made her the most beautiful of the Henderson sisters. He had just begun sitting by her at church picnics and making up silly reasons to stop by her house, just so he could see her. As he went to sleep in his cabin each night, Edward longed to stroke her auburn hair and hold her in his arms. Finally, he wrote to Papa, asking him to help make this dream come true.

After nearly a year, a telegraph came with a plan to make his life complete. Mr. Henderson had agreed to send his daughter to Edward in America. Because she was a hard-working young woman with a good mind for business, she would work alongside Edward for a year to help the mining business grow. By then both families could afford to come to America for their wedding.

Edward's heart soared with joy as he spent the next month trying to make the cabin into a home. He bought a cot for him to sleep on in the living area and tried to make his former bedroom suitable for a woman. Floral cloth from flour sacks replaced the burlap-bag curtains covering the grimy window. He arranged dried sage from the meadow into a tin-can vase on the nightstand.

At last, the day he had been waiting for his whole life arrived. With a bouquet of fresh-picked daisies in hand, he left for the train depot. Steam billowed and wheels screeched as the train crawled to a stop. Edward scanned every window looking for Ingrid's glowing hair and smile.

His heart beat with eager anticipation, then stopped with a sinking thud. Not Ingrid, but her older sister Marta, stepped down from the train. She stood shyly before him, her eyes cast down.

Edward only stared — dumbfounded. Then with shaking

hands he offered Marta the bouquet. "Welcome," he whispered, his eyes burning. A smile etched across her plain face.

"I was pleased when Papa said you sent for me," Marta said, looking into his eyes briefly, before dropping her head again.

"I'll get your bags," Edward said with a fake smile. Together they headed for the buggy.

Mr. Henderson and Papa were right. Marta did have a great grasp of business. While Edward worked the mine, she worked the office. From her makeshift desk in one corner of the living area, she kept detailed records of all claim activity. Within six months, their assets doubled.

Her delicious meals and quiet smile graced the cabin with a wonderful woman's touch. *But the wrong woman*, Edward mourned as he collapsed onto his cot each night. *Why did they send Marta*? Would he ever see Ingrid again? Was his lifelong dream to have her as his wife forsaken?

For a year, Marta and Edward worked and played and laughed, but never loved. Once, Marta had kissed Edward on the cheek before retiring to her room. He only smiled awkwardly. From then on, she seemed content with their exhilarating hikes in the mountains and long talks on the porch after suppers. One spring afternoon, torrential rains washed down the hillside, eroding the entrance to their mine. Furiously, Edward filled sand bags and stacked them in the water's path. Soaked and exhausted, his frantic efforts seemed futile. Suddenly there was Marta at his side holding the next burlap bag open. Edward shoveled sand inside, then with the strength of any man, Marta hurled it onto the pile and opened another bag. For hours they worked, knee-deep in mud, until the rains diminished. Hand in hand, they walked back to the cabin. Over warm soup Edward sighed,

"I never could have saved the mine without you. Thank you, Marta."

"You're welcome," she answered with her usual smile, then went quietly to her room.

A few days later, a telegraph came announcing the arrival of the Henderson and Wellman families next week. As much as he tried to stifle it, the thought of seeing Ingrid again started Edward's heart beating in the old familiar way.

Together, he and Marta went to the train station. They watched as their families exited the train at the far end of the platform. When Ingrid appeared, Marta turned to Edward. "Go to her," she said.

Astonished, Edward stammered, "What do you mean?"

"Edward, I have always known I was not the Henderson girl you intended to send for. I had watched you flirt with Ingrid at the church picnics." She nodded toward her sister descending the train steps. "I know it is she, not me, you desire for your wife."

"But ..."

Marta placed her fingers over his lips. "Shhh," she hushed him. "I do love you, Edward. I always have. And because of that, all I really want is your happiness. Go to her."

He took her hand from his face and held it. As she gazed up at him, he saw for the first time how very beautiful she was. He recalled their walks in the meadows, their quiet evenings before the fire, her working beside him with the sandbags. It was then he realized what he had known for months.

"No, Marta. It is *you* I want." Sweeping her into his arms, he kissed her with all the love bursting inside him. Their families gathered around them chorusing, "We are here for the wedding!"

LeAnn Thieman

Belonging

With the freeway ahead of us and home behind, the photographer and I left on a three-day newspaper assignment.

We were bound for the Columbia Gorge: where the Columbia River carves a mile-wide path between Washington and Oregon; where windsurfers come from across the country to dance across waves created by "nuclear winds;" where I would be far away from the world of nine-to-five, and deadlines, and routines, and errands, and rushing kids to baseball practices, and having to make sure my socks weren't left on the bedroom floor. Far away from the *R* word — "responsibility."

Frankly, it had not been the perfect farewell. Our family was running on empty. Our '81 car was showing signs of automotive Alzheimer's. We were all tired, cranky and trying to shake colds. My eight-year-old son tried to perk us up with his off-key version of a song from a Broadway musical. It didn't work.

I had been busy trying to get ready for the trip; my wife Sally had been busy fretting because my three days of freedom were going to cost her three days of extra responsibility.

"Daddy, are you coming to hear my class sing Thursday night?" Jason, my eight-year-old son, asked amid the chaos of my departure. Had I been Bill Cosby, I would have gotten a funny expression on my face, said "Well, of course", and everyone would have lived happily ever after—or at least for a half an hour. But I didn't feel much like Bill Cosby that morning.

"No Jason, I'm going to be out of town," I said. "Sorry." Giving Sally a quick kiss, I was on my way.

Now, hours later, I was far away from family, free from the clutter, the runny noses, the demands on my time. Knowing little about each other, the photographer and I shared a bit about ourselves as we drove. Roughly my age — mid-thirties — he was married but had no children. He and his wife had seen too many situations where couples with children had found themselves strapped down, scurrying for babysitters and forced to give up spontaneous trips. He told he how he and his wife had recently taken a trip to the Gorge by themselves. My mind did a double take. *By themselves? What was that like?*

I vaguely remembered that kind of freedom. Taking off when the mood hit. No pleas for horseback rides about the time you're ready to crash for the night. No tornado-swept rooms. Besides having no children, the photographer had no six-month-old french fries on the floor of his car, no Superman action figure legs on his dashboard and no chocolate-smeared road maps in his glove box. *Where had I gone wrong?*

For the next couple of days, despite a threat of rain, we explored the Gorge—thousand-foot-walls of basalt rising on either side of the Columbia, fluorescent-clad sail-boarders, like neon gnats, carving wakes in the water. If the land and water were intriguing, so were the windsurfers.

There were thousands of them, nearly all of them baby

boomers, spending their days on the water, their nights on the town, their mornings in bed. Every fourth car had a board on top. License plates from all over the country dotted the streets.

Some of these "board-heads" were follow-the-wind free spirits who lived out of the back of vans; others were well-established yuppies who were here for a weekend or vacation. In the evenings, the river's hub town turned into Oregon's version of a California beach town: boomers eating, drinking, and being merry, lost in a world of frivolity and freedom.

For me, seeing this group was like discovering a lost, ancient tribe. *You mean, while I was busy trying to put on jammed bike chains, these people were jamming to the rock beat of dance clubs? While I was depositing paychecks to be spent on groceries and orthodontic bills and college funds, these people were deciding what color sailboards to buy? Where had I gone wrong?*

On our last night, the cloudy weather continued, which irked the photographer and mirrored the mood that had overcome me; we both needed sunshine, only for different reasons.

As I stared from the motel room at the river below, I felt a sort of emptiness, as if I didn't belong. Not here. Not home. Not anywhere. Just as the winds of the Gorge were whipping the river into whitecaps, so were the winds of freedom buffeting my beliefs. Faith. Marriage. Children. Work. I had anchored my life on such things, and yet now found myself slipping from that fixed position. *Had I made a mistake? Had I sold out to the rigors of responsibility? Someday, when I was older, would I suddenly face the bitter-cold reality of regret, wishing I had gone with the wind?*

I was getting ready for bed when I spotted it—a card in my suitcase, buried beneath some clothes. It was from Sally. The card featured cows—my wife's big on bovines—and simply stated, "I'll love you till the cows come home."

I stared at the card for minutes, and I repeated the words. I looked at the same handwriting that I'd seen on love letters in college, on a marriage certificate, on two birth certificates, on a will.

As I went to bed, there was no need to call the front desk and ask for a wake-up call; I'd already gotten one. The card bore through my hardened heart, convicted my selfish conscience, refocused my blurry perspective. I knew exactly where I needed to be.

The next day, after a two-hour interview, six-hour drive and three-block sprint, I arrived at my son's school, anxious and out of breath. The singing program had started twenty minutes before; had I missed Jason's song? I rushed into the cafeteria. It was jammed. Almost frantically, I weaved my way through a crowd of parents clogging the entrance, to where I could finally get a glimpse of the kids on stage.

That's when I heard them: twenty-five first-grade voices trying desperately to hit notes that were five years away. My eyes searched this collage of kids, looking for Jason. Finally, I spotted him. Front row, as usual, squished between a couple of girls whose germs, judging by the look on his face, were crawling over him like picnic ants.

He was singing, all right, but with less enthusiasm than when he's been told to clean his room. Suddenly, his eyes shifted my way and his face lit up with the kind of smile a father only gets to see in a grade-school singing program when his eyes meet his child's. He had seen me, a moment that will forever stay frozen in my memory.

Later, through a sea of faces, I caught sight of Sally and our other son. After the program, amid a mass of parent-child humanity, the four of us rendezvoused, nearly oblivious to the commotion surrounding us.

I felt no emptiness, only connectedness. How could one man be so blessed?

In the days to come, I resumed my part in life as a bike-fixer and breadwinner, husband and father, roles that would cause a windsurfer to yawn.

But for all the excitement of riding the wind, I decided, I'll take the front-row smile of my eight-year-old son any day.

And for all the freedom of life in the Gorge, I'll take the responsibility of caring for the woman who vowed to love me till the cows come home.

Bob Welch

Someone to Have

If I can stop one heart from breaking, I shall not live in vain.

Emily Dickinson

Every mother wants to see her daughter happy and loved. And every daughter wants to live happily ever after. So it was hard for my daughter Jackie and me when she became a single mom. We both had to face the fact that her life was not the picture we'd had of how things "should" be.

And then, as if things weren't bad enough, Jackie decided to move away with her two-year-old son, Kristopher, hoping to begin a new life. Even though the move would mean that we would be many miles apart and that I would miss her and Kristopher very much, I knew that my daughter had made the right decision.

Jackie was a nurse, and she got a job working evenings in the local hospital. Eventually, she became involved with a young man. "He's wonderful, Mom," she would report. And even though she sounded fine, I was skeptical. *What were this man's intentions with my daughter? Would he accept her son? Would he treat her with kindness and love, or would he only add more hurt and heartache to her life*? No matter how much I tried to put these questions out of my mind, they would not go away.

Then, something every parent and grandparent dreads happened: Little Kristopher became very ill. He cried and complained of leg pain whenever he was carried or touched. After several agonizing days, the doctors diagnosed his problem—osteomyelitis, infection of the bone and it was serious. The infection seemed to be spreading, and he was hospitalized so he could undergo immediate surgery.

After the operation, Kristopher was brought back to his room, and attached to an IV. Tubes ran in and out of his tiny hips to irrigate the treated area. But despite fluids and antibiotics, he continued to run a high temperature. Kristopher lost weight, had no appetite and became a sad-looking little boy.

The doctors told us that more surgery was needed to stop the infection, and once again, his body had to undergo the painful procedure. Afterward, Kristopher lay in his crib, attached to so many tubes that he couldn't be moved, picked up, held or rocked in his mother's arms.

Each night when Jackie had to go back to work, I would make the long drive to see Kristopher. I could only stay a few hours, because it would take me several hours to drive back home. Each time when I prepared to leave, Kristopher would cry, "Please Grandma, don't leave. 'Cause if you do, I won't have anybody to have." And each time, it would break my heart to hear his pleas. But I knew I had to leave, so I would tell him I loved him and promise to return soon.

One evening, as I approached my grandson's room in the hospital for my nightly visit, I could hear someone talking to Kristopher. It sounded like a man's voice. As I got closer, I could hear the voice more clearly—it was steady and kind, and speaking to Kristopher in comforting tones. *Who could be here talking to my grandson like that*? I wondered.

I entered the room, and what I saw took my breath away.

There, lying in the crib, was the young man my daughter had been telling me about all along. His six-foot frame was curved as small as he could make himself; his broad back was pressed against the crib bars; and his long arms were wrapped around Kristopher, cuddling him like a precious bundle.

The young man looked up at me with a gentle smile of explanation and said softly, "Babies need to be held. Since we can't take him out of this crib, I decided to climb in and hold him."

Tears of happiness filled my eyes. I knew my prayers had been answered. My daughter had, indeed, found a man with a tender, compassionate heart. And Kristopher had gotten his wish: finally, he had "somebody to have".

Kristopher is now twenty years old and totally recovered. And my daughter's fine young man, John, became the best stepdad a boy could ever have.

Maxine M. Davis

A Love Story with God

When I was young, we had a neighbor down the street in the cantonment of Poona (in India), a Mr. Dalal, whom nobody liked. He was stooped and gray, very thin, and he greeted everyone with a sour, pained expression. Curiously, he had a small, vivacious wife — his exact opposite — who adored him. They were always together, and if I happened to pass them on the way to school, Mrs. Dalal would wave to me from underneath her blue sari, all the time keeping a loving eye on her husband, who would be tapping his way down the sidewalk with his cane.

"They are like Rama and Sita," my grandmother said admiringly behind their backs. This I very much doubted, since Rama and Sita were divine incarnations of man and woman, and the most perfect lovers in Indian mythology. When Rama strung his bow it caused lightning and thunder, while Sita was beauty itself. Being eleven and obsessed with cricket, I had little time for either Rama and Sita or the Dalals, until a shadow passed over our household. Mr. Dalal lay dying just a few doors away from us.

My grandmother paid a visit to his bungalow and came back looking somber and pale. "Only a few hours," she told my mother. Small boys can be callous about death, and I resented Mr. Dalal for the time he had poked his cane at me and ordered me to pick up a package he had dropped on the sidewalk. Years later, when I had entered medical school, I realized that Mr. Dalal had been suffering from angina, and his weak heart had not permitted him even to bend over. Severe chest pain accounted for the twisted expression on his face, and now it had brought him to death's door.

Of course, Mr. Dalal's dying was the talk of the neighborhood. That day my grandmother informed us that Mrs. Dalal had decided to die in her husband's place. She was praying fervently for this wish. Our family was stunned, except for my father, who was a cardiologist. He kept quiet, only assuring us that Mr. Dalal had no hope of recovery from his infarction. A week later this prediction was confounded when an extremely frail Mr. Dalal and his wife appeared again on the street. Mrs. Dalal, very much alive, waved from beneath her blue sari, looking as cheerful as ever, as if somehow changed.

My grandmother waited, and only a few months passed before Mrs. Dalal fell sick. A minor cold turned to pneumonia, and in those days when penicillin was not so readily available or believed in by common people, she died suddenly, in the middle of the night.

"Like Rama and Sita," my grandmother murmured, wearing a look on her face that could be mistaken for triumph. She described the last scene between husband and wife, when Mr. Dalal took off his prayer beads and laid them tenderly around his wife's neck before she passed. "That is a real love story," she said. "Only love can work such a miracle."

"No," I protested, standing impatiently by the stove. "Mrs. Dalal is dead. You call that love, but now they both have nothing." My father had already told me, in his measured, clinical voice, that Mr. Dalal's survival had been a fluke, not a miracle. He could be expected to die within the year.

"You just don't understand," my grandmother reproached me. "Who do you think gave Mrs. Dalal her wish? When she loved her husband, she was loving God, and now she is with him. Every real love story is a love story with God."

This story isn't about Mrs. Dalal. A Westerner would be skeptical that she had achieved anything of value by dying for her husband, assuming that was what had happened. The point of the story lies in my grandmother's deepest beliefs:

A man and a woman can reflect divine love in their love for each other. Loving your beloved is the way you love God. Human love survives death.

If you could hold the same beliefs, your love would contain a profound power and meaning.

Deepak Chopra, M. D.

Taking Pictures

I will cherish forever a particular Saturday in April 1997 with my son. Torey was five years old and just beginning to adjust to the new arrangement since my divorce from his mother. It was a relatively calm process with each of us going our own way and nothing being contested. I found myself spending more quality time with Torey now. I could see him during the week when I called ahead, and he stayed with me every other weekend. I would not say life was perfect, but I realize it could have been a lot worse. The only worry that still nagged at me was that somehow, the divorce would influence Torey to believe that happy marriages weren't possible, and I didn't want that for him.

I picked Torey up at school as usual that Friday afternoon. I told him I had a surprise for him tomorrow, but would say no more. He was bursting with anticipation and begging for hints. I finally told him we were going somewhere and that was the last hint. He then began to guess, like kids do: the park, the playground, the beach, and on and on. He even guessed that we were going to see his grandparents, who now lived in Miami, or his best friend, Trenton Stimes, who moved to California last year.

When the barrage of questions failed to get him any closer to knowing what he was after, he started his con artist routine. I almost told him at that point, but instead I said I would give him one more clue. "You'll have to bring the Polaroid camera because you will want lots of pictures." Somehow this seemed to settle him down.

I suppose he thought that if I figured he would like to have some pictures, then it must be a neat place to go, or maybe he just enjoyed the idea of using the new Polaroid. Either way, he was content until the next morning. At 8:00 A.M. sharp, he was ready to go. He did not even try to find out where we were headed. He had the camera case strapped around his shoulder and was hurrying me every step of the way. He was truly anxious to get there, wherever it was.

As I drove, I kept turning my head so I could see his eyes when we approached the sign that said, "Lowry Park Zoo." Torey had never been to a zoo before, but had mentioned it several times. His excitement thrilled me. It was better than watching him at Christmas, or when we brought his puppy Snoop home for the first time.

There was a small line at the entryway of the park, and Torey displayed his impatience by stepping out of line and stretching his neck to see every possible sight. I looked ahead and saw what was causing the backup. An elderly couple walking very slowly. They were side by side, holding on to one another with one hand, and the railing with the other hand, which made passing impossible as they went along the wooden trail.

I was afraid Torey was going to say something about the old couple that might embarrass all of us since he was in such a hurry, so I began talking to him about the animals to keep him occupied. Soon, Torey was completely engrossed in the animals, as he ran from one habitat to the next. Somewhere near the orangutan, he remembered the camera.

"Dad! I have to take some pictures! Will you help me?"

I took the shoulder strap off, opened the case, and removed the camera. I then realized that there was only one exposure left on the film in the camera and no spare roll. I explained to Torey he would have to look at all the animals first, then decide what he wanted a picture of, and go take it.

He was mildly upset at first, but the excitement of being there took over and he began to concentrate on the animals again. After touring the entire area, we stopped at the concession stand for some refreshments.

I asked Torey, while we were drinking our sodas, if he knew what he wanted to take his picture of.

He nodded and said, "Oh, yes! Can I go take the picture now?"

I asked him what he had in mind, but he smiled shyly and would not tell me. I figured he was getting back at me for keeping the zoo a secret. So, I finally told him he could go ahead and take the picture, if he could do it without going out of my sight.

He pointed to a spot near the chimpanzees and said, "Can I go over there?"

I nodded and looked at him suspiciously because I knew he was up to something. The chimpanzees were not on his list of favorites. Torey ran to the spot he had pointed to and looked back at me for approval. I nodded my consent.

I saw him raise the camera and snap his picture, but I could not tell what it was he was aiming at due to a small group of people in the way. He ran back to me with the camera as the picture was still developing. He did not want to let me see it at first, but realized it was hopeless to keep it from me forever, and handed it to me for my inspection.

My mouth fell open in astonishment when I looked down

at the developing picture of the elderly couple we had encountered at the entrance. They had their arms around each other and were smiling at Torey.

"Aren't they awesome?" he glowed. "Today is their fifty-first anniversary, and they are still in love. I heard 'em say it."

In that moment I knew, perhaps for the first time since the divorce, that everything was going to be all right. I knew Torey understood that his mother and I will never have a fifty-first anniversary, but that in his mind we are both very special.

I knew Torey somehow realized, even at the age of five, that those folks who do stay together for fifty years or more must be extra special, special enough to take a picture of. And I knew that what Torey chose to remember from his outing that day was a snapshot of true and lasting love.

Ken Grote

The Wink

In marriage you are neither the husband nor the wife; you are the love between two.

Nisargadatta

Not so very long ago, my husband of thirteen years admitted he'd had second thoughts about marrying me. The afternoon before our wedding, he stopped by the hall where our reception was to be held to drop something off. My parents were already there. Mom, renowned for her talents in the kitchen, had taken it upon herself to prepare a simple, but delicious meal for no less than 150 guests. When my soon-to-be husband went in, he found my father placidly sitting by the door to the kitchen and my mother ranting and raving at the poor man. Dad sat there as Mom ticked off her list of grievances against him. Everything from being short a jar of pickles to the ham having been sliced too thin. It was all his fault.

Those acquainted with my parents would probably testify to the fact that they had a somewhat odd marriage. And in all honesty, most would classify Mom as harpy and Dad as henpecked.

As an only child, and labeled a "change-of-life baby" by my parents, I grew up witnessing their peculiar relationship. At the time of my birth, they had already been married twenty-plus years. I remember wondering if other parents conducted their marriages this way as well. As the years passed, I grew older and began to study the interaction between other couples. The more I studied other relationships, the more I wondered why on earth my parents had married each other, let alone stayed together when divorce is as common as changing the oil in your car.

When I was sixteen, Mom, a diabetic, became seriously ill and was hospitalized for nearly ten days. I came home from my part-time job one afternoon and found Dad sitting at the kitchen table, playing game after game of solitaire. Every few minutes he'd glance at the clock. He hadn't eaten dinner yet, probably because making coffee was the extent of his skills in the kitchen. I made him a hot meal, and he resumed his solitaire. The phone rang, and I answered in the living room.

"Hello, dear."

"Hi, Mom. I hope you're feeling better than this morning when I was up there."

"Lots better. Is your dad still home or has he left?"

"Nope, he's still here."

"Did he stop and get something to eat? I sent him home. He needs to get some rest. He looks so tired. I told him to stop and pick up a hamburger or something. The food in this hospital is awful. Your father shouldn't have to eat this stuff. It's bad enough I have to. I told him not to come back until after six."

"No, I don't think he picked anything up, but I just cooked him dinner."

"Thanks, sweetie. I've gotta go. They want to take some

blood. See you in the morning."

I went back into the kitchen to finish cleaning up.

"That was Mom. I told her you'd eaten."

He checked the clock again: six o'clock on the dot. "Thanks for dinner, honey. That was just as good as if Mom had made it. I've got to get back to the hospital."

He gathered his deck of cards, put them in their box and left.

I remember the events of that day long ago. Not because I noted anything special at the time, but because of my mother's illness and the glowing compliment to my cooking by my father.

As I look back, I realize a great deal about my parents' relationship was demonstrated by their actions during those trying days: my mother's concern for my father even though she herself was seriously ill and my father counting the minutes until he could return to her side. Both acts spoke volumes. These two people shared much more than the world could ever know.

The insight I've gained is priceless. No two relationships are alike. It would be like comparing two leaves from the same tree. On the surface, they both appear the same, but it's the tiny, undefinable differences that make the two unique.

What might seem like an odd union to you or me is perfectly ordinary to the couple involved. Relationships are about what you put in and what you take out. And the only people who can judge the worth of what they receive are the people in the commitment. Mostly I believe love is a personal thing; it can best be valued by the person you give it to.

My husband told me that on that long-ago day, the day before our wedding when he wondered what on earth he was getting himself into and nearly backed out, one thing stopped him. When he stood up from behind the bar, he glanced at my poor, beleaguered, browbeaten father, my mother's haranguing echoing across the hall, and my father winked at him and smiled.

After nearly fifty years of marriage, Dad very suddenly passed away ten years ago. Mom suffered a massive stroke that left her wheelchair-bound only two months after Dad left us. Mom continued on for another six years. She stayed and greeted both of her grandchildren before she left to be with Dad.

There's no doubt in my mind that as soon as Mom passed through the pearly gates and saw Dad, she probably scolded him because he needed a haircut, or his pants pressed. And I'm sure Dad glanced over at Saint Peter, winked and smiled.

Karen Culver

The Little Red Boots

Watch. Wait. Time will unfold and fulfill its purpose.

Marianne Williamson

When my granddaughter, Tate, celebrated her fifth birthday recently, her mother gave her a very special present — a pair of red cowgirl boots that had belonged to her when she was a little girl. As Tate slipped on the little red boots, she began to dance across the room in excitement. My mind flashed back to the afternoon my daughter-in-law, Kelly, showed me the little red boots and told me about the first day she had worn them. You see, not only did Kelly experience the thrill of wearing her first pair of real cowgirl boots back then, but she also experienced the thrill of meeting her first love.

He was her first "older man" — she was five and he was seven! He lived in the city, and his father had brought him to Kelly's grandfather's farm one Saturday afternoon to ride the horses. Kelly sat on the top fence rail, watching her grandfather saddle her pony. She was proud of her shiny new red boots and was trying really hard not to get them dirty.

Just then, the city boy came over to say hello. He smiled at Kelly and admired her red cowgirl boots. It must have been love at first sight, because Kelly found herself offering to let him ride her pony. She had never let anyone ride her pony before.

Kelly's grandfather sold the horse farm later that year, and she never saw the little boy again. But for some reason, she never forgot that magical moment when she was five, and she thought of the cute city boy every time she put on her red cowgirl boots. When Kelly outgrew the boots, her mother decided not to throw them out, but to pack them away. After all, Kelly had loved the little red boots so much.

Many years passed. Kelly grew up into a beautiful young woman, and met my son, Marty. They married and had their daughter, Tate. One day, while Kelly was rummaging through some old boxes in preparation for a garage sale, she found the little red boots. Fond memories flooded into her heart. "I used to love these boots," she recalled with a smile. "I think I'll give them to Tate for her birthday."

Tate's laughter brought me back to the present, and I watched as my son scooped his giggling daughter up in his arms and danced around the room, with her red birthday boots on her feet. "I sure like your new cowgirl boots, baby," he told her. "In fact, for some reason, they remind me of the day I rode my very first pony. I wasn't much older than you."

"Is this a true story, Daddy? Or a make-believe one? Does it have a happy ending? I like stories with happy endings," Tate said. She loved to hear her Daddy tell stories about his childhood and begged him to tell her about his first pony ride. Marty laughed at Tate's never-ending questions and sat down in the big recliner as Tate climbed onto his lap.

"Once upon a time," he began, "when I was seven years old, I lived in the big city of St. Louis, Missouri. And do you know what I wanted more than anything in the world? A horse! I told my dad that when I grew up I wanted to be a real cowboy. That summer my dad took me to a farm not very far from here and let me ride a real pony. I remember that there was a little girl on that farm, sitting on a fence, and she was wearing new red cowgirl boots just like yours."

Kelly sat listening to Marty telling their daughter about his first pony ride. When he got to the part about the red boots, her eyes grew wide in amazement, and her heart filled with wonder: Marty had been the cute city boy she'd met back when she was only five years old!

"Marty," she said, her voice trembling, "I was that little girl. That was my grandfather's farm. And those are the same red boots!"

Tate sat happily in her Daddy's lap, unaware that in that magical moment, her parents realized that they had met as children and that even back then they had felt the special connection between their hearts.

Jeannie S. Williams

"Of course you realize there is a fifteen-year waiting period."

Reprinted by permission of Dave Carpenter.

The Real Family Circus

For cartoonist Bil Keane, being a family man has paid off. He uses his own wife, daughter and four sons as models for the characters in his popular feature, "The Family Circus". In fact, he sometimes mixes them up.

In 1962, for example, Keane realized that the fictional Jeffy, though only a toddler, was too old for some of the baby situations—diapers, baby food, highchair, etc.

The cartoon needed an infant, and he thought it would be a good idea to show Mom pregnant and then have the baby born. "My wife was out working in the garden," recalls Keane. "I ran out of my studio and asked for her advice: 'Thel, what would you think of adding a new baby to the family?'

"'Well all right,' she answered, 'but let me finish the weeding first.'"

William E. Smart

"I think they're goin' through a phase."

Reprinted by permission of Bil Keane.

All the Days of Your Life

The best minute you spend is the one you invest in your family.

Ken Blanchard

My wife Joan and I were on vacation at a ranch near San Antonio, Texas. For three days we played tennis from morning till sundown, and we even got in a few rounds of golf. Nights were spent around a campfire, trading stories with friends.

On the fourth day Joan started to limp, holding her hip in pain. But this didn't stop her, and we played our hearts out until our last day there.

As a friend drove us to the airport for our trip back to New York, he said, "I don't like the look of that limp Joanie," and cautioned her to see a doctor.

Two days later our internist, Dr. Jack Bornstein, made an appointment for Joan to see a radiologist. She was in the X-ray room for about a half-hour. Then we sat in the doctor's office, waiting.

When the doctor returned, he smiled at Joan and said he was still waiting for the plates to dry. Almost as an afterthought, he said, "Mr. Simon, I have some things to go over with you. Could you come inside?"

I shrugged to Joan and followed him into a back room with X-rays on the wall. He pointed to a small gray area the size of a nickel. "This is her left hipbone. This dark gray area worries me."

I could feel my heartbeat quickening. "What do you mean, worries you? What do you think it is?"

"It looks like a small tumor. It's possibly benign, but we won't know until we do a biopsy."

When the doctor and I returned, Joan was sitting there. The doctor explained to her in carefully chosen words what he had told me. He would set up an appointment at Lenox Hill Hospital for a biopsy. It was a simple procedure in which they'd take a bone sample from her hip. After the tests they'd know better how to treat it.

This was in 1971 when cancer was a word still spoken in hushed voices. But the words "treat this" and "simple procedure" gave us cause to think that there really wasn't any concern.

I was nervous, but I couldn't believe anything was seriously wrong with Joan. We had been married nineteen years, and she looked robustly healthy and as beautiful as I had ever known her.

That night at dinner we said nothing to worry Ellen and Nancy, our two girls. Joan told them she might be out the next day when they came home from school because she had to take some tests for "this pesky leg of mine". That was all.

Later Joan got into bed next to me. "Are you worried?" she asked.

"Worried? No. Not at all."

"Would you tell me if you were?"

"Probably not. But I am not worried."

She turned on her side and closed her eyes. "Would you rub my back? It still hurts."

I rubbed her back as gently as I could.

The next day I was in the Lenox Hill waiting room with Joan's mother, Helen, when the surgeon appeared. "Mr. Simon?" he said.

I followed him down the hall to the privacy of a cold, back stairway. Sitting on the third step, he asked me to sit next to him.

"It's not good," he began. "What do you mean? The biopsy?"

"In examining her before the procedure, I found a malignant tumor in her breast. It's cancer, and it's already metastasized. I didn't remove her breast."

The words were coming too fast, with too many emotions bouncing around in my brain to accept what he was saying. What was the prognosis? I heard it all in one devastating statement: "She has about a year. A year and a half at most."

A hole opened up underneath me. The fall was far and dark and unending. I could not breathe, and I could not stop sobbing. He put his hand on my arm and said he was sorry.

"Does she know?" I finally asked.

"I told her it was breast cancer. I did not tell her how long she has. That's as much a family matter as it is medical one."

"What do I tell her?"

"I would give her some hope. She'll know herself when the time comes. If I were you, I'd say that we caught the cancer early and that we got it all. If you can handle it, keep it from the children for a while. That's up to you, of course." He said he would do what he could to slow things down.

Joan was wheeled into her room, and the doctor went in. I saw Helen in the hallway. It wasn't fair to keep the truth from her. Besides, I knew that I couldn't get through it on my own, that I'd need an ally.

Helen's eyes looked into mine. I burst into tears and held onto her. She sobbed, saying over and over, "I knew it. I knew it all along."

I told her everything and explained how the doctor thought we should handle this. "It's just between us," I said. "I don't want anyone else to know. Not Ellen. Not Nancy. Not until it's time."

She nodded as the doctor summoned us into Joan's room. My wife was sitting up in bed, a hopeful smile on her face. "The doctor said they caught it early," she said. "They got it all. Isn't that wonderful?"

I nodded and kissed her. I could feel her body relax in my arms. From that moment I lived out a conspiracy of silence. Yet I still believed, no matter what I had been told, that Joan would beat the odds.

Joan started radiation treatments. As the weeks passed and her pain lessened, her spirits rose. I got so much in the habit of keeping up my own spirits that I didn't know if I was pretending or believing. The lie became the truth. Not the real truth, but one that gets you through day to day.

At home I worked on my new play, *The Sunshine Boys*, letting it swallow up all my other thoughts. The hours I sat over the typewriter were my refuge. Joan stayed in bed, writing poetry — something she had not done since college, almost twenty years before.

I wanted to get something for Joan that would deflect the shadow that hung over her. I thought of the dream house she'd always wanted.

We had friends in Bedford, New York, about an hour's drive from the city. I rented a car and drove up, telling Joan I had meetings that day about some film projects. I walked into a real-estate office, and within an hour I'd seen a dozen houses. About 3 P.M., we turned onto a wooded area with a lovely little home sitting on a knoll. I saw a wooden footbridge over a stream. Beyond it the sun shimmered on a lake. "It's Blue Heron Lake," said the agent. "I'll show you."

He took me across the bridge to a small pier with a boathouse. A rowboat was tired to the rail. The lake seemed enormous.

I barely looked at the house before I made an offer, then went to his office and signed some papers. If Joan were happy here, who knew what miracles could occur?

Driving home, I wondered what Joan would think of my buying a house without her ever seeing it. It was so unlike me to do something like this. I walked into the bedroom, unable to conceal the huge smile on my face. She smiled back. "What are you so happy about?"

"I did something crazy today. Maybe something wonderful."

"Are you going to tell me?"

"I bought a house. On a lake. Do you think I'm crazy?"

The smile on her face was worth everything. "I don't believe it! Are you telling me the truth?"

We talked all night about the house. Nancy and Ellen were beside themselves with joy. When I turned out the lights, I wondered, *Does she know why I did it so quickly*? But even if she did suspect, her mind was now consumed with living in the country on a place so perfectly named as Blue Heron Lake.

I began to have the reverse of nightmares. My dreams were happy—of a healthy Joan, of meeting her for the first time at summer camp in the Pocono Mountains, of the laughter we shared sitting in Washington Square Park with our older daughter, Ellen, still in a baby carriage. I awoke feeling wonderful until I turned and saw Joan sleeping beside me, and the awakening became the nightmare.

She rarely let on to her own feelings. She never asked questions, and I soon learned to stop asking, "How are you feeling?" She still couldn't get around without a cane, and I could see she didn't want me to help her. Still, when she was walking down the stairs, my hand was always an inch away from her arm.

At the next appointment with the oncologist, I was not prepared for what he said.

"Well, Mrs. Simon, everything looks good. The tumor is going into remission."

An enormous smile of relief crossed Joan's face. I could barely believe my ears. What was happening here? Was the cancer gone?

I no longer knew what to believe except that today the sun was shining and that Joan and I were going to leave for her first visit to the house in Bedford. When we arrived, she was beaming with excitement. "I'll show you the house in a minute," I said. "First comes the lake."

Joan stood on the dock, looking at the boathouse and the water. I could see by her expression that it took her back to when she was her happiest: growing up in the Poconos, taking a rowboat out at night and swimming in the dark, cool waters.

"I'm going to get rid of this cane," she said. "I'm going to swim in the lake. And I'm going to catch the biggest fish and cook it for dinner."

And that's exactly what she did.

By summer Joan was out in a boat fishing with Ellen and Nancy, teaching them what she learned as a girl. In the afternoons we played tennis. She was banging them across the net with power and speed. "Damn it!" she'd yell. "Hit the ball like you want to win!"

It was wonderful to see her like this again. The cane was gone. The limp was gone. We had our lives back. Had God granted us a reprieve?

At the end of the summer, Joan was still free of all signs of cancer. We went to Manhattan, and I started rehearsals on *The Sunshine Boys*. I was glad now I had never told Ellen and Nancy about Joan's recent battles, and I prayed I would never have to.

After the play opened, Joan and I took the girls to Florida. Suddenly the limp was back again. Joan held on to the railing when climbing steps, breathed a little harder, moved a little more slowly. A few days later the pain got sharper, and she could no longer get around without the cane.

Radiation treatments started again in Manhattan. At dinner Joan would use the word "treatments" but never mentioned radiology. She just tossed it off as that "bad leg" of hers. The girls seemed to accept it.

Finally one weekend in the middle of the night, Joan turned to me and whispered, "I'm so scared." I tried to assuage her fears, but we both knew the only true comfort I could give her was to hold her tightly until she fell asleep.

Joan's health was not improving, but radiation relieved the pain. In the spring the warm sun and fresh air put color back in her cheeks. Her smile returned, yet it was not the smile I had known all these years. It reflected a new attitude — not exactly acceptance but rather understanding, as if she had made a pact with someone that was going to get her through this.

I saw her walking in the woods with Nancy, who was ten, telling her how the flowers kept replenishing themselves and that even when a flower dies, it inevitably comes back in a new place. She was telling Nancy in her own way what I couldn't bring myself to say.

I was outside the house when I heard her cry of pain. I rushed into the bedroom and found her unable to move. I helped her into bed, then called Jack Bornstein, who said to get her into Lenox Hill.

I phoned for an ambulance, and Joan asked me to call her mother. The doctors in the hospital told me Joan would need to stay about a week. Two weeks came and went. A month went by. When I met Dr. Bornstein in the hall, I saw the glum look on his face. "What's happening?" I asked.

"The cancer is spreading through her like wildfire," he said. "Faster than we can treat it. We'll do everything we can to make her comfortable. Let's not give up hope."

Joan did not want any visitors, except for family. Even I couldn't go into her room without first knocking. The nurse would open the door a crack and whisper, "Joanie wants a few minutes to get ready."

"Even for me?"

"Especially for you."

When the door opened, Joan was sitting in bed, smiling her best smile, hair tied back in the ponytail she had worn when I first met her. She would talk about the girls, my work, even make plans for when she got out of the hospital.

One night at home I sat with Ellen at the kitchen table. Her fifteen-year-old face looked at me apprehensively. "I should have told you this before," I said, "You know Mom is really sick."

She nodded.

"I don't know how long she'll last. The doctors say it could be as long as August or even ...."

"I knew she was sick, I knew she was going to die. I just didn't know when." Her eyes welled up with tears, and as I reached across the table to touch her hand, all her sorrow came pouring out. I told her I wouldn't say anything yet to Nancy, who was at camp. She was only two hours away, and I could bring her back before anything happened.

The phone rang on the table next to my bed. It was 3:10 A. M., July 11. A voice told me — softly — that Joan had passed away in her sleep.

She was forty years old.

I sat up in bed, trying to compose myself, then woke Ellen. It came sooner than we expected, and the finality of it hadn't sunk in yet. The depth of the loss comes later, when the sun rises and you realize that this new day and all the days of your life to come will be without Joan.

I made the arrangements to bring Nancy home from camp. This was the day I finally told her, and it was too late. Of all the regrets I've ever had, what I most regret was not telling her sooner. It took her years to tell me she was angry and confused. Yet she never blamed me.

We drove home from the cemetery with Joan's mother sitting between her grandchildren. I looked at their faces and at the countryside passing by. At age forty-six, with two young daughters, I felt empty and frightened. The one thing we did have was each other.

Neil Simon

Tender Moments

Saturday morning, the moment she woke up, Kay thought of the new man she had met the night before and the coming telephone call. Her eyes opened instantly. An image of David Dickson sprang full-blown to her mind—his looks, his charm—and she smiled with sudden euphoria. She had fallen in love. And she was going to hear from him today.

Jumping up from the bed, she ran out to the landing and leaned over the railing—a long-legged, pretty girl, nineteen years old. "Mom!" she yelled down. "I'm expecting a very important call! If it comes, I'll be in the shower!" She waited. "*MOM*!" A distant "all right" came from the kitchen.

A little later, dressed in jeans and a shirt, she entered the kitchen and kissed her mother on the cheek. There was a book under her arm.

Her mother said, "How was the party last night?"

"I had a fine time." The wildly inadequate statement made her feel guilty. She had heard often of mother-daughter relationships in which the two were "like sisters" together and told each other everything. But neither of them could do that, although they loved each other deeply. Her mother had been raised in a strict household in which emotional restraint had been ingrained in her. "Your mother," Kay's father had once sighed, "plays things very close to the vest. When I first met her I called her 'Miss Buttoned-Up' and she hasn't changed much over the years."

Now Kay said, "No breakfast for me. I'm going outside for some fresh air."

In the backyard Kay tried to read her novel but an hour passed, rich with daydreams, interrupted only by frequent glances at her watch.

Sitting there, it was as if her body had become one huge ear that strained like a bird dog's for a sound that would not come. Why didn't it come? she fretted.

It was late morning when her friend Emily arrived for a visit. Kay felt the pressure inside her easing as another chair was brought out and placed next to her own. "Guess what," she said to her friend. "I think I'm in love." Her voice was rich with drama.

"No!" Emily cried out. "Who with?"

During the next few minutes Emily listened as Kay poured out her disclosures; David's every expression was detailed, every word he had uttered was now reviewed for possible hidden meanings. "There was a strong physical reaction between us. High-Octane. Spontaneous Combustion."

Suddenly she flopped back in her chair, overwhelmed by frustration. "What's the matter with him? If he was so attracted to me, why hasn't he called by now?"

They gazed at each other pensively, members of the same sisterhood. They talked a little longer, then Emily left. It was lunchtime.

Kay could not eat. Her fifteen-year-old brother, Steve, had come home from batting practice and now his strident voice affected her nerves in a terrible way.

Her eyes turned for relief to her mother who was, as usual, eating quietly, her eyes lowered.

Her mother had always held a fascinating strangeness for her. A loving woman, yes. But she kept her love deep inside herself, finding it difficult to reveal in word or gesture. Her father could grab his children in bear hugs, but she couldn't do anything like that. "It's not in my nature," she would explain simply if teased about it.

Miss Buttoned-Up, Kay thought now. Did she ever give Pop the eye when they met? The thought seemed preposterous. Yet how had her parents gotten together?

She excused herself and went into the backyard again. She felt, for the first time, a chill of foreboding. How could she be sure he would call? It was already mid-afternoon.

Suddenly her mother emerged from the screen door and joined her.

"Emily looks good," she said. "I saw her through the window this morning." She hesitated. "The two of you sure had a lot to talk about."

Kay looked up swiftly and caught an expression that erased itself instantly from her mother's face. But what had it been? Jealousy? No, not jealousy, but — wistfulness, that was it. Her mother wanted her daughter to talk to her as she had talked with her friend.

Kay felt a sharp pang. For a moment, standing there, a dozen words pushed up in her throat; she wanted to say them, to enclose her mother in her own world. But it was only for a moment.

She said awkwardly, "Well, we hadn't seen each other for a while."

"Sure," her mother said. She straightened. "I'm going into town to do a little shopping. I'll see you later."

After her mother left, she went inside. At the archway to the living room she stood still, looking at the phone.

Suddenly a hatred for it seized her. *Ring*, she thought savagely; *ring, you rotten black thing, why don't you ring*?

Her father came home early; Steve returned from a movie; her mother appeared again. Suddenly the house was full, and Kay, to her horror, found them all congregated in the living room. Suppose David called now, she thought in anguish, with all of them right on top of the telephone? How could she laugh provocatively or maybe say something daring, with them listening?

Suddenly she could not bear it. She went upstairs and into her room where she shut the door and fell down on the bed. Weak tears gathered under her closed eyelids. Whatever made me think he would call? She thought. I'm too vulnerable, too trusting about men; I must be on my guard from now on.

Hearing her name called, she went into the dinette and found her mother sitting at the table, looking down at what appeared to be an old snapshot. The lowering sun made a halo of light around her head.

"Kay," she said, "look what I found this morning. I've been meaning to show it to you all day." She handed the snapshot to her daughter.

"Why, it's Pop!" Kay said in surprise. "How good-looking he was!"

She looked up at her mother. Something stilled instantly inside her. A change had come over her mother. "Yes, he was," her mother said. "He was very handsome. I was just crazy about him."

Kay did not move. The little statement — so innocuous coming from someone else — stupefied her.

She said foolishly, "Were you?" Her mother — just crazy about someone! Saying it out loud!

"Oh, Lord, yes." The words came haltingly. "I loved him so much I couldn't see straight." Her hands were clasped tightly together on the tabletop. "He lived with your Aunt May and Uncle Ed around the corner from our house, you know. On summer evenings like this I used to sit on our porch and pray that he'd come by, because then he might ask me to walk with him." She looked down at her hands. "Sometimes he'd come two nights in a row and sometimes he'd let a week go by—oh, he gave me fits, I can tell you." She looked up slowly at Kay. "When he did come up the steps and sit next to me on the glider I'd be in the clouds. But I suffered too. I had this hang-up about my hips," her mother said. "I thought they were too big for the rest of me. So when he was there I used to grab a cushion and put it on my lap to hide my hips."

Kay was shaken. Her mother was suddenly opening one of the little secret doors inside her mind and letting her daughter look inside.

Her mother went on, "Girls in my college class had a saying then. 'Give him The Ooh-la-la.'" She smiled wanly. "Oh, how I wanted to give your father The Ooh-la-la! But I couldn't." She nodded. "It wasn't my nature."

Kay swallowed. "Well, you must have given out *some* signals. He married you."

"I guess I did. In my way. Me and my big hips."

They were silent, looking at each other. It came to Kay that her mother was waiting for something. Her eyes were big in her face. *Tell me*, they were saying. *Now tell me things too. I'm your friend, like Emily. And I've known all day what you were going through.*

Her mother gazed down at the table. With her head bent over, the arch of her white neck looked thin and very young.

"Mom," Kay blurted out, "I think I'm in love the way you were with Pop."

Her mother's head shot up. "No kidding," she said eagerly. "Who is he?" They began to talk. Her mother listened and asked all the right questions and said all the right words and sighed or exclaimed at all the right times. A richness seemed to slowly gather and swell in the air between them until they were both breathing with one breath, and in the breathing something warm and astonishing enfolded them together.

It seemed to Kay that after that talk a little lens had turned inside her head and she was seeing everything through a different perspective. The telephone call no longer carried the urgency it had before; if it came, she thought, it would be wonderful; if it didn't, well—she wouldn't kill herself. Because of this new calmness, her appetite came roaring back; she ate her supper ravenously and gazed at her brother with a kindlier eye. And when she helped her mother in the kitchen afterward, she said, "You know, I think keeping your emotions to yourself, like we do, kind of heats them up out of proportion." She frowned. "Actually, I don't know if I'm really in love. It could be just a sudden crush."

"He bowled you over," her mother said.

"Exactly. But that doesn't necessarily mean love. Now..."

The telephone rang inside.

They both stood motionless as statues, looking at each other. Then Kay went inside the living room and picked up the receiver. Her heart was suddenly pounding. "Hello?" she said.

"Hello." A young man's voice. "May I speak to Kay, please?"

"This is Kay."

"I thought it was. This is David Dickson. We met last

night."

"Oh—David. How are you?"

"Fine. Look, are you doing anything tonight?"

"Not a thing."

"Then suppose I pick you up in about a half an hour. Okay?"

"Fine."

She hung up. For a few seconds she stood there, dazed. And then she went back to the kitchen where her mother stood with her back to her at the sink.

"Mom," Kay said. All the excitement was back; she could hardly speak. "That was my call. He's coming over in a little while."

Her mother turned around. Her face shone. Suddenly she winked. "Give him 'The Ooh-la-la.'"

"Oh, you can depend on it!" Kay burst out laughing.

Her mother did too. Suddenly they were both laughing helplessly together. Recovering, key said, "I'd better go up and change."

"Kay."

Kay faced her mother. They looked at each other. And suddenly Kay knew what she had to do, what she wanted more than anything else to do.

She walked back to her mother. Their arms went around each other and they held each other tightly, their eyes closed, their cheeks pressed together. *My mother*, Kay thought, *My friend*.

Then, as if by secret code, they broke apart. Kay turned, went into the hall and started bouncing up the stairs taking them two at a time. There was singing inside her head.

Florence Jane Soman

An Unbreakable Bond

The human spirit is stronger than anything that can happen to it.

C. C. Scott

The young couple stands at the front of the church, his arm tenderly about her waist. Before the gathering of family and friends, they light five white candles. They share a kiss that puts a catch in the throats of onlookers.

This could be Cliff and Regina Ellis's wedding. They are certainly demonstrating their commitment.

But no. This is a memorial service for their five-year-old daughter, Alexandra, who had battled cancer for two years.

The day before she died, her parents helped her out of this world just as they'd welcomed her into it — by getting into the bathtub and cuddling her close in the warm, safe tub.

They spoke to her of dolphins, just like the one she'd swum with in Hawaii weeks before. They tucked her into their big bed in a quiet upstairs room, lit candles, played soft music, sang her favorite songs quietly and held her close. She said good-bye to her kitten, Simba, her three-year-old brother, Zachary, and five generations of family and friends. When she stopped breathing, they spent several more hours just sitting with her, and then they let her go.

At just thirty-one and twenty-nine years old, Cliff and Regina are an unusual young couple. Strong. Loving. Wise beyond their years. While a child's terminal illness stresses a marriage terribly, Alex's long fight and death has further cemented theirs.

Reflecting on their daughter's death and its effects two months later, they decided that their cement is made up of *commitment*: to each other; to being the parents Zach deserves; to the foundation they've established to provide information and support to other children with cancer; and commitment that allowed them to hang in there for this terrible, topsy-turvy year, where one moment found them appreciating the sunset, and the next, wondering how life can be so cruel.

Regina Rathburn and Cliff Ellis met in high school in the early 1980s; she was a freshman and he a senior. They dated off and on, getting serious in her senior year. They seemed to be soul mates, clicking with each other as they did with no one else. Cliff was "funny, sensitive, warm"; Regina was "beautiful, with a really strong personality."

When they married in 1988, they wanted several children—the kind of family that Regina knew, where people talk things out, laugh and cry together. "I was always realistic," Regina says. "I knew marriage took a lot of hard work. I never had the expectation it'd be sweet and wonderful. If we were going to grow and change, we'd have to make an effort."

Alexandra was born soon after, a perfect baby who developed breathing problems after birth. When she finally came home, they climbed into a warm bathtub with their daughter, safe in fate's hands. Three years later, Zach joined them. Their dreams were coming true, with plenty of time for their children as they managed their business.

Then Alex was diagnosed with cancer on her spine. For two and a half years, they fought the good fight, complete with chemotherapy. Cliff shaved his head to match his bald daughter's "chemo cut."

Late in the winter, the cancer came back. Alex declined a bone-marrow transplant; no more hospitals, she begged. She wanted to go to Hawaii and swim with a dolphin. So they did.

Neither parent knew how the other would react when the end came. Would they be the same people? Could they even love each other after such a loss? Yet as she lay dying in her parents' big bed, Alexandra had given them a priceless gift:

"She took my hands and my husband's hands," says her mother. "And she connected them to each other over the top of her tiny body. It was as if her last act here on earth was to create an unbreakable bond between them.

"In that moment, I looked at Cliff and thought, *God, he's so beautiful*! What a devoted father he's been. I saw in him this love, this incredible giving. We were there for her—100 percent teamwork. We honored our hearts, our daughter, our relationship—just like we did with her birth."

Cliff and Regina's eyes lock across their living room as they recall that unforgettable night.

"And I looked at Regina," says Cliff, "and couldn't imagine loving her more. I was drawn even closer to her—it was unbelievable."

Two months later, they endure. This is what keeps them together:

Knowing that grief is a solitary act, they give each other

space.

They understand that marriage — especially one under stress—has its ups and downs; some days are simply down days and not a reason to leave.

They agree that children are their first job—and their first joy. Procrastinate on anything but make time for your children, they urge other parents.

Having knowledge—hard won and unusual for people so young—that life is short and to be savored, they spend their limited time only with people or activities they enjoy and find meaningful.

They appreciate that time changes people, and they encourage each other to grow.

They acknowledge that even in the bleakest times, there are gifts to be discovered.

"I thought Alex's death was going to ravage us—that losing her would be losing myself," admits Regina. "I didn't know who I was anymore. But Cliff said something that is the deepest truth of our marriage: Whoever we are, we'll be together."

Jann Mitchell

7

THE FLAME THAT STILL BURNS

Those who have never known the deep intimacy and hence the companionship of happy mutual love have missed the best thing that life has to give.

Bertrand Russell

Just Like New

Love doesn't just sit there, like a stone; it has to be made, like bread, remade all the time, made new.

Ursula K. Le Guin

Years ago my husband, Charlie, and I had some marital problems. Growing family responsibilities and financial worries took a toll on us, and we began arguing frequently, often late into the night. Even going out together for dinner was strained and full of forced conversation.

But neither of us could take the step that would end our eleven-year marriage and bring heartbreak to our three young children. Deep down we knew we still loved each other, so we pledged to work it out.

The year that followed was hard. Charlie and I had grown neglectful about expressing ourselves, and for too long we had let small differences and disappointments build between us. We had stored up reserves of anger and resentment that pushed us apart. But through countless discussions and a lot of prayer, we began to close the gulf. The more honest we were, the closer we became.

When I felt we were reaching solid ground, I asked my husband to give me an "eternity ring". I had bought the advertising hype hook, line and sinker: *Show her you'd marry her all over again.* It was not so much the ring I wanted; it was the reassurance I thought it would bring.

We went shopping on a beautiful summer day, my birthday. We left the kids with their grandparents and had a leisurely lunch before walking hand in hand along Jeweler's Row in Philadelphia. Finally, I found a ring I liked. While waiting for it to be adjusted, the jeweler took my left hand and peered at my engagement ring. "May I clean it for you?" he asked.

Charlie hunched over and leaned on the glass case. "It really doesn't sparkle like it used to," he said. I slipped the ring off my finger.

A few minutes later the jeweler was back. The ring shone like new!

On the drive home, I didn't take my eyes off it. I forgot all about the eternity ring. I just couldn't believe how this old ring suddenly sparkled the way it had the day Charlie gave it to me. I had taken it for granted these last years, but with a little polish it could still make my heart beat fast. And that's the way it is with a marriage. You have to work at keeping it polished and new, or else the grime of the passing years will hide the joy.

I put my hand on the seat between us and spread my fingers. Charlie covered my hand with his. As we pulled into the driveway, I said a prayer of thanks to God for helping me see the sparkle in something old when I thought I needed something new.

Anita Gogno

My Girl, My Wife

I entered Northwestern University in the fall of 1941—a shy, skinny, ill-dressed boy on a $300 scholarship from the Winnetka Community Theater. For the first two or three days in my theater course, I sat behind a girl named Lydia Clarke. All I saw was her tumbling mane of black Irish hair, which made me tremble. She bent over her desk, talking notes. I sat bemused, taking note only of her.

Between classes I made terse, offhand remarks — "Hi there. How ya doin'?" But I couldn't figure out how to advance the relationship. I'd never even been on a date. Girls expected to be taken out and bought hamburgers and Cokes and taken home in cars. I didn't have any money. I didn't drive a car or know how to dance. Girls? I didn't have a clue.

Fate, as they say, took a hand: Lydia and I were cast in the same bill of plays. I was in *Francesca da Rimini*, playing a medieval lover, all tights and curled hair and daggers at the belt. Lydia was in a moody English piece called The Madras House. During dress rehearsal—could she have been nudging fate along? Lydia asked me how to speak her opening line. She told me she was to enter and say, "Minnie, my frog is dead!"

Well, *of course* I knew how that line should be read. I had firm ideas about all the performances. This was conversation

I knew. I just had no idea how to stop.

On opening night my medieval bit was first, and I decided I was terrible. As I brooded in a corner of the dressing room, Lydia came in and said, "I thought you were marvelous!"

Cary Grant would have thought of twenty funny or engaging replies. I stuck out my tongue.

In an infinity of female wisdom, Lydia neither walked out nor hit me. Finally I said in a strangled voice, "What I mean is, ah, I would like to talk to you about it. Could we go and ah, have some coffee?"

Yes, she would like that (this to the music of the spheres). But later as we walked to the coffee shop, I realized I had no money. Not a nickel. I couldn't tell the celestial beauty beside me. All I could do was silently pray that I'd find a pal I could hit up for a loan. I did: Bill Sweeney, who lent me a quarter. May his name be written in the Golden Book.

Lydia and I had tea, because it would last longer (you got more hot water free). We sat there for some two hours, talking about everything. After I left her at the dorm, I ran home along the dark streets, saying, "I love her, I love her," over and over. I did, too.

Never doubt that this can happen. I'd barely spoken to her before that night, but I knew absolutely. What are the odds: one in a hundred, a thousand? It happened to me.

The fall passed in a hazy mix of work and love. Then, on December 7, 1941, the Japanese attacked Pearl Harbor. Every healthy male between eighteen and forty-five knew where he'd be before long: in uniform.

I enlisted in the Army Air Forces. During the six months before I was called up, Lydia and I continued to share classes, act and work in stage crews together. "In love" is an inadequate description for me. Try "obsessed". But that was from my end. I don't think Lydia was even in love at that point. She kept me at arm's length, waiting to see if I might ripen into an actual human being.

But she did go out with me, so she must have been drawn to me a little. Since I had no money, we seldom went out on real dates. We walked along the lakefront a lot. I remember once it snowed, and she took my arm. I never moved my elbow the whole forty minutes we walked, with the flakes whirling down, coating her glove and the sleeve of my jacket. In the spring we often stood beside a lilac bush at school, embracing for ten minutes at a time.

By my last weeks on campus, I was preoccupied with getting Lydia into bed or married to me. She rejected both options with adamantine resolve. She had no intention of getting pregnant or wed: she was determined to get her degree.

Desperately, I fell back on the ploy soldiers have used for centuries. "You realize you may never see me again. We must have something to carry in our hearts! It may be years, it may be never!" It was a heart-breaking performance, not least because I meant it, but it never dented her resolve.

One afternoon we were down in the school basement, silk-screening a set of theater posters. "I got a letter from this boy I knew in high school," Lydia said. "He's coming to town for a few days. Pete."

"Pete?"

"I thought I might see him. He's going in the Navy."

"The *Navy*?"

"We might have dinner ...with other people, of course. At that place on Ridge Road. Not a date."

"No! I mean, of course, not a date. Sure, I guess ...sure." I had blown it, but all was not lost. She might not be willing to marry me, yet, but I was not going to lose this girl five days before I check in for World War Ⅱ! The night of Pete's visit, I bullied a friend into letting me borrow his car. "For one hour, for God's sake. Of course I have a license!!" (I didn't.)

All the way to the restaurant where the nefarious Pete was plotting to steal my girl, I rehearsed a speech designed to win her heart. I avoided disaster driving the car and strode confidently into a restaurant, where I saw Lydia seated at a large table. Everyone turned to look at me ...and I forgot my speech. Every word.

The silence lengthened. Stepping to the table, I took Lydia's hand and said, "come with me." *And she did.*

I believe with all my heart that the rest of my life began with that moment. That boyish, quixotic disruption of a dinner is the most important single action I've ever taken. I remain proud of it and eternally grateful to my girl, as she sure became, irreversibly, when she stood and walked out of the restaurant, holding my hand.

After I left for basic training, I redoubled my effort to get Lydia to marry me. "Just think, darling," I wrote, "if we're married and I get killed, you get $10,000 free and clear." This appeal, eminently rational to my Scots soul, failed to move her.

Exhausted by the grind of basic training, I gave up even mentioning marriage in my letters. One day I shambled back to my barracks after hours on the obstacle course to find a yellow envelope on my bunk. "HAVE DECIDED TO ACCEPT YOUR PROPOSAL," the telegram said. "LOVE LYDIA."

So she came down to the piney woods of Greensboro, North Carolina, to marry me. A two-day pass was the most I could wangle. I raced into town, where I got us a room and spent my private's pay on a $12 ring.

I was a gangly kid in uniform. But Lydia, in a marvelous violet bridal suit, was a vision that still shimmers in my mind. As we walked to the church, a shower opened over us. Who cared? We ran laughing up the steps and inside to the altar.

Lydia and I have now celebrated our golden wedding anniversary. That's a long time. But half a century, two children, and one wondrous grandson later, it seems more than a time-tick since I stood beside my girl — my wife — in that Carolina church.

Charlton Heston

Wednesdays

The great doing of little things makes the great life.

Eugenia Price

She is my wife, my lover, my best friend. For over fourteen years, our marriage has endured and grown. I can honestly state that after all this time together, my love for Patricia has not diminished in the slightest way. In fact, through each passing day, I find myself more and more enraptured by her beauty. The best times of my life are the times we spend together, whether sitting quietly watching television or enjoying an afternoon at a San Diego Chargers game.

There is no secret to why our marriage has lasted while so many others have failed. There is no formula for success that I can offer, other than to express that the most important feature of our relationship is that it has never lost the sense of romance that bloomed when we first met. Too often marriage kills the romance that was born in the courtship of a relationship. To me, I have always felt that I am still courting Patricia, and therefore the romance has never died.

Romance is not something that can be taught or copied.

One can only be romantic through another. Patricia, my wife of fourteen years, has instilled the romance in me. I am romantic because of her. Patricia has always brought out the best in me. The many aspects of our romance are too numerous to mention. However, there is one special romantic interlude that I began over fifteen years ago.

Before we were married, Patricia and I could not see each other as much as we would have liked during the week. The weekends always went too fast, and the days in between dragged on forever. I decided that I needed to do something to make the weekdays go faster, or at least to give us something to look forward to during the week.

And so it began one Wednesday some fifteen years ago: I bought a card and gave it to Patricia. There was no special occasion. The card was just an expression of how much I loved her and how much I was thinking about her. I picked Wednesday for no special reason other than it was middle of the week.

Since that day, I have never missed a Wednesday—Patricia has received a card from me every Wednesday, every week, every month, every year.

The purchase of the card each week in not done out of habit. It is my romantic mission each week to find the right card. At times, my search takes me to many different card stores to find that perfect offering. I have been known to spend a considerable amount of time in front of the card displays, reading up to a dozen different cards before I choose the right one. The picture and the words in the card must have specific meaning to me and must remind me in some way of Patricia and our life together. The card needs to evoke an emotion in me. I know that if a card brings a tear of happiness to my eyes, I have found the right one.

Patricia awakens each Wednesday morning to find her card, and even though she knows it will be there, she still lights up with excitement when she tears open the envelope and reads what is inside. And I still get just as excited giving each card to her.

At the foot of our bed is a brass chest that is filled with all of the greeting cards Patricia has received from me over the past fifteen years, hundreds and hundreds of cards, each one full of just as much love as the next. I can only hope that our life together will last long enough for me to fill ten brass chests with my weekly messages of love, affection and most of all thanks for the joy Patricia has brought to my life.

David A. Manzi

Forever Young

As long as one can admire and love, then one is young forever.

Pablo Casals

Something very strange has happened over the course of my twenty-six-year marriage. My parents have grown older. Our children are ready to leave the nest. But I have not aged. I know the years have passed because I can feel the losses. Gone are the size-twelve jeans and platform shoes. Gone is the eager face of a young girl ready to meet any challenge. But somehow, like Tinkerbell, I have been suspended in time. Because in the eyes and soul of my husband ... I am still, and will always be ... eighteen, as carefree and whimsical as the day we met.

He still calls me his "cutie". He takes me to scary movies, where we sit in a theater filled with screaming teenagers. We hold hands and share popcorn, just as we did so many years ago. We still chase fire engines and eat at diners and listen to sixties rock and roll.

"You would look good in that," he says, pointing to a beautiful girl walking in the mall. She has blond hair flowing down the middle of her back and is wearing a tank top and short-shorts. Did I mention she's about twenty? I want to laugh out loud, but I know better. He's serious.

Every July, he takes me to the country fair. On a hot summer night, we stroll across dusty fairgrounds taking in the sights and sounds. We eat corn on the cob, and he buys me tacky souvenirs. Pitchmen call out to us from booths along the midway. He throws darts at a board of balloons, trying year after year to win the giant stuffed bear. While others our age are stopping to rest on benches, we're riding the rides. Up, down and around, we're holding on tight as the creaking wheels of the roller coaster make their final loop. As the evening hours come to an end, we're at our favorite place, high on top of the Ferris wheel, sharing pink cotton candy and looking out at a sea of colorful neon lights below.

Sometimes I wonder if he realizes that I have passed four decades. That the children I bore could have children of their own. Doesn't he notice the beginning gray hairs? The lines around my eyes? Does he sense my insecurities? Hear my knees crack when I bend? I watch him ...watching me ...with young playful eyes, and know that he does not.

In four more decades, I often wonder where we will be. I know we'll be together, but where? In a retirement home? Living with our children? Somehow, these images do not fit. Only one picture is constant and clear. I close my eyes and look far into the future ...and I see us ...an old man and his cutie. I have white hair. His face is wrinkled. We are not sitting in front of a building watching the world go by. Instead we are high atop a Ferris wheel, holding hands and sharing pink cotton candy under a July moon.

Shari Cohen

I Still Love You

Twelve feet or so off the east edge of State Road 103, which runs north-south through the town of Newbury, New Hampshire (population fifteen hundred, more or less), there sits a squat brown-gray slab of rock roughly the height of a man. Its southern face is flat, nearly smooth, at a billboard angle toward the traffic coming north.

About twenty-five years ago, across from the rock on the west side of the road, there sat a tidy white cedar-shingled house in whose backyard, as it is remembered, a dozen chickens pecked about. Their eggs made breakfasts (and a tiny sideline business) for a family named the Rules whose daughter Gretchen was pretty, smart, wistful and sixteen.

There was a boy—a shy boy, also wistful, whose name is forgotten today — who pined for Gretchen Rule. He cast about for ways to tell her or show her—without telling or showing himself — then hit upon the rock: "CHICKEN FARMER, I LOVE YOU," he wrote on it, in eight-inch-high, spray-painted letters, one moonlit, high-starred night—or so the story goes. And the girl saw and guessed the author (though it was only, really, a guess)—and the town and the passing motorists smiled, made their own guesses, and went on about their ways.

The message endured for years, though brambles grew up

to obscure it, and the letters, once so bold and white, began to fade.

Gretchen Rule went away to Harvard, then on to life. The boy, whoever he was—or is—became a man. The rock grew into a relic, a love note out of time.

One night—ten, perhaps twelve years ago (no one saw it happen, and no one today can say for sure)—the brambles were cut away. And the message was repainted and renewed: "CHICKEN FARMER, I STILL LOVE YOU."

The rock became a landmark. "It's your first left past Chicken Rock," the locals were wont to say. "Chicken", "love" and "farmer" were the first words one Newbury kindergartner—today a teenager—learned to read. Sunapee-bound skiers headed north from Boston spun tales of unrequited love. And every year or two, barely noticed, the letters would be freshened and the brambles cut away.

Then, late last April, an unknown caller complained of "graffiti" to the Newbury office of the New Hampshire Department of Transportation. By nightfall the same day, a three-foot square of rust-colored primer was all that was left of a shy boy's long-ago love. The *Concord Monitor* offered its requiem: "Love Message to Chicken Farmer Is No More."

A week passed. Then, with the coming of dawn on April 30, a Wednesday, the new sun rose on New Hampshire's stubbornest love: "CHICKEN FARMER, I STILL LOVE YOU."

The same message, the same eight-inch letters. But bolder this time: thicker-lettered, and painted rather than sprayed.

In Newbury the townspeople, inspired now as never before, took steps to ensure that their landmark would live on. "A Petition for Status Quo to the State of New Hampshire Department of Transportation," they called it and filled it with signatures—192 signers in the space of a day. The DOT responded with a letter. The Chicken Rock's message would be forever safe.

And somewhere, surely, a shy, fortyish man must have smiled.

Geoffrey Douglas

Just a Tuesday

One blustery Tuesday in the early 1950s, a good friend of ours stopped in to tell us of the birth of his new daughter. He asked my husband, Harold, to ride with him to the hospital. They said I should expect them back for supper.

The two stopped at the florist to pick out a pot of tulips for the new mother, and it occurred to my love to bring his wife tulips, too. He also decided to buy two dozen red roses for good measure and charged everything to our account, which I keep open for funerals, et cetera. (I guess he thought this was an et cetera.)

After the hospital visit, they stopped at Gatto's Inn for a quick beer, taking the flowers in with them so that they wouldn't wilt in the car. One thing led to another and soon the regulars at the bar were inquiring about the red roses and tulips. Caught off guard and a little embarrassed, Harold replied, "They're my Dot's anniversary gift."

But it was not our anniversary nor my birthday. Just a Tuesday. One regular after another sent my husband and his friend a drink in celebration of his anniversary. Around 9:30, the regulars ribbed him for celebrating alone. "My wife was tied up until ten o'clock," he replied. "She's joining me here for a steak dinner in the Pine Room." He promptly ordered steak dinners, not only for us, but for all the bar regulars. The innkeeper gladly set the banquet room for eighteen.

Now the problem arose—how to get me there. It was not my favorite spot, the hour was late, he had missed supper, and I was probably worried and cross.

My beloved called a taxi and told the driver, who was a friend, to go to Dublin, tell Dot he was in trouble at Gatto's, and come at once. I was in my nightgown and housecoat with my hair up in ugly metal curlers when the taxi driver pulled in. I threw on a coat, pulled my boots over my slippers and rushed out.

The bar was empty when we arrived at Gatto's. "My God," I said. "It must be something really serious." A waitress led me into the darkened banquet room. "Surprise! Surprise!" Harold stood up and pulled out my chair. He kissed my cheek and whispered, "I'll explain later." You just bet he would.

Well, roses are roses, and steak is steak, and married life is for better or worse. I smelled the roses, smiled at my strange guests and kicked my husband soundly under the table. I had never dined with these people before and probably never would again, yet I knew their wishes were sincere. I even danced the "Anniversary Waltz" in my nightclothes and boots to celebrate the fact that it was just a Tuesday.

Dorothy Walker

"Alright, Harold, what did you do?"

Reprinted by permission of Dave Carpenter.

The Loving Compliment

The applause of a single human being is of great consequence.

Samuel Johnson

Nearly every one of us is starving to be appreciated, to be the recipient of that most supreme compliment—that we are loved. We need others to recognize our strengths or sometimes just to prop us up in the places where we tend to lean a little. Honest compliments are simple and cost nothing to give, but we must not underestimate their worth.

Mark Twain once said he could go for two months on a good compliment. The most loving compliment I've ever heard of was given by Joseph Choate, former ambassador to Great Britain. When asked who he would like to be if he could come back to earth again after he died, he replied without an instant's hesitation, "Mrs. Choate's second husband."

Leo Buscaglia

My Home Is Where My Husband Is

"I took my wedding vows seriously," Dame Margot Fonteyn gently explained near the end of her accomplished life. "For richer, for poorer, in sickness and in health." When the prima ballerina of Britain's Royal Ballet married the darkly handsome Panamanian diplomat Roberto Arias in 1955, however, she had no idea how her affections would be tested.

Fonteyn was an eighteen-year-old dancer and Arias a nineteen-year-old law student when they met at a party in Cambridge, England, in 1937. The next morning, "I got up and I walked across the room and had this really strange sensation," Fonteyn later recalled. "Then it came into my mind about people walking on air when they're in love." For the following two summers, they would rendezvous in that university town, taking long walks beside the river where the reticent boy known as Tito "did manage to tell me that his father had been the president of Panama". But then, in 1939, World War Ⅱ broke out, Tito was called home and she did not see him again for fourteen years.

Fonteyn, the daughter of the chief engineer of the British Cigarette Company and a half-Brazilian mother, went on to a life of glamour and adulation. There were sailing parties with Laurence Olivier, dinners with David Niven and dressing rooms filled with flowers. Then, in New York City in 1953, during a highly acclaimed tour with the Royal Ballet at the old Metropolitan Opera House, an assistant handed Fonteyn the card of a gentleman caller. "Roberto E. Arias," it read, "Ambassador for Panama to the United Nations." A now portly Tito, separated from his wife of six years and the father of three young children, was ushered into her dressing room. "He sat down on the settee, not saying anything much," Fonteyn remembered. "He just sort of stared at me." The next day he arrived for breakfast at her hotel, where, "Suddenly he said, 'You know, you're going to marry me and be very happy.'" Fonteyn's response: "You're crazy."

But Arias showered her with roses, diamonds and a mink coat, and pursued her on stops along her U. S. tour. Ultimately, Fonteyn wrote in a 1976 autobiography, her ardent suitor "rescued the human heart trapped inside the ballerina". On February 6, 1955, she married him in the Panamanian consulate in Paris amid an explosion of flashbulbs.

On their return from a honeymoon in the Bahamas, Arias immediately took up his new post as Panama's ambassador to Great Britain. Fonteyn, who maintained a grueling performance schedule, took on the additional role of ambassador's wife. "For the first time in my life," she would later say, "I knew who I was."

And wherever in the world Fonteyn danced, there were always red roses waiting from her husband. Then, on June 8, 1964, while she was rehearsing in England, came news of the event that would change their world forever: Arias, at the end of a political campaign in Panama, had been shot five times by a rival and was paralyzed from the neck down.

A shaken Fonteyn flew to his bedside and later helped nurse him through a near-fatal 108-degree fever. "She quite literally kept him alive," says close friend, dancer Joy Williams Brown. "She put the will back into him that he was going to pull through." Eight months after the shooting, as his wife took forty-three curtain calls after dancing *Romeo and Juliet* in London, Arias watched from a stretcher in the wings.

Throughout her many performances in the following years—and a renowned stage partnership with Rudolf Nureyev — Fonteyn's primary concern remained her husband, who had lost none of his sparkling intelligence in the attack. Others saw the tragedy as a cross to bear, but not Fonteyn. "I feel it's rather a fair division," she said. "He thinks. I move." When a friend wondered how she could manage it all, Fonteyn had a simple answer. "You see," she said, "I love him."

In 1980, at age sixty, Fonteyn finally retired, and the couple settled into the simple, four-room house with a corrugated metal roof that they had built on a ranch outside Panama City. There, with her five beloved dogs and four hundred head of cattle, Fonteyn was content to dote on Arias. In those years, she later told a reporter, "I once asked my husband, 'Who shall I take care of when you're gone?'" There was little time to answer the question. In 1991, Fonteyn, at the age of seventy-one, succumbed to bone cancer, less than two years after Arias had died of colon cancer. In the end it all seemed fitting. During a triumphal performance of *Swan Lake* in New York City nearly two decades earlier, a reporter had asked Fonteyn where she made her home. "My home," she replied, "is where my husband is."

People magazine

Baby, You Are ...

My sunny sky,
my favorite high,
my bed so warm,
my port in a storm,
my sweetest gift,
my emotional lift,
my best friend
until the end,
my inspiration,
my destination,
my shining light,
my day and night,
my heart healer,
my anger chiller,
my pain reliever,
my spring fever,
my gem so rare,
my answered prayer,
my heart and soul,
my life made whole,
my merry-go-'round,
my "up" when I'm down,

my best chance,
my last dance,
my best shot,
my sweet kumquat,
my energizer,
my appetizer,
my morning sun,
my evening fun,
my dancing partner,
my heart's gardener,
my source of laughter,
my everafter,
my heaven sent,
for who I'm meant,
my burning fire,
my greatest desire,
my soul mate,
my sweet fate,
my dream lover,
my "before all others,"
my confidence,
my common sense,
my reason why
until I die.

Just in case you didn't know.

David L. Weatherford

On Our Twentieth Wedding Anniversary

There is only one serious question. And that is: ...how to make love stay?

Tim Robbins

I smile when someone defines bigamy as having one spouse too many and monogamy as being the same thing. Instead, I think of marriage as a lifetime communication adventure. It has certainly been that with my husband, Marty.

Marty and I have been together for over twenty full, rich years.

He is, I would say with complete affection, just an ordinary kind of guy, in a very down-to-earth way. For instance, recently I told Marty I was thinking of taking up painting. He glanced at me, and without missing a beat, asked: "Semigloss or latex?"

That's Marty.

I remember in the months before our twentieth wedding anniversary, I began to think about our marriage and wonder if, indeed, it was all it should be. Nothing was wrong, mind you. But there just didn't seem to be any "newness" in our relationship anymore. I remembered the long-ago magic of being in a new relationship — the excitement of meeting someone you didn't know anything about and slowly discovering all the adorable details of his personality; the joy of finding out what you had in common; the first date, the first touch, the first kiss, the first snuggle, the first *everything*.

One morning, my well-worn husband and I were up early taking our customary walk of about four miles. Even though the scenery was beautiful, my mind was elsewhere. I was thinking about all the things that seemed to be missing after twenty years of marriage, and if, indeed, I was missing out on new things I should be experiencing. We had just reached the two-mile point in our walk, a shady spot where two cedar trees create a natural secluded private arch above us. And as we were about to turn around, my husband reached over, took me in his arms and kissed me.

I was so busy thinking about all the "new" things I was missing out on, his kiss totally caught me by surprise.

And there in the middle of a hot, sticky, sweaty, exercise-panting kiss, I was suddenly flooded with an awareness of the cumulative gifts of twenty years of living with Marty. We had comforted each other through the deaths of three parents and two brothers. We had seen his son graduate from Virginia Tech. We had camped from Nova Scotia to the Canadian Rockies. We had shared songs with my family in Ireland one Fourth of July, and we had hiked along the Bay in Anchorage, Alaska. We had shared a lot of potatoes, a lot of sunrises and a lot of life.

I did not have this special level of sharing with any other human being — only with my husband. And right now, we *were* sharing something new. A walk, a sweet, safe, comfortable companionship that offered new love each day, and a kiss that had never happened before and would never happen again. This moment *was* new, as each moment always would be.

That day, our twentieth anniversary took on a completely different meaning, one that has stayed with me every day since then — inside our oldest commitments can lie our newest celebrations.

Maggie Bedrosian

CLOSE TO HOME JOHN McPHERSON

Smile at the One You Love

Mother Teresa often gives people unexpected advice. When a group of Americans, many in the teaching profession, visited her in Calcutta, they asked her for some advice to take home to their families.

"Smile at your wives," she told them, "Smile at your husbands."

Thinking that perhaps the counsel was simplistic, coming from an unmarried person, one of them asked, "Are you married?"

"Yes," she replied, to their surprise, "and I find it hard sometimes to smile at Jesus. He can be very demanding."

Eileen Egan

Above All, Love

Flowers grow out of dark moments.

Corita Kent

Real-life death scenes aren't like the movies. My husband, too tall for a regulation bed, lay with his feet sticking out of the covers. I stood clinging to his toes as though that would save his life. I clung so that if I failed to save him from falling off the cliff of the present, of the here and now, we'd go together. That's how it was in the nether-world of the intensive care unit where a freak accident had brought my husband to lie connected to tubes and things that went beep in the night.

It seemed that the entire world had turned into night. Cold and black. No place you'd volunteer to enter. Doctors tried to be kind. Their eyes said: "This is out of our hands. There's nothing more we can do." Their eyes asked: "Are you strong enough for this?" The surprise was that their eyes also asked, "Are we?" A nurse with a soft Jamaican lilt placed a pink blanket over my shoulders. Someone whispered, "It's just a matter of minutes."

Just a matter of minutes of tell each other anything we had ever forgotten to say. Just a few minutes to take an accounting of our days together:Had we loved well enough?

It is not unusual for one experiencing massive internal bleeding to be as my husband was—pain-free and completely conscious. I have been told since that this is a good way to die. Perhaps this is true in the sense that we were able to speak to each other,to stare into each other's eyes. To be intensely present. I am too young to regard any way as a "good"way to die. But that night I began to learn that there are good ways to live.

Suddenly in the cold, outer-space atmosphere of that room, it seemed so foolish that, like many overcommitted, overworked women, I had spent so much time fussing about priorities. When you look in the face of death, what becomes perfectly clear and suddenly simple is that there is only one priority. And that is love.

The gift for my husband and me in that time of terror and heartbreak in intensive care was that our love was revealed to us. Moments of darkness provide sharp and astounding clarity. The gift was the realization that we did not have to make up for lost time. We knew that we had loved each other with a focus and fire that had fueled our days. We had set about lives together to make certain that they would be just that — together. Our offices were within walking distance of our home so that we could eat three meals a day in each other's company. We had slept in the same bed each night, even when there had been a terrible fight and one of us would have preferred the solitary comfort of another room. In sleep there is forgiveness—and an arm or leg that would reach out to find solace in touch.

Ours had not been a romance full of extravagant gifts,

Rice Pudding

Sheila stomped into the staff room, her uniform bespattered with someone's dinner. "I don't know how you do it!" She fumed to Helen, the nurse supervising the evening shift. Sheila slumped into a chair and looked morosely at her crumpled lunch bag. "Mrs. Svoboda just threw her tray at me again, and she's so agitated I don't know how I'll be able to clean her up before bed. Why don't you have so much trouble with her?"

Helen smiled sympathetically. "I've had my share of rough nights with her, too. But I've been here longer and, of course, I knew her husband."

"Yeah, Troy. I've heard about him. It's about the only word I can understand when she gets going."

Helen looked quietly at the young nursing student. How could she explain what she saw beneath the aging exteriors of the nursing home residents they cared for? Sheila was only here for the summer. Was that enough time to learn to love the unlovable?

"Sheila," she began hesitantly. "I know it's hard to work with people like Mrs. Svoboda. She's rude, uncooperative and packs a mean left hook." Sheila smiled ruefully. "But there's more to her than the dementia you see every day." Helen got up to pour another cup of coffee. "I'd like to tell you about when I first met the Svobodas."

"When Mrs. Svoboda was admitted she wasn't as bad as she is now, but she was still pretty spicy. She used to give me grief over the smallest things — her tea wasn't hot enough, her bed wasn't made up right. On her bad days she'd accuse us all of stealing her things. I had no patience with her, until one day her husband happened to be there during bath time. I was gearing up for the usual fight with her when he asked if he could help. 'Sure,' I said gratefully. She was okay until I started lowering the lift into the tub. Good thing the safety restraints were on because she began kicking and screaming.

"I began washing her quickly, anxious to get it over with, when Troy laid his hand on my arm. 'Give her a moment to get used to the water,' he asked. Then he began talking softly in Russian. After a few moments she became calm and seemed to listen to him. Very gently, he took the cloth and soap from me and washed each of her hands. Then slowly and carefully, he washed her arms and shoulders, working his way over the wrinkled, sallow skin. Each touch was a caress, each movement a promise, and I suddenly became aware that I was intruding on a rare moment of intimacy. After a while, she closed her eyes and relaxed into the warm water. 'My beautiful Nadja,' the old man murmured. 'You are so beautiful.' To my surprise, Mrs. Svoboda opened her eyes and murmured back, 'My beautiful Troy.' Even more astonishing, she had tears in her eyes!

"Mr. Svoboda reclined the lift and released her hair into the water. The old woman sighed with pleasure as he stroked and lathered and rinsed. Then, he kissed her temple. 'All done, my beauty. Time to get out.'

"I had to stay with them, even though they didn't need

me. But I'd caught a glimpse of the well-loved woman who hid deep within the ruin of old age. I'd never thought of her that way before. I'd never even learned her first name."

Sheila was quiet as she stirred her yogurt without looking up. Helen took a deep breath and continued her story.

"Mrs. Svoboda stayed calm that whole afternoon. Her husband helped me dress her and feed her lunch. She complained about the food and at one point knocked over her soup. Mr. Svoboda patiently cleaned it up and waited until her tantrum was over. Then he slowly fed her the rest of her meal and talked to her until she was ready to go to bed.

"I was concerned about the old man. He looked completely exhausted. I asked him why he insisted on doing so much himself when we were paid to do it. He turned to me and said simply, 'Because I love her.'

" 'But you're wearing yourself out,' "I answered.

" 'You don't understand,' he continued. 'We've been married for almost forty-nine years. When we started out, life on the farm was harder than you can imagine. The drought killed our crops, and there wasn't enough pasture for the cattle. Our children were small, and I didn't know how we were going to survive the winter. I felt so helpless, and it made me angry. I was very hard to live with that year. Nadja put up with my moods, and left me alone, but one night I blew up at the supper table. She'd made our favorite treat, rice pudding, and all I could think about was how much sugar and milk she'd used.'

" 'Suddenly, I just couldn't take it. I picked up my bowl and threw it against the wall, and stormed out to the barn. I don't know how long I stayed there, but around sundown, Nadja came out to find me. "Troy," she said, "you are not alone in your troubles. I promised to stand beside you through everything life brought our way. But if you won't let me, then you have to go." She had tears in her eyes, but her voice was firm. "You are not yourself right now, but when you are ready to be with us again, we are here." Then she kissed my cheek and walked back to the house.

" 'I stayed in the barn that night, and the next day I headed into town to look for a job. There was nothing, of course, but I kept looking. After about a week, I was ready to give up. I felt a complete failure, at farming, as a man. I started for home, not knowing if I'd be welcome, but I didn't have anywhere else to go. When she saw me coming down the lane, Nadja came out running, her apron strings flying. She threw her arms around me and I began to weep. I clung to her like a newborn baby. She just stroked my head and held me. Then we went in the house, as if nothing had ever happened.'

" 'If she could stay committed to me during my worst times, during the hardest times of our life, the least I can do is comfort her now. And remind her of the good times we had. We always smiled at each other when we ate rice pudding, and it's one of the few things she still remembers.' "

Helen was quiet. Suddenly Sheila pushed back her chair. "My break is over," she said, dabbing at the tears that rolled down her cheeks. "And I know an old lady who needs another dinner." She smiled at Helen. "If I ask them nicely, I'll bet the kitchen can rustle up a dish of rice pudding for her, too."

Roxanne Willems Snopek

Remember Africa?

Where the heart that doth not keep within its inmost core,
Some fond remembrance hidden deep, of days that are no more?

Ellen Howarth

"Who are you?" Frank demanded when Ruth walked into the room. She sighed and eased gently down on the bed next to him, folding his age-shrunken hand in hers. He recoiled from her uncertainly, fear widening his eyes.

"I'm Ruth, your wife," she said, forcing a polite smile and patting his hand.

His eyebrows shot upward as he bolted upright in bed. "Wife?" "We've been married forty years, Frank."

"No." Frank shook his head vigorously. "No, I don't remember you."

Ruth nodded and closed her eyes. It was a conversation they had had nearly every day during the past few months. The illness had not much weakened Frank's body, but his mind faded, day to day, like color from an oft-washed cloth.

"That's okay, dear," Ruth answered. "I love you whether

you know me or not. "She adjusted the pillow between his back and the wooden headboard, then straightened the covers around his waist. "Oh Frank, we've had so many wonderful years. We've sure had a good life together."

He smiled back at her tentatively, eyes still clouded in confusion. "Was I a good husband?"

she chuckled. "You devil," she said, pinching his cheek softly. "The best. You were always kind and gentle and lots of fun. Even now, you try, don't you?"

He nodded. Her words seemed to reassure him. He looked around the room, as if desperately searching for clues. "Our family ...?"

Ruth hesitated. "We never had children, Frank. We tried, but we couldn't. But we have so many friends and loved ones. You've lived eighty-two good, long years now. People have always loved you, Frank. And you've touched so many lives." "Hmmm."

He nodded, but his eyes kept that faraway gaze, unable to connect with any familiar faces. "Well, what did we do?"

"Well, mister, we worked. We worked hard and we built up your family business and we went to church and we enjoyed ourselves just fine. And we traveled all over the world."

"Oh?" His eyes danced, just a flicker of light. "Where?"

"Everywhere, Frank. We went to so many beautiful places. Do you remember Edinburgh, Frank? The castles and the countryside of Scotland? You loved how green it was, even when we were freezing. And you wore this silly plaid cap that made me laugh." She searched his eyes, but the light had passed.

Frank slipped back down on the pillow and stared at the ceiling. His profile was nearly the same as her first sight of him forty years earlier, as he stood in her doorway, coming to pick her up for a ride to church camp. When she opened that door, his eyes had grown wide with interest, and he gave her that devilish grin she'd come to love so much. Now his mouth was drawn tight, grim with irritation.

"And Japan. Remember Tokyo, Frank? Remember the lights and those crowded streets and the temples? How you bought all those tiny mechanical toys and the radio as small as your fingernail?"

She held up his hand to show him, but his eyes were squeezed tight, his mind fruitlessly searching for his memories. He shook his head, a frown deepening on his face.

A moment passed. He blinked and stared at her again, at the face he had awakened to every morning for four decades.

His eyes narrowed. "Who are you?" He asked, his voice edged with fear.

She drew a long, steady breath, looking into his bewildered eyes. "Africa, Frank," she said slowly. She took his hand back, gripping it tightly. "Do you remember our travels through Africa?"

"Africa," he repeated quietly.

"We saw animals," she ventured softly.

"Lions," he answered. She sat silently, waiting.

"We saw lions," he said, pulling himself up slowly beside her. "We sat in the Land Rover and the lions were surrounding us, coming right up to us. And there were elephants and a huge one with the huge tusk that came crashing out of the bush right at us ..."

Ruth nodded, smiling back at him.

"You were there with me. You were sitting next to me." His eyes were clearing, shining; she could feel the tears begin to well in her own.

"And the flamingos," he said, his voice rising. "We stood at the edge of the lake and watched them fly. There were so many of them, it was just like a pink cloud rising up from the water."

His words slowed, and his eyes closed.

"Frank ..." she said, and he sat still, not moving, not answering.

"Frank, remember the night in Uganda, when the children sang to us? We were in that little village near the river ..."

"The children! Yes," he said, opening his eyes again. "They were so young, so sweet ..."

"And their round little faces all lit up ..."

" ...they were all holding candles! And afterward, we ate in that man's home, with the dirt floor. We sat in the candlelight, and they brought us the food in those huge black bowls ...."

"Remember how strange that food looked?"

Frank laughed, then groaned. "We didn't know if it was raw, or worms, or what. And, and ...were we with missionaries?"

She nodded. "Yes, we were visiting missionaries who had a church in the village."

"Yes, yes," he said. "I can see them now. And the missionary told us how he prayed before he ate. He prayed, 'Lord, I'll put it down if you keep it down!'"

As they laughed, she took in every detail—the blueness of his eyes, the curve of his cheekbones, the wrinkles surrounding his smile.

Then Frank looked toward the window, where sunlight streamed in through a crack in the curtains. "Ruth," he asked worriedly, "why am I in bed so late this morning?"

"You're not well today, Frank."

"I am feeling tired," he said, yawning. He slid back down onto his pillow, smiling dreamily up at her. "Ruth, what were those waterfalls?"

"Victoria Falls?"

"Yes, Victoria Falls. Ruth, I remember standing there, feeling the spray from the falls, and you were scared and holding onto my arm so tight. And you said it was the most beautiful sight you had ever seen. And I told you no, you were still more beautiful to me."

He curled up and kissed her softly on the cheek. She was shaking, holding as tight to his arm as she had at the edge of the falls.

"And you still are beautiful."

"You are something else, mister," she laughed.

"I love you, Ruth."

"And I love you, Frank."

His eyes were blinking, fading.

"Why don't you dream about those waterfalls?" Ruth said. "I'll be right here."

With that, he gave a sigh and relaxed, his sparse gray hair flattening against the pillow.

Ruth pulled the covers up around his chest and kissed him, listening to the rise and fall of his breathing. His mind was drifting back in the fog, away from her and the world they had shared. When he woke, he would again recoil from her. And she knew the sight of his face and the warmth of his skin were a gift, a brief glimpse too soon lost to memory. Someday, even the vast continent would not have the power to bring him back to her.

Jo Beth McDaniel

A Sign of His Love

It never occurred to me that our airline tickets were to be round-trip for me and one-way for Don. We were on our way to Houston for open heart surgery, Don's third operation. But he was otherwise healthy and robust, and only sixty-one years old. His doctor felt confident that he would come through this valve replacement just fine. Others had survived two or more heart operations. Don would, too.

The day of the operation came. A very long day. Six hours into the procedure, the doctor came out to tell me that they could not get Don off the heart-lung machine. His heart would not kick back in. A left-ventricle assist was put in. After two days with this implanted machine, it had to be removed. He remained in a coma for five days on every conceivable life support. The morning that the doctors shook their heads and said it looked like we were losing the battle, I went in at the usual time, held his hand and told him how much I loved him, that I knew he was struggling to come back, but I needed to release him to do whatever he needed to do. "I'll always love you," I said. "I want you to know that if you have to go. I'll be all right." That night he died.

Back home to Denver—my loving brother accompanied me. My children came for the funeral, offering wonderful, loving support. Still, I was totally lost. I had found Don again, after parting from him in college thirty years ago, each of us leading our own lives, me in Houston, Don in Denver. I was divorced, and running across a letter and picture of this college sweetheart, I felt compelled to write him. A "hello across thirty years". I found his name in the Denver phone book and sent the letter. And I held my breath. He replied, and he told me his wife had just died two months prior to my letter. We corresponded and finally decided to meet again. What a reunion. We fell into the same easy, comfortable love we had known so many years ago. We married in April, two years after meeting again. I moved to Denver. We had six gentle, wonderful years together. We had planned on many, many more.

It was the day before the funeral and I was sitting out on my back patio, feeling like my life had ended too. More than anything, I wanted assurance that Don was okay now, that he was out of pain, at peace and that his spirit would always be near at hand. "Show me," I pleaded. "Give me a sign, please."

Don had planted a rosebush for me that summer that was supposed to bear yellow roses. He had always called me his "yellow rose of Texas". The plant had so far been disappointing as it had not produced one bud in three months. Now my gaze landed on that rosebush. Startled, not believing what I was seeing, I got up and went closer for a better look. One stem had many perfect buds on it, just opening. There were six perfect yellow buds, one for each year of our union. Tears welled in my eyes as I whispered a "thank you". A perfect yellow rosebud rested in Don's hands thc next day at his funeral.

Patricia Forbes

The Waiting

Another day had passed. Another day of waiting. I sat staring at a wall-mounted TV in the small dark room. Attractive wallpaper and drapes hid in the shadows. The lone window, facing a brick wall, was cheerless in daylight and offered nothing at night. The medicinal and disinfectant smells no longer distinguished themselves. When had I stopped noticing them?

Visiting hours were over for another night. How many more nights? How much longer would I have to watch my Jerry, who was both my husband and my best friend, struggle against the merciless disease that was destroying us?

As I listened to his pattern of shallow gasps, I absently combed my hair with my fingers and wondered how our life together could end here. Almost twenty-four years ago, I had promised God I would never leave Jerry until one of us died. The eighteen-year-old playing bride in a white dress had thought death only happened to those who allowed it to happen. The tired forty-two-year-old was now praying that God would soon release her weary husband from his suffering. How could someone so healthy and energetic have fallen victim to this monster of an illness? Lymphoma. Most of our family and friends had never even heard of it.

I shifted in the hide-a-bed chair I had slept in for the last month. The room before this one had a recliner. The ICU waiting area, where I had earlier spent three nights, was obviously designed to discourage waiting. It had padded chairs with wooden arms. It had been impossible to combine three chairs for a bed. It was good to be back on 4th West, where our nurses understood my waiting.

Hearing the tap-tap of high heels fade to soft crepe echoes, I opened the door to the hallway just to convince myself that there was still a world out there. The other times here had been different. We had still had some hope for another remission, or even a cure. The other times we had been able to talk, to laugh, and to encourage each other. More than a month had now passed since he had spoken or followed me around the room with his eyes. He could no longer even let me know that he heard or understood my whispers:

"Sweetheart, you're still the most important person in the world to me."

"I won't leave you. I promise."

"If you don't see me, I'm in a chair or in the hall or in the bathroom. I'll be right back."

"You don't have to keep fighting for me. I know you're tired. It will be okay."

"I won't leave you. I promise."

But a vacant stare had replaced the twinkle in those brown eyes. Waiting. The waiting was over for the family across the hall. A stroke victim, seventy-eight, had lain still and silent in her bed for weeks. Her "No Code" status had been posted so that no heroic measures would be taken to further traumatize her passing. Tonight a good mother who had lived a long and fulfilling life had slipped quietly away. However, her children, children-in-law, and grandchildren had been anything but quiet. Their wailing stampede to and from the waiting area had sent nurses scurrying to dose the doors of other patients. "Oh, no!" "She's dead!" "Oh, no!" "Go get John!" "Go get Frank!" "Oh, no, no!" How could they have so little concern for those of us still waiting? Waiting.

Trying to escape their hysteria, I had turned up the television volume and phoned my closest friend.

"Betty, talk to me. Tell me what you did today. Start talking and don't stop until I tell you to." Betty has always been a better friend than I deserve. Without a question, she began and continued until her calm voice slowed the pounding in my chest.

Still waiting, I tried to think. I tried to plan. What if I couldn't handle that inevitable moment? Could I get a promise from our nurses? "Please help me if you are here when it happens. I think I can be calm, but, if I can't, lock me in a bathroom or stuff a towel in my mouth. If I lose all dignity, please don't let me upset others."

Restless and fighting the constant worry over our children and their pain, I sought a temporary escape. A walk to the vending machine would take me to a south window. A real window that would allow me a glimpse of streetlights, traffic, people, a distant shopping center — the life we used to live. I whispered to Jerry that I was going for a Pepsi.

Looking out into the night, I ached for my girls. My mother, who should have been enjoying bus trips with other senior citizens, was managing our home. Carol, twenty-two years old, had dropped out of college. She was making her own decisions, and some of them troubled me. Mary, in fifth grade, was truly her father's child in looks and interests, and she missed the attention he had always shown her. I had neglected her during much of Jerry's illness, but especially in the past six months. Our spirited little elf was having a problem at school, but I was here, waiting, and she was there. She was only ten. I would have her for a long time. Surely I would have time to make it up to her. Surely.

Sighing heavily, I turned away from the window to see a young woman, short, sandy-haired and smiling. Her arms were full with a canvas tote, a purse, and a brown paper grocery bag. Clearly, she had spent the day with a patient.

She pressed the elevator call button and faced me. "Well, I'm going home."

My self-pity began to overwhelm me. She would be going home to her husband and children. She would be planning for Thanksgiving next week. She had seen the leaves change color this year. And, after spending one day in the hospital, she thought she was tired. It was just too much to bear. I felt so helpless and exhausted that I couldn't just smile and nod. I had to tell her, "I haven't been home for more than six weeks."

She walked forward, shifted her bags, tilted her head, and asked me, "What's wrong?"

"My husband is dying." She immediately put her free arm around me and held me as my tears spilled. Over her shoulder I could see doors parting. A soft *ding* sounded. "Your elevator." I motioned.

She released me and looked into my eyes. "Never mind. Is there anything I can do for you? Is there anything you need?"

I shook my head and sent her on her way.

And wherever you are, dear nameless, faceless stranger, I want to thank you. How could I have said I needed nothing? The hug you gave me was exactly what I needed. Your comfort renewed me for my last two days of waiting.

Ann W. Compton

The Angel's Gift

There is a land of the living and a land of the dead, and the bridge is love.

Thornton Wilder

Gretchen and her husband, Fred, had had a long and happy marriage, but Fred had recently died. And although Gretchen had a son and four grandchildren who loved her very much, one does not easily recover from such a momentous loss.

During the first few months, Gretchen had been numb with grief and unable to weep. But she had progressed beyond the initial shock stage, and now, it seemed, crying was all she did. "I was beginning to dread meeting anyone," she recalls, "because I was so afraid that I would burst into tears in the middle of an ordinary conversation." People had been very kind, but Gretchen didn't want anyone pitying her and she didn't want her sorrow to make others uncomfortable.

On this Sunday, Gretchen went to church by herself and selected an empty pew. She saw no familiar faces, and she was relieved. At least if her anguish threatened to overwhelm her, she could slip out quietly.

As she sat in the pew, she thought again of Fred, and desolation and grief swept in waves across her spirit. "I could hardly keep from crying out," she says. It was hard to endure such continuous mourning. Would it ever end? In another moment, she was going to weep ...

Suddenly, a small boy entered the pew and sat next to Gretchen. She eyed him through her tears. He had light-brown hair, was neatly dressed in a little brown suit and appeared to be about six years old. And he was looking up at her in the most familiar way, smiling as if he knew her.

It was peculiar. Children rarely attended church alone in this particular congregation, especially at such an early hour. Where could his family be? Even stranger was the fact that, although the youngster had picked up the church prayer book to read, he kept edging toward Gretchen. "He moved nearer and nearer, very casually. He would read, then look up, catch my eye and beam. His whole attitude made it clear that he had come to keep me company. "What a darling child!

As the little boy snuggled close to Gretchen, something else began to happen. She felt her heart lighten. Somehow, although she hadn't believed such a thing would ever happen again she began to feel, yes, happy. It was only a fleeting emotion, like a brief little kiss, but she felt it.

And she would be happy again. She knew it now without question. "A time to mourn and a time to dance ..." Gretchen was still very much in mourning but the love and sweetness in the little boy's face had given her a glimpse of a better time yet to come.

But who was this child? Gretchen looked down at him, and again he smiled at her in that intimate and penetrating manner. She must know him ... Why else would he be behaving this way? Of course. He was probably the son of a younger neighbor or friend who, aware of Gretchen's loss and seeing her sitting alone, had sent her little boy up to share the pew. Gretchen would have to thank his parents for their thoughtfulness. She would watch where the child went after the service.

As the service ended, Gretchen and the boy left the pew and headed for the front door. There were people around, but not a huge crowd, and the child was right next to Gretchen. "What is your name?" She asked him. "Do I know your mother?"

But instead of answering, he looked up at her for one last smile. And then, as Gretchen's eyes scanned the crowd to find someone searching for him, the child vanished. He was there—and then simply wasn't. Gretchen didn't see him go, but when she glanced down, the spot next to her was vacant.

"I kept looking for him among the people until everyone had left, but I never saw him again, nor did I meet anyone who knew him or had sent him."

But after that Sunday, Gretchen never felt quite so alone again. Gradually the truth seemed to come upon her—that an ordinary child, no matter how charming, would not have been able to lift her spirits in that mysterious and welcome way. Instead, the child had been sent by someone who understood her suffering and was reaching out to comfort and heal her. Perhaps it was Fred.

Joan Wester Anderson

Love After Divorce

When you look for the good in others, you discover the best in yourself.

Martin Walsh

He was stretched out in the casket with small metal seagull silhouettes adorning the sides. Flowers in a myriad of colors covered the coffin and filled the surrounding walls. There were banners with"Rest in Peace" and "In Sympathy" draped across the stands of blooms. The conflicting fragrances of the flowers and a warm roomful of people added to the heavy feeling of hushed anticipation. Death's recognition created a surrealistic picture.

The service was about to begin, and the organ's melancholy music faded away. Several relatives had taken the podium to pay tribute, speak eloquently and tell vignettes of times past. Comments from the clergy elicited tears and chuckles. Then the minister asked for any additional impromptu remarks from the mourners.

At I rose and spoke to identify myself as "Bonnie, the deceased's ex-wife", I was aware of the "whoosh" of air as every head spun around to see me standing in the back of the room. No one was more surprised than I that I stood to speak! Although my senses were numbed by grief, I could feel the palpable tension created by the mourners' concerns for what I could or would say. They, too, had heard stories of bitter and angry ex-spouses spewing forth a vitriolic eulogy in such a situation!

During our marriage, Greg and I had become intimate friends and had shared many rich experiences. The reasons and memories related to the divorce had become unimportant as we became even more companionable friends after the breakup.

I had recently suffered during a particularly painful emotional crisis, and Greg and his fiancée had become loyal supporters. We still owned property together, and the three of us worked and played in mutual cooperation, respect and fondness.

The minister had told the gathered friends and family about Greg's earlier years and his young-adult adventures. Then, in a ten-second duration of time, he had briskly referred to our sixteen-year marriage, and then went on to other memorializations. I simply could not let this moment go by without paying tribute to the richness and span of our shared time.

With a tear-stained face and with choking sobs, I spoke briefly but with love and affection of our history and association. I poked fun at our beloved Greg and how he liked to "innocently" stir things up between his fiancée and me. I assured them that he didn't get far, for we both knew well his impishness.

The multiples of staring eyes began to soften as they started to listen to my gentle words. Smiles began to form at the ends of pinched lips. I could see and feel the warmth and acceptance pouring out to me, and I was comforted by the affection that was renewed by those who began to recognize me after many years.

After the service, many of Greg's longtime friends and family came to me to extend hugs and kind words about my sharing of memories. For just a few moments, we were all taken back to our younger years and relationships so full of hope and glorious anticipation. It was a fitting memorial to a man far too full of youth and life to die so soon.

Genuine love doesn't have to suffer a fatality in a divorce. Our going our separate ways was right. But after the prerequisite time apart, we were able to come back together in a fondness that served us better than did our marriage. I am grateful for our willingness and ability to transcend the severance and to create something better. My publicly honoring Greg at his funeral was an affirmation of a truth I deeply believe in: Although the form of a relationship may change, the love doesn't ever have to die.

Bonnie Furman

The Dance

You don't get to choose how you're going to die, or when. You can only decide how you're going to live. Now.

Joan Baez

Dar and I loved to dance. It was probably the first thing we did together, long before we would share our lives. We grew up in a small Oregon mountain community where dances were held almost every Saturday night, sometimes at the Grange Hall, sometimes at the home of Nelson Nye. Nelson and his family loved music and dancing so much that they added a special room to their house, large enough to accommodate at least three sets of square dances. Once a month or more, they invited the entire community to a dance. Nelson played the fiddle and his daughter, Hope, played the piano while the rest of us danced.

In those days, the entire family went together—including the grandparents, the farmers and loggers, the schoolteachers and the store owner. We danced to songs such as "Golden Slippers" and "Red Wing", side-by-side with contemporary ones like "Red Sails in the Sunset" and "It's a Sin to Tell a Lie".

Smaller children always had a place to sleep among the coats, close at hand, when they tired. It was a family affair, one of the few entertainments in a small mountain town climbing slowly out of the Great Depression.

Dar was seventeen, and I was twelve, when we first danced. He was one of the best dancers on the floor, and so was I. We always jitterbugged. No slow dancing for us, nothing remotely romantic. Our fathers would stand along the wall and watch. They weren't friends. They didn't talk to each other, not even a casual conversation. Both good dancers themselves, they were proud of their kids. Every once in a while, Dar's dad would smile a little, shake his head and say, to no one in particular, but so my dad could hear, "Boy, my kid can sure dance."

My dad never blinked an eye; he acted like he'd never heard. But a while later he would say, to no one in particular, "That girl of mine can sure dance." And being of the old school, they never told us we were that good or had stirred that tiny bit of boastful rivalry along the wall.

Our dancing together stopped for five years while Dar was in the South Pacific in World War Ⅱ. During those five years, I grew up. When we met again, Dar was twenty-two, and I was almost eighteen. We began to date — and dance again.

This time it was for ourselves — finding our moves, our turns, our rhythms — adjusting, anticipating, enjoying. We were as good together as we remembered, and this time we added slow dancing to our repertoire.

For us, the metaphor fits. Life is a dance, a movement of rhythms, directions, stumbles, missteps, at times slow and precise, or fast and wild and joyous. We did all the steps.

Two nights before Dar died, the family was with us as they had been for several days — two sons and their wives and four of our eight grandchildren. We all ate dinner together, and Dar sat with us. He hadn't been able to eat for several weeks, but he enjoyed it all — told jokes, kidded the boys about their cribbage playing, played with two-year-old Jacob.

Afterward, while the girls were cleaning up the kitchen, I put on a Nat King Cole tape, *Unforgettable*. Dar took me in his arms, weak as he was, and we danced.

We held each other and danced and smiled. No tears for us. We were doing what we had loved to do for more than fifty years, and if fate had so ordained, would have gone on doing for fifty more. It was our last dance — forever unforgettable. I wouldn't have missed it for the world.

Thelda Bevens

Sarah's Last Request

I may have all knowledge and understand all secrets; I may have all the faith needed to move mountains—but if I have no love, I am nothing.

1 Cor. 13:2

Death lay heavy on Sarah. Her doctor, one of the few who made house calls, had just left her room when he told her husband, Frank, the inevitable news: "Sarah has only a few hours to live. If your children want to see her one last time, they need to come as quickly as possible. Frank, let me say it again: We are dealing with only a few hours. I'm so sorry. Call me if you need me." With those words burning in his mind, Frank feebly stuck out his hand to the doctor. "Thanks, Doc. I'll call you."

"A few hours," echoed through the canyons of Frank's mind as he watched the kind doctor drive away. Night was rapidly approaching as Frank moved swiftly, alone to the backyard. There with hunched shoulders and bowed head he wept from the depths of a broken heart. How would he live without Sarah? How would he manage without his companion?She had been such a splendid wife and mother. It was Sarah who had taken the children to church. It was Sarah who had been the rock in times of crisis. It was Sarah who had mended the children's bruises, scratches, sprained ankles and broken hearts. Her motherly kisses had mended many a childhood illness. It was Sarah who had made him a better man. When he was able to choke back his tears, he moved back into the house and asked his daughter to summon the other children who lived only short distances away. Within a brief period of time all of them had arrived, three daughters and two sons. "They're here, Sarah," Frank told her. "They're all here."

Sarah's breathing was more labored. Cancer had reduced the lovely, healthy woman to a mere skeleton, but her fighting spirit was still present. "Frank, I want to spend a few minutes with each of the children, alone," Sarah stated weakly. Frank moved quickly as he responded, "I'll get them now, Sarah."

Frank assembled the children, all in their twenties and thirties, in the long hall outside Sarah's bedroom. Each went in and closed the door to spend a little time alone with Mama. Sarah spoke lovingly to each of them, and as she spoke, she told each one how special he or she had been to her as a son or daughter. Each son, each daughter had a precious few minutes with that loving mother as life ebbed quickly away.

When Sarah completed her visit with the last child, the minister arrived. Frank greeted him at the door and ushered him to Sarah's bedside. Sarah and the pastor talked for a few minutes about her family, heaven, faith and lack of fear. She was ready to go on to heaven, but she hated to leave her family—especially Frank. At that point in time Sarah, Frank, the minister and the children held hands and prayed. Frank accompanied the pastor to the door, telling him, "It will be a little while, preacher. The doctor says it will be just a matter of hours now—short hours, I suspect."

When the minister had gone, Sarah whispered to her children in the room, "Get Daddy. I have talked to everybody but him." In a moment, the children cleared the bedroom, and Frank came back. When they were alone, Sarah slowly, surely, sincerely put forth her last request to her loving husband. "Frank, you have been a good husband and father. You have stuck by me through these last months of suffering, and I love you even more for it. However, there is one thing that is worrying me badly. You have never been to church with the children and me. I know you are a good man. I have asked each of the children to meet me in heaven because I want us to be together again as a family. You are the only one now that I am worried about. Frank, I cannot die without knowing that you have made your peace with God." Hot tears of love and compassion streamed down Sarah's cheeks.

Frank was a self-made man who operated his own little business. He was a no-nonsense person who worked long hours, and Frank had acquired his meager possessions the hard way. With five children to support and educate, he and Sarah had not accumulated much of the world's goods. Also, Frank was not much for emotionalism, and sometimes he felt that the church services were a bit emotional for him. In reality, he had never made much time for God.

"Frank," Sarah continued, "please tell me that you will be with me and the children in heaven. Please Frank, make your peace with God." Frank's heart melted with Sarah's kind words, and tears gushed from his eyes as the big man with the rough hands knelt slowly by her bed. Frank reached out, took Sarah's frail hand in his, and uttered a prayer of forgiveness and love that touched the heart of God.

Frank rose from his knees, sat on the edge of the bed, gently took the frail, small body of his precious wife in his arms and held her once more. They wept openly together, and from deep within Frank said, "I'll be there, Sarah. I'll meet you in heaven. We'll be a family again. Don't worry. I'll be there, Sarah. I promise. I promise."

"Now I can die in peace," Sarah whispered to him. Easily he laid her down on the bed and called the children into the room. Frank moved alone to the backyard to his favorite crying spot and purged his soul with tears once more. After that, he moved back to Sarah's room to be with the children for their death watch.

Sarah's breathing was lighter and lighter, and as she lay dying, Frank whispered in her ear, "I love you, Sarah, and I'll be there." Angels of mercy came and swept her away, and as Sarah passed from earth to heaven, she smiled.

Death lay heavy on Sarah, but she was at peace because the man she had loved for so many years had promised, "I'll be there, Sarah. I'll be there."

Ray L. Lundy

One More Kiss from Rose

The one thing we can never get enough of is love. And the one thing we never give enough of is love.

Henry Miller

Mr. Kenney returned to our unit of the hospital frequently. He was a retired executive, a widower, and cancer had taken its toll over the last three years. The cancer had metastasized from his colon to all of his vital organs. This would probably be his last admission, and I believe he knew it.

Some patients are known to be "problems" because of behavior changes that often accompany major diseases. When people are suffering, they aren't aware of what they say or do to people, and frequently they lash out at the first person who enters their room.

All things considered, every nurse is well aware of these circumstances. The more experienced nurses have acquired knowledge in how to handle such cases. Of course, this is where I come in—the "new kid on the block," in a manner of speaking. For days, the other nurses talked about Mr. Kenney at report, and there were special staff meetings to decide how to handle his outrageous behavior. Everyone tried to spend as little time as possible while in his room. Sometimes he threw things at the nurses and other staff members, if they so much as looked at him the wrong way.

One evening, while on a particularly busy shift, we had more than our share of emergency admissions on the already overcrowded medical-surgical unit. Mr. Kenney picked this same evening to refuse his medications and decided to throw every large object that was well within his reach, while cursing at the top of his lungs. I could hardly believe that a terminally ill man of eighty-one could reach that volume and cause so much damage.

While I cautiously entered his room, I started talking. "What can I do for you, Mr. Kenney? What seems to be the problem? There is such a ruckus in here that even the visitors are terrified. I don't know what to think of it. The other patients are trying to get to sleep."

An annoyed Mr. Kenney put down his next projectile (that seemed to be aimed at me!) and asked me to sit in the chair next to his bed for a minute. Knowing I didn't really have the time, I still said, "Okay."

As I sat on the edge of the chair, Mr. Kenney proceeded to share some of his life with me. He started by saying, "No one understands how hard it is. How long it has been since I felt well. It has been so long since ... since ... anyone has even taken the time to really look at me, to listen to me ... and to care."

A long silence followed, and I wondered if this wouldn't be the best time to politely leave, but I didn't have the heart. Something told me to stay with this man.

After what seemed like an hour, he finally said, "It has been so long since I have had my Rose with me. My lovely, sweet Rose. We would always kiss good night, and that made everything better. No matter what happened that day, Rose's kiss always made everything better. Oh, God, how I would give anything for one more kiss from Rose. "Then Mr. Kenney started crying.

He held onto my hand and said, "I know you must think I'm crazy, but I know my life is almost over. I look forward to being with my Rose again. My life is hell this way! I really appreciate your taking the time to listen—to really listen to me. I know you are terribly busy. I know you care."

"I don't mind at all. While I prepare to give you your medication, is there anything else that I can do for you?"

"Please—call me Joseph," he said as he rolled over very cooperatively. I gave him his injections, and he thought for a few moments before answering my question. As I was almost finished, he finally said, "There is one last favor you could do for me."

"What is it, Joseph?" I asked.

Then he leaned over the side of the bed, and said in a hushed voice, "Could you just give me a good-night kiss? Rose's kisses always made everything better. Could you just give me a kiss good night? Please? Oh, God, how I would give anything for one more kiss from Rose."

So I did—I walked over and placed a huge kiss on his cheek. It felt right to kiss a dying man in the place of his "Rose"!

During report the next day, the nurses said Mr. Kenney had slipped peacefully away during the night. It is wonderful to know how strong true love can be—to be inseparable, even after death. I was so honored that Mr. Kenney asked me to give him one more kiss from Rose.

Laura Lagana

Life Without Michael

Memory is the gift from God which death cannot destroy.

Kahlil Gibran

I learned a lot from Michael Landon. Today I believe that my strength comes from him. Weeks before he died, he wrote his parting advice to me in a Mother's Day wish book. It's very special to me and I read it often. In it he said, "Be strong. Be solid. Live life, love it and be happy." Michael once told me, "Don't grieve too long." I'm trying, but losing someone like Michael is something that stays with you forever.

When you lose someone you love, you struggle with it every day. At first, our five-year-old, Sean, had a tough time talking about his father. Just recently he began watching Michael on television again and admitting how much he misses him. Still, this morning he told me he missed his daddy so much his stomach hurt. Jennifer is eight and it's been rough for her, too. All three of us are in therapy. We just take life day by day.

The children and I visit the cemetery often. We bring

Michael letters, usually just to tell him about what we're feeling and what is happening in our lives. But I really don't feel as close to him there as I do at home, where there are pictures of him in every room and his clothes are still in his closet, just as he left them. This is where Michael most loved to be. I expect him to walk through the door any minute. Sometimes, especially when I go up to bed at night, I wish he was waiting upstairs and we could just sit down and discuss the day's events.

I first met Michael when I was nineteen and hired as a stand-in on *Little House on the Prairie*. Seeing the way he treated everybody, I developed a terrible crush. One night, two years after I'd joined the show, he came to my apartment after a party on the set. From that moment on, we were wildly in love.

Michael and I were married on Valentine's Day, 1983. As a husband, he was the best — strong, caring, supportive, witty and fun to be around. Michael was also a homebody. Every day before he left the studio, he'd call and ask what we needed from the market. He'd show up with a bag of goodies in his arms. Michael loved to cook, and on many nights he'd take over the kitchen. His specialties were Italian dishes like spaghetti with sausage and chicken cacciatore.

He was as good a father as he was a husband. I used to love to watch him with the children, especially on vacations. In Hawaii, he taught them to skip stones across the water and got as excited as the children did when they discovered a beautiful shell or a tiny hermit crab. He would spend hours, literally hours, playing in the ocean with Sean and Jennifer. Everything was just perfect. Michael loved our life and his work. He'd always been incredibly healthy. We were looking forward to growing old together.

Then in February 1991, he began having abdominal pains. It was always tough to get Michael to see a doctor. Finally I made an appointment, and he was examined for an ulcer. Nothing was found, but they put him on some medicine that helped for a while.

In early April, the pain resurfaced. Four days later — April 5—we had the results of the biopsy: pancreatic cancer that had metastasized to the liver.

Looking back, I now believe Michael knew even then that he wasn't going to make it. Pancreatic cancer is swift and lethal, with a five-year survival rate of only 3 percent. I was angry, stunned. Why was this happening? Michael looked at it more pragmatically, as he did everything in his life. From the moment he was diagnosed until the day he died, he was never angry. Once he told me, "It's not God who does it. It's the disease. God doesn't give you cancer." For Michael, death wasn't something to fear, but he didn't want to die. He didn't want to leave everyone he loved.

We leveled with the kids from the beginning. Michael and I called his older children to tell them what was going on, and then we sat down with our two little ones. We told them that Daddy had a very serious type of cancer and that Daddy was going to do the best he could to fight it, but there were no guarantees. Sean was very calm. I'm not sure he really understood. Jennifer, too, seemed to take it well, but later there were indications she was suffering inside — stomachaches, headaches and anxiety attacks.

These first moments were before the storm, the hurricane of media that surrounded us as soon as news of Michael's disease hit the press. Photographers staked out our home and the hospital. They climbed over our walls and peeked in our windows. The tabloids came out with bizarre stories.

Almost every week, they printed a new fabrication. Once they said Michael had only four weeks to live. Another time, they claimed the cancer had spread to his colon. Neither was true. At the same time, the public responded with compassion and love. We received a flood of letters — twelve thousand a week. Michael was deeply moved, and he told me, "This is the first time I've realized how many lives I've touched."

In less than a month, the cancer doubled in size. For the first time, I think both of us realized Michael was probably going to die. That afternoon, we held each other. I lay my head on his lap and cried. Michael stroked my hair and whispered, "I know, I know."

Although he had resisted at first, Michael finally agreed to undergo experimental chemotherapy. He hated the idea, and I don't think he would have done it if it wasn't for the children and me. He was making a final effort to survive.

Michael's health continued to deteriorate, however, and by Father's Day, June 16, it was obvious to all of us that we wouldn't have him with us much longer. In past years, we bought Michael gifts like tennis rackets. This year there were pajamas and beautiful homemade cards. The whole family showed up to see him.

Shortly after Father's Day, Michael told me that he only had a week to live. That last week, Michael's health continued to fail. Then, on Sunday morning, June 30, the nurse told me they believed the end was near, so I called the children and Michael's best friends to the house. Since the doctors had increased his morphine and Percocet, Michael was drowsy and drifted in and out of consciousness. Throughout the last day, each of us said our private good-byes and let Michael know that it was okay. If he was ready to die, it was all right to let go.

The next morning, Michael was in a dreamlike state, and we were all in the bedroom again when he suddenly sat up in bed and said, "Hi. I love you guys." Then a little while later, Michael asked the others to leave so we could be alone. Looking back, I believe he was ready to die, and he really didn't want it to happen in front of the whole family.

I stayed with Michael, waiting for the inevitable. Sometimes he drifted off into almost a trance. At one point I asked him, "Do you know who I am?" He looked at me and answered, "Yeah." I said, "I love you." He answered, "I love you, too." Those were his last words. A moment later, he stopped breathing.

I felt stunned and stayed with Michael for a little while before I went downstairs to tell the others that he had died. There was, however, little time for contemplation. As if they somehow knew, we heard the swirl of helicopters overhead as the press circled in. Suddenly we heard screaming outside. Jennifer had climbed to the top of the swing set and was shouting, "Not my daddy. Not my daddy. I don't want my daddy to die." I told the others to let her be, because I wanted her to be able to get it out. Soon she climbed down and was sobbing in my arms.

A while later, the undertaker arrived. When they carried Michael's body out, I knew he was never coming back. That was the finality of it—Michael was gone.

That night, both children slept with me. Jennifer and I wore two of Michael's shirts to bed with us. I felt like I didn't belong anywhere, like I just didn't fit in anymore. I was completely lost, lonely.

The best thing I could do was leave, so I took the kids away for four weeks in Hawaii. We went to a place Michael and I loved. It was hard, because he wasn't there. But it was even tougher coming home, knowing that Michael wouldn't be waiting for us.

We're getting better, but it all takes time. The children still sleep with me sometimes, though not as often as in the beginning. They just seem to need to be hugged more often. And I continue to have some very difficult moments. A few days ago, I was on the expressway and got off at the wrong exit. I ended up at the studio. That was where the children and I would go visit Daddy. It was such a part of our lives. But Michael is gone, and all of our lives are changing.

It's odd, but before Michael died, I was frightened of death. I used to worry about illness or sometimes just getting on an airplane. Now I'm no longer afraid. Life is too short. You never know, so you'd better make the best of every moment.

When I think about Michael, what I remember most is how he relished life and how fiercely he loved his family. Ours was a good marriage: Michael was always there for me, and I was always there for him. He told me once, after he'd been diagnosed, that win or lose he could handle whatever happened. He said, "I've had an incredible life, great happiness." I miss Michael every day, but I know wherever he is, he's happy and well—and that someday I'll see him again.

Cindy Landon
with Kathryn Casey

One Last Good-Bye

I have sought to come near you, I have called to you with all my heart; and when I went out toward you I found you coming toward me.

Judah Halevi

The hospital room, hushed and dim, had come to seem somehow unreal to me as the day slowly passed, as though I were witnessing a tableau within a darkened theater. Yet the scene was sadly real — my brother, sister and myself, each lost in our own thoughts, silently looking on as our mother, sitting at our father's bedside and holding his hand, talked softly to him even though he was not conscious. Our father, after years of patiently withstanding the pain and indignities of a terminal illness, was near the end of his struggle, and had slipped quietly into a coma early that morning. We knew the hour of his death was at hand.

Mother stopped talking to Dad, and I noticed that she was looking at her wedding rings and smiling gently. I smiled, too, knowing that she was thinking of the ritual that had lasted for the forty years of their marriage. Mother, energetic and never still, was forever ending up with her engagement and wedding rings twisted and disarranged. Dad, always calm and orderly, would take her hand and gently and carefully straighten the rings until they were back in place. Although very sensitive and loving, the words "I love you" didn't come easily to him, so he expressed his feelings in many small ways, such as this, through the years.

After a long pause, Mother turned to us and said in a small sad voice, "I knew your father would be leaving us soon, but he slipped away so suddenly that I didn't have the chance to tell him good-bye, and that I love him one last time."

Bowing my head, I longed to pray for a miracle that would allow them to share their love one final time, but my heart was so full that the words wouldn't come.

Now, we knew we just had to wait. As the night wore on, one by one each of us had nodded off, and the room was silent. Suddenly, we were startled from sleep. Mother had begun to cry. Fearing the worst, we rose to our feet to comfort her in her sorrow. But to our surprise, we realized that her tears were tears of joy. For as we followed her gaze, we saw that she was still holding our father's hand, but that somehow, his other hand had moved slightly and was gently resting on Mother's.

Smiling through her tears, she explained: "For just a moment, he looked right at me." She paused, looking back at her hand. "Then," she whispered in a voice choked with emotion, "he straightened my rings."

Father died an hour later. But God, in his infinite wisdom, had known what was in our heart before any of us could ask him for it. Our prayer was answered in a way that we all will cherish for the rest of our lives.

Mother had received her good-bye.

Karen Corkern Babb

Across the years
I will walk with you—
in deep, green forests;
on shores of sand:
and when our time
on earth is through
in heaven, too,
you will have
my hand.

Robert Sexton

Who Is Jack Canfield?

Jack Canfield is one of America's leading experts in the development of human potential and personal effectiveness. He is both a dynamic, entertaining speaker and a highly sought-after trainer. Jack has a wonderful ability to inform and inspire audiences toward increased levels of self-esteem and peak performance.

He is the author and narrator of several bestselling audio- and videocassette programs, including *Self-Esteem and Peak Performance*, *How to Build High Self-Esteem*, *Self-Esteem in the Classroom* and *Chicken Soup for the Soul-Live*. He is regularly seen on television shows such as *Good Morning America*, *20/20* and *NBC Nightly News*. Jack has coauthored numerous books, including the *Chicken Soup for the Soul* series, *Dare to Win* and *The Aladdin Factor* (all with Mark Victor Hansen), *100 Ways to Build Self-Concept in the Classroom* (with Harold C. Wells) and *Heart at Work* (with Jacqueline Miller).

Jack is a regularly featured speaker for professional associations, school districts, government agencies, churches, hospitals, sales organizations and corporations. His clients have included the American Dental Association, the American Management Association, AT & T, Campbell Soup, Clairol, Domino's Pizza, GE, ITT, Hartford Insurance,

Johnson & Johnson, the Million Dollar Roundtable, NCR, New England Telephone, Re/Max, Scott Paper, TRW and Virgin Records. Jack is also on the faculty of Income Builders International, a school for entrepreneurs.

Jack conducts an annual eight-day Training of Trainers program in the areas of self-esteem and peak performance. It attracts educators, counselors, parenting trainers, corporate trainers, professional speakers, ministers and others interested in developing their speaking and seminar-leading skills.

For further information about Jack's books, tapes and training programs, or to schedule him for a presentation, please contact:

Self-Esteem Seminars
P. O. Box 30880 • Santa Barbara, CA 93130
phone: 805-563-2935 • fax: 805-563-2945
Web site: *http://www.chickensoup.com*

Who Is Mark Victor Hansen?

Mark Victor Hansen is a professional speaker who, in the last twenty years, has made over four thousand presentations to more than 2 million people in thirty-two countries. His presentations cover sales excellence and strategies; personal empowerment and development; and how to triple your income and double your time off.

Mark has spent a lifetime dedicated to his mission of making a profound and positive difference in people's lives. Throughout his career, he has inspired hundreds of thousands of people to create a more powerful and purposeful future for themselves while stimulating the sale of billions of dollars worth of goods and services.

Mark is a prolific writer and has authored *Future Diary*, *How to Achieve Total Prosperity* and *The Miracle of Tithing*. He is coauthor of the *Chicken Soup for the Soul* series, *Dare to Win* and *The Aladdin Factor* (all with Jack Canfield) and *The Master Motivator* (with Joe Batten).

Mark has also produced a complete library of personal empowerment audio- and videocassette programs that have enabled his listeners to recognize and use their innate abilities in their business and personal lives. His message has made him a popular television and radio personality, with appearances on ABC, NBC, CBS, HBO, PBS and CNN. He has also appeared on the cover of numerous magazines, including *Success*, *Entrepreneur* and *Changes*.

Mark is a big man with a heart and spirit to match—an inspiration to all who seek to better themselves.

For further information about Mark write:

MVH & Associates
P. O. Box 7665
Newport Beach, CA 92658
phone: 714-759-9304 or 800-433-2314
fax: 714-722-6912
Web site: *http://www.chickensoup.com*

Who Is Barbara De Angelis ,Ph. D. ?

Barbara De Angelis, Ph. D. , is internationally recognized as one of the foremost experts on human relations and personal growth. As a bestselling author, popular television personality and sought-after motivational speaker, she has reached millions of people worldwide with her positive messages about love, happiness and the search for meaning in our lives.

Barbara is the author of nine bestselling books which have sold over 4 million copies and been published in twenty languages. Her first book, *How to Make Love All the Time*, was a national bestseller. Her next two books, *Secrets About Men Every Woman Should Know* and *Are You the One for Me?*, were #1 on the *New York Times* bestseller list for months. Her fourth book, *Real Moments*, also became an overnight *New York Times* bestseller and was followed by *Real Moments for Lovers*. Her most recent books are *Passion*, *Confidence*, *Ask Barbara* and *The Real Rules*.

Barbara appeared weekly for two years on CNN as their Newsnight relationship expert dispensing advice via satellite all over the world. She has hosted her own daily television show for CBS TV and her own popular radio talk show in Los Angeles. She has also been a frequent guest on *Oprah*, *Leeza*, *Geraldo* and *Politically Incorrect*. Barbara's first television infomercial, *Making Love Work*, which she wrote and produced, won numerous awards and is the most successful relationship program of its kind. It is used by half a million people throughout the world.

For twelve years, Barbara was the founder and executive director of the Los Angeles Personal Growth Center. She received her master's degree in psychology from Sierra University in Los Angeles and her doctorate in psychology from Columbia Pacific University in San Francisco. Barbara is known for sharing her vitality, warmth, humor and inspirational presence with her audiences.

For further information about Barbara's books and tapes, or to schedule her for a presentation, please contact:

Shakti Communications
12021 Wilshire Boulevard, Suite 607
Los Angeles, CA 90025
800-682-LOVE
e-mail: *shakti97@aol.com*

Who Are Mark and Chrissy Donnelly?

A husband and wife who exemplify the kind of loving couple these *Chicken Soup* stories portray, Mark and Chrissy Donnelly began their marriage with a decision to spend as much time together as possible—both in work and in spare time. Mark recounts how, during their honeymoon in Hawaii, they planned dozens of ways to leave their separate jobs and begin to work together on meaningful projects. Compiling a book of stories about loving couples was just one of the ideas.

Of the *Couple's Soul* project, Mark and Chrissy say they were drawn even closer together through the experience of meeting other loving couples and reading their stories, even the hundreds that were not chosen for the final book. As a result, the Donnellys now strive to minimize their time apart and continue learning new ways to practice love and commitment in their daily lives.

Active contributors to the success of the *Chicken Soup* series, Mark and Chrissy are currently at work on four other *Chicken Soup* titles: *Chicken Soup for the Golfer's Soul*, *Chicken Soup for the Father's Soul*, *Chicken Soup for the Family Soul* and *Chicken Soup for the Friend's Soul*. Mark also serves as president of The Donnelly Marketing Group, expanding the *Chicken Soup* message to people around the world through special projects. Mark is former vice president of marketing for his family's successful building materials business. Chrissy was formerly a CPA with Price Waterhouse.

The couple make their home in Paradise Valley, Arizona. Mark and Chrissy can be reached at:

3104 E. Camelback Rd. Suite 531 • Phoenix, AZ 85016
phone: 602-604-4422 • fax: 602-508-8912
e-mail: *soup4 soul@home.com*

What People Are Saying About ...

"Every couple owes it to themselves to read *Chicken Soup for the Couple's Soul*. You will be inspired, you will be entertained, you'll learn to better understand your partner, and you'll come away feeling more in love than ever before!"

Marie Osmond
TV talk show host, *Donny & Marie*
cofounder, Children's Miracle Network

"The world needs more love, and *Chicken Soup for the Couple's Soul* gives us a beautiful glimpse into the difference love can make in our lives."

Deepak Chopra, M. D.
author, *The Path of Love*
educational director, The Chopra Center of Well Being

"The love in this book will make your heart sing! I highly recommend it."

Susan Jeffers, Ph. D.
author, *Opening Our Hearts to Men*

"*Chicken Soup for the Couple's Soul* is the most touching

collection of stories about love, romance and relationships written in many decades. It will elevate the spirits of readers of all ages. Whether you are already in love or have yet to meet that special someone, you will be carried to new heights by the warm and sensitive romantic experiences shared in these pages."

Terry M. Walker
publisher, *American Bride Magazine*

"What a delight to sit down and read something that is truly good for you. My wife and I know that we are in this marriage for the long haul and find great comfort in reading about others who feel the same way. Thank you for putting together so many wonderful stories that show the ups and the downs, the trials as well as the rewards of being married. Our three children thank you too!"

John R. Schneider
cofounder, Children's Miracle Network
actor, *Dukes of Hazard*

"Don't forget to bring along a copy of *Chicken Soup for the Couple's Soul* to read on your honeymoon or romantic getaway. This wonderful collection of stories makes great reading for newlyweds or any couple in love."

Adam Sandow
president, *Honeymoon Magazine*

"Just when I thought I'd heard every romantic marriage proposal and declaration of love, *Chicken Soup for the Couple's Soul* comes along. What uplifting, heartfelt stories to inspire romance and make you truly appreciate the loved ones in your life."

Cynthia C. Muchnick
author, *101 Ways to Pop the Question* and
Will you Marry Me? The World's Most Romantic Proposals

英文版《心灵鸡汤》系列丛书

《关于工作》工作的人是快乐的，但也　是多感的。18.00 元

《象牙塔里的日子》美国大学生情感生活的真实再现。19.00元

《致天下有情人》沐浴着爱情雨露的人让世界更精彩。19.00 元

《女人心语》事业、家庭、爱情中的美国当代女性心语。19.00 元

《心灵鸡汤》第　三　辑 19.00 元

《心灵鸡汤》第　二　辑 19.00 元

《豆蔻年华》当代美国青少年的情感故事。亲情、友情、爱情伴随着成长的历程。19.00 元

《心灵鸡汤》第　一　辑 18.00 元